Intercultural Voices in Contemporary British Literature

Also by Lars Ole Sauerberg
FACT INTO FICTION
THE PRACTICE OF LITERARY CRITICISM (*editor*)
SECRET AGENTS IN FICTION
VERSIONS OF THE PAST – VISIONS OF THE FUTURE

Intercultural Voices in Contemporary British Literature

The Implosion of Empire

Lars Ole Sauerberg

palgrave

© Lars Ole Sauerberg 2001
All rights reserved. No reproduction, copy or transmission of
this publication may be made without written permission.

No paragraph of this publication may be reproduced, copied or
transmitted save with written permission or in accordance with
the provisions of the Copyright, Designs and Patents Act 1988,
or under the terms of any licence permitting limited copying
issued by the Copyright Licensing Agency, 90 Tottenham Court
Road, London W1T 4LP.

Any person who does any unauthorised act in relation to this
publication may be liable to criminal prosecution and civil
claims for damages.

The author has asserted his right to be identified
as the author of this work in accordance with the
Copyright, Designs and Patents Act 1988.

First published 2001 by
PALGRAVE
Houndmills, Basingstoke, Hampshire RG21 6XS and
175 Fifth Avenue, New York, N.Y. 10010
Companies and representatives throughout the world

PALGRAVE is the new global academic imprint of
St. Martin's Press LLC Scholarly and Reference Division and
Palgrave Publishers Ltd (formerly Macmillan Press Ltd).

ISBN 0-333-80170-9

This book is printed on paper suitable for recycling and
made from fully managed and sustained forest sources.

A catalogue record for this book is available
from the British Library.

Library of Congress Cataloging-in-Publication Data
Sauerberg, Lars Ole, 1950–
Intercultural voices in contemporary British literature: the implosion
of empire / by Lars Ole Sauerberg.
    p. cm
    Includes bibliographical references (p.) and index.
    ISBN 0-333-80170-9
    1. English literature—Minority authors—History and criticism.
2. English literature—20th century—History and criticism.
3. Intercultural communication in literature. 4. Postcolonialism—
Great Britain. 5. Multiculturalism in literature. 6. Decolonisation
in literature. 7. Ethnic groups in literature. 8. Minorities in
literature. I. Title.

PR120.M55 S28 2001
820'.9'355—dc21

2001045175

Printed and bound in Great Britain by
Antony Rowe Ltd, Chippenham, Wiltshire

To Mette

The situations of Conrad, Eliot, James, Auden, and Isherwood are in certain ways exemplary of what has happened to English literature in the twentieth century. It is both English, and it is not. It is both British and it is not. What really matters is that English literature, rather than being confined to an insular Poets' Corner, now belongs in and to a wider world.

(Sanders, *The Short Oxford History of English Literature*, 1994:15)

Contents

Preface	viii
Introduction	1
1 Literary Britain between Imperial Legacy and Regional Devolution	12
2 Imperial Aftermath in British Post-World War Two Fiction	33
3 Verbal (Pre)Occupations	54
4 Wholly Female, Partly Foreign	83
5 In the Great Tradition – but with a Difference	109
6 Global Villagers	137
7 Adopting and Adapting Crime Fiction	162
8 Critical Perspective	189
Notes	213
References	219
Index	223

Preface

The process from idea to book has also in this case been one of constant revision and adjustment. The original concept was to present a study of what has been happening in British literature of the late twentieth century as a result of stimuli from cultures formerly of the British Empire and now independent but decidedly oriented – 'sucked' – towards Britain in a post-Imperial implosive dynamics. Hence, in the subtitle, 'Implosion of Empire', to begin with signifying the literary exposition of the formerly colonial other in British literature. However, as the project progressed, it became increasingly clear to me that the state of British culture towards the end of the twentieth century is very much that of a transitional culture, for which a past of wider spaces and undisputed influence represents a highly complex legacy. Not only did the Empire implode, with Britain again after half a millennium a national state in a European context, the implosion coincided with searches in different contexts for new identities politically, culturally and socially, in combination opening up for new and complex creative energies in literature.

The following persons and institutions have been helpful at different stages of work on this book, and I want to express to them my gratitude: Professor Susan Bassnett of Warwick University, The British Council (in Copenhagen and London), Mary Enright at the Poetry Library on the South Bank, Maxim Jakubowski of Murder One bookshop in Charing Cross Rd, London, Judith Cutler of the Crime Writers Association, UK. The University of Southern Denmark, formerly Odense University, I wish to thank for having granted me 'time out' from teaching obligations without the prospect of which a research and writing project like this would indeed be meaningless, but with the daily burdens of which, as we in the trade all know, its implementation would be well nigh impossible.

University of Southern Denmark   LARS OLE SAUERBERG

Introduction

> Hundreds of citizens have written to Tony Blair from every part of Britain urging that 'God Save the Queen' is replaced by a 'more appropriate' tune [for sports events]. 'Their general opinion is "England, get your own national anthem; 'God Save the Queen' is a British song"', explained a Downing Street insider.
> (*The Observer*, 5 March 2000, News Section, p. 6)

The face of a person is displayed on the cover of the last twentieth-century issue of *New Writing*, 8 (1999), the annual sample anthology of new writing published by Vintage in association with the British Council. The image is clearly a composite one, signalling a person partly North-West European, partly Indian, partly African, partly Asian. Peter Blake's identikit image speaks very eloquently a message put into words in the introduction by editors Tibor Fischer and Lawrence Norfolk, when they rejoice in the state of Balkanisation in modern British literature. They have discovered a 'new imaginative mobility' in the capacity of British writers to take up subjects and themes of an outlandish nature with the result that 'British writing today appears as effective when treating of Algiers or Ulan Bator as it always has been when dissecting the *mores* of the Shire Counties or the All Saints Road' (Fischer and Norfolk, 1999:xiii). Writers' Britain has become a 'cultural entrepôt, a place of flux and reflux, differently but intricately connected to both Europe and the United States, historically and more problematically to the Indian subcontinent and Africa' (ibid.).

But also within Britain certain trends suggesting upheaval are discernible, since the balance is currently being shifted in favour of Scotland, Northern Ireland and Wales, with England proper apparently lagging behind, judging by the proportion of regional contributions to *New Writing*, 8.

However, the increasingly cosmopolitan characteristics suggested by Fischer and Norfolk have been forming over a period considerably longer than just the one year dealt with. Arguably, since the early 1980s it has become increasingly difficult to consider British literature in terms of 'national' and 'mainstream' in the traditional senses of the words. Indeed, what has been happening in British literature over the last couple of decades of the twentieth century parallels the increasing contestation of the very term 'British' as an adequate designation of national identity.

In *fin-de-vingtième-siecle* British literature we have a situation in which the traditional lineage of a literature predominantly English – in the twentieth century very much influenced by Continental European and American brands of modernism – is being partly insulated as in itself regional, partly used as stepping stone or foil for literary efforts deliberately different from but at the same time distinctly aware of this very strong and widely influential tradition. Such literary efforts can be seen in the mass of literature written 'back' by the former Empire and in a lot of the literature written in declared difference from the English tradition in Scotland, Wales and Northern Ireland. Also inside England 'proper' there is an increasingly marked sense of regional difference, especially in the north.

It is the contention of this study that in the period under consideration – the last two decades of the twentieth century – it is possible to see UK literature both as fragmenting into regional writings and in the process of being reforged into something new, transcending traditional, regional boundaries. English, that is *sans* Irish, Scottish, and Welsh, literature has indeed come under attack as a canon of specifically political and cultural interests overlapping with those of the British Empire. The response has been the 'reduction' of the canon into a literary tradition narrowly and consistently applying to England. Outside England the literary reaction has often been to wryly adopt the familiar patterns in writings critical of what they have traditionally represented. However, in this paradoxical situation of both having to acknowledge and discard a literary tradition of unique historical significance because it is so entrenched and widespread, writers have responded with a heightened sense of their own personal situations, regarding social, political and social belonging, and with an equally heightened sense of the English – or British as the distinction is usually ignored in everyday parlance – literary tradition at their disposal, and produced literature energised by both at the same time. The result is a literature which merges rather than dissolves traditions and experiences and in which we often feel that the publisher's British imprint is only an address of convenience for writers looking beyond region and nation or, conversely, insisting on the purely local.

With oil discoveries in the North Sea boosting already well-entrenched Scottish hopes for independence from Westminster with the promise of a sufficiently sound independent economy, the tendency towards regionalisation has been especially strong in Scotland. The first effective step towards Scottish devolution was taken when Prime Minister Tony Blair's election promises to create a higher degree of self-rule in northern and western Britain were carried out in the spring of 1999. Welsh nationalists have been eager to join up, although there a failing economy due to the closing down of mines with no natural resources to replace them has given less optimism for a self-sustaining economy. In Northern Ireland there seems, at the moment of writing, to be hopes for peaceful coexistence after almost a century of bitter troubles, with perhaps the EU membership of the UK and Ireland the best guarantee of a positive and mutually beneficial relationship between the two national states, and with the Stormont parliament seeing itself on an equal, quasi-independent footing with the Scots and the Welsh. Literally in the midst of these urges for a degree of regional autonomy, England has begun to see itself as only part of the British Isles, but then also with an increasing sense of a cultural identity of its own. Although since taking office Tony Blair has been eager to persuade the English that the north–south divide is a thing of the past, there is still a widespread sense of difference between north and south in England. This difference is basically an economic divide, with the decline of the formerly heavily industrialised north having left its mark on culture. If the culture of the south has been cosmopolitan, outgoing and all-embracing, the culture of the north seems poised between attitudes of impotence and cries of defiance. So regionalism, both relating to the UK as a whole with England, Northern Ireland, Scotland and Wales, and to England with its North East, North West, Yorkshire and Humbershire, East Midlands, West Midlands, East, South East, South West and London (Britain 2000, 1999:10), is very much an economic issue with a demographic history determined by resource access and commercial exchange.

With Britain breaking up into regions, and with the constant threefold external interaction-cum-pressure from the former imperial dominions, from the European Union and from the USA, nationalistic endeavours in favour of an old-style Britain seem anachronistic. Only among more or less militant Unionist protestants in Northern Ireland does it seem possible to measure a degree of national loyalty towards the concept of a United Kingdom.

As the receptacle of numerous British passport holders from all over the world where the Union Jack used to signify British sovereignty, the demographic basis of Britain's social and cultural fabric has been changing radically. For all practical purposes today's Britain is a multicultural society, having developed into such in a comparatively short time. With a generally peaceful and nonviolent history of retreat from Empire, Britain has attempted to replace world leadership with political consultancy functions and the maintenance of trading and market interests. So Britain is still very much globally engaged. As a half-hearted member of an EEC which was turned into the much more tightly-knit quasi-federalist organisation of the EU by the Maastricht Treaty of 1992, Britain has had endless trouble at home and on the European continent since 1972, with economic need countering emotional reservations about pan-European collaboration on such an unheard-of scale. Having cultivated a special relationship with the USA since World War Two, and because of the shared language, Britain has been more closely attached to the former transatlantic colony than any other European nation. The cultural exchanges between the two countries have been considerable since the 1960s, with Britain, like the rest of the world, increasingly at the receiving end of a life-style trade.

All in all, however, Britain's position towards the end of the twentieth century is unique. No other country in the West is facing so many simultaneous challenges affecting its economy, its social texture and its culture. No wonder that British literature can no longer be spoken of in terms of homogeneity and monoculture.

Modern British (a term also here used to apply to Northern Irish) fiction is indeed characterised by a variety of thematic concerns which challenge and rework the manner and morals, the *'mores* of the Shire Counties or the All Saints Road' focus of much traditional, mainstream 'English Literature'. The influx of writing talent from the former Empire, combined with an increasing cosmopolitan orientation in the writing community, are factors of seminal importance. But also an enhanced feeling of regional loyalty is making itself felt in the literature written in Britain. But it is not only a question of regionalism in the narrow, geographical sense, since the regional is only one angle of a perspective comprising the historical, the social and the cultural. To speak, for instance, of a specifically Northern Irish literary identity soon proves futile, since on the one hand the literature of that region is subject to constant influential interchange with the literature of Ireland, and on the other, London – and via London the wider world – is the magnet for (Northern) Irish writers as it is for writers from the rest of the UK – indeed from all over the former Empire. Not only do we have to do with a state of geographical flux, but we also have to take into account dynamics both determined by geography and history and overriding them at the same time. Social identities are formed in response both to local conditions and to such universal categories as gender and the sense of belonging which may be found under the labels of ethnicity and regional or local: there are Scots – male and female, rich and poor, of long standing or recently arrived – in Scotland, and there are Scots in the rest of the UK, also male and female, rich and poor, and with varieties of family origins. Addressing works of modern British literature in which the borderline between the traditional and the new is being constantly redrawn, the critic needs correspondingly flexible tools.

It is the main point of this study to address some significant literary developments that may be attributed to a sense of cultural transition and multiplicity in literature relating to Britain and, in the process of discussing relevant works, to consider adequate, hence rewarding, critical endeavours. I have wanted to tilt the perspective towards a consideration of what impacts a changing geopolitical situation in combination with a changing regional orientation has had on the literary scene relating to Britain, with special focus on literature displaying a marked sensibility to the shift of Britain from an insular to a global culture and/or from a centralised culture to a decentralised culture complex.

Some would, no doubt, suggest that such a project belongs within a critical context of post-colonial studies or criticism. Putting off my arguments until the final chapter, I shall restrict myself to declaring initially that post-colonial studies and criticism seem better suited to deal with issues of a different kind from those proposed in the present study, although areas of overlap are not hard to find. Post-colonial studies is a fast-developing late twentieth-century cross-disciplinary area of activities within (literary) historiography and literary criticism. The critical orientation has largely been preoccupied with the effects of the European cultural hegemony on the rest of the world. Approaching the manifestations of colonialism and Empire from a critical consideration of enforced social, political and cultural values on geopolitically weak targets, post-colonial studies have favoured a centrifugal approach (what London, Madrid, Lisbon, Paris, Berlin, Rome and Copenhagen did to the world in terms of colonisation and ensuing decolonisation) rather than the complementary opposite (what colonisation and decolonisation did to London, Madrid, Lisbon, Paris, Berlin, Rome and Copenhagen). Whereas it is tempting to apply to the current intercultural situation in the UK the principles of post-colonial theory and criticism, which have so successfully dealt with the literature of the former imperial dominions, the post-colonial approach, tending to rest on an ideological basis of opposition ('hegemony', 'subaltern' and so on), allows only insufficiently and schematically for the actual complexity and variety in contemporary literature written in or relating to the British Isles, and may even be misleading when the object of critical interest refuses to be typecast accordingly. Original insights in post-colonial criticism, and here I am thinking first and foremost of Edward Said, Homi K. Bhabha and Gayatri Chakravorty Spivak, and the enthusiasm and energy with which the post-colonial approach has been advocated and disseminated by, for instance, Bill Ashcroft, Garreth Griffiths and Helen Tiffin, have certainly been major forces in literary and cultural criticism since the 1970s. Also the present study stands in general debt to the suggestions of both post-colonial and other kinds of contemporary critical activities. But the close attachment of college dynamics and academic careers to developments in criticism has a way of consolidating and institutionalising the fresh and new. In that process empires of thought are built, not so much by the originators as by their devoted followers, who desire the gospels not only to be preached, but to be presented in well-edited form and in well-built churches.

Contemporary literature written within or in relation to Britain presents an astounding variety of thematic foci and formal alignments. If the state-of-the-nation novel used to be the preserve of born-and-bred Britons from well-ensconced middle-class positions, social criticism in novel form has found new and controversial voices in, for instance, Hanif Kureishi. Many of the most striking achievements in fiction have been made by writers very much aware of themselves as British in all but the usual, historico-geographical lineage sense of the designation. Besides Kureishi, authors like Timothy Mo, Kazuo Ishiguro, William Boyd and Salman Rushdie come to mind immediately. In poetry one can appreciate the voice not only of a versatile David Dabydeen shifting deftly between Caribbean and standard English, but also of British poets with immigrant backgrounds (John Agard, Moniza Alvi, Imtiaz Dharker, Linton Kwesi Johnson, Jackie Kay and Mimi Khalvati, to name but a few representative writers), a circumstance which clearly influences their work while at the same time they are pursuing other, and nationally neutral, goals such as issues to do with gender, family and age.

A good many writers with a British lineage have written themselves into positions best described as cosmopolitan. This applies to Julian Barnes, John Berger, Martin Amis, Lawrence Norfolk,

Nicolas Shakespeare and Ian McEwan, who all seem to prefer the transnational perspective either in their choice of settings or in their sources of influence. Clearly, this is a form of interculturalism which has always been at work in the form of influence received and given, but which is articulated explicitly by such writers as those mentioned, and which seems to have been very much enhanced by Britain's changing geopolitical situation, along with the general development into global village existential conditions, to which media-related activities are especially sensitive.

I have chosen to approach my subject inductively, with each of the first seven chapters taking up a literary subject I have felt to be directly related to Britain's changing situation after Empire, with the last two decades of the twentieth century predominantly in focus. Methodologically I have tried to let myself be guided by the 'invitations' explicit or implicit in the material, although I make use of various critical tools often honed for other, and perhaps more systematic and deductive, critical projects. It may be true that a contemporary view of things always has difficulties in seeing patterns and systems, and that such only emerge in the rear-view mirror. But it seems that what most critical voices agree to be the situation in the last few decades of the twentieth century is the plurality of interests, emphases and approaches, in literature as well as in criticism. So I feel congenial with the epoch under consideration in my decision to refrain from system building or theory imperialism. Nonetheless, as my subject in general and my foci have been the objects of various kinds of critical attention, I have felt it within my self-chosen remit to touch on some areas of a theoretical nature in a last chapter, which functions rather as a coda than as a last-minute theoretical justification.

In the first chapter, 'Literary Britain between Imperial Legacy and Regional Devolution', it will be pointed out that the book is not intended as a general literary history, but as a set of possible literary–historical selections in recognition of the impossibility of the validity of a grand centre-assuming narrative. It seems more to the point to write an account of some of the 'small' and decentred literary histories at present making up literary activities in Britain. So my attention will be primarily directed towards the last two decades of the twentieth century and to literature with a bearing on Britain, although that bearing may often seem to be the very impetus of the writer's creative projects. At the same time it will be argued that a change of critical perspective in the direction of the intercultural/transnational/transcultural is a much-needed addition – and corrective – to much current criticism practised along conventional lines. Marked presence of 'compound voice', understood as a writerly position emerging thematically in the literary text in the form of divided national/ethnic loyalties or otherwise foregrounded problematisations of Britishness in relation to writer and text, has served as a criterion for the selection of texts as well as a simple methodological tool.

The second chapter, 'Imperial Aftermath in British Post-World War Two Fiction', will deal with literary responses to the retreat from Empire. With the British commitment to decolonisation after the war, the inter-war criticism of and qualms about Empire voiced famously by E.M. Forster and George Orwell must be said to have met with a constructive response. Just as Britain had to cope with a new geopolitical situation, post-war fiction dealing with Empire had to readjust and respond to a situation in which the fact of 'loss' of Empire received more attention than the canonised fiction of the period evidences, ranging from pragmatic to nostalgic positions in an attempt to come to terms with not only the changed policy but also with the imperial past as a whole.

Perhaps the best indication of a split ethnic awareness is the linguistic versatility of a number of contemporary writers. The third chapter, 'Verbal (Pre)Occupations', brings into focus a number of writers who have used poetry as their medium to express a divided loyalty. For them the recourse to variants of English is a well-orchestrated effort to highlight problems to do with the situation of the immigrant. Attention to language is here not only the most clearly marked form of identification, but also an instrument of great symbolic and stylistic power.

Contemporary British poetry has numerous examples of texts written by women who give voice to concerns to do with ethnicity and cultural differences. At the same time, however, such texts rarely focus altogether on ethnic questions, but bring together problems to do with gender, family and class. The fourth chapter,

'Wholly Female, Partly Foreign', is intended to show the interdependence of ethnic and gender awarenesses in relation to a generic medium that traditionally places in the foreground the personal and intimate.

Some of the most respected and admired novelists of the last couple of decades have published novels clearly in Leavis's great tradition. Although such novelists are British by upbringing and education, their intercultural backgrounds provide them with an experience different from those of a one-faceted British lineage. In the fifth chapter – 'In the Great Tradition – but with a Difference' – a point will be made of demonstrating the extent to which Leavis's notion of a 'great tradition' in English fiction may be said to inform novels with thematic emphases on alienation from the notion of a British national consensus identity.

One of the literary reactions to a changing international situation with increasingly less emphasis on the national state has been for writers of the UK to set their works elsewhere, or to juxtapose Britain with the European continent or the USA. Julian Barnes has focused on France, D.M. Thomas on Russia, Martin Amis on the USA, Nicolas Shakespeare on Latin America, while John Berger has sought peasant roots and values in the French–Italian Alps, Bruce Chatwin has renewed the travelogue and Maureen Duffy has explored journeys in time and space, as have Penelope Lively and Ian McEwan. Having been placed more or less in the British mainstream, writers such as these have nonetheless responded to a change in the national climate with transpositions and expansions of settings and themes. This will be the focus of Chapter 6, 'Global Villagers'.

Crime fiction is very sensitive to social change. With its tradition of reflecting all the potentially significant elements of a banal and trivial everyday world, it follows stirrings in the body politic like a seismograph. Also a media-versatile genre long ago established across national boundaries, it is a truly international genre. Immigrant groups, as described in Chapter 7, 'Adopting and Adapting Crime Fiction', also have taken up the genre and adapted its formula to their specific environments and experiences, and mainstream British crime fiction gives increasing attention to intercultural Britain.

The concluding chapter, 'Critical Perspective', is a discussion of the critical and theoretical issues run into or explicitly or implicitly invoked in a study like this one, which sets out without subscribing to a ready-made critical credo apart from the conviction that, in the midst of so much and so varied contemporary creative vigour and with a writerly tendency to seek out interfaces rather than solid bastions, the very thought of a critical Procrustean bed seems an insult to the subject.

The building of the British Empire may be compared to an explosion, although a slow one. An explosion is the result of tremendous concentrated force seeking an outlet. An implosion generates energy by the need to fill a suddenly occurring vacuum, which I have found an appropriate metaphor of the situation faced by a Britain voided of Empire, leaving that 'space' for filling, not surprisingly with the global inheritance left by the explosion. In this book, then, 'implosion' signifies that new and complex creative literary energy visible in texts bearing witness to cultural condensation and diversification in a multicultural, inescapably ex-Empire-marked Britain responding to immigration, globalisation and regionalisation. In consequence I have found it to the point to extend the domain of the multicultural from encounters solely in terms of ethnicity to the designation of cultural encounters generally, in terms of ethnicity, gender, social groups, history and genre – in short where an awareness of impacts that 'disturb' traditional notions contributes to a changing landscape in literary Britain. In that widened perspective of cultural interaction 'intercultural' seems a more appropriate term than 'multicultural', despite the general currency of the latter. I have chosen not to attempt to cover the whole field on which the implosion has left its mark. Instead I have preferred to focus on literary phenomena in the last couple of decades of the twentieth century in which the implosion is a prominent feature in terms of what I call 'compound voice', that is the placing in the foreground of a literary awareness of cultural transition or multiplicity in terms of interaction.

1
Literary Britain between Imperial Legacy and Regional Devolution

'So the much vaunted Anglo-Saxon race...?'
'Is a myth. The northern half of Britain is more Danish and Celtic; and even in the south', he shrugged, 'I doubt very much whether our Anglo-Saxon ancestry would make up one part in four. We are, quite simply, a nation of European immigrants with new graftings being added all the time. A genetic river, if you like, fed by any number of streams.'

(Rutherfurd, 1997:826)

In the 3 July 1992 issue of the French newspaper *Le Monde*, Olivier Mongin, editor of the journal *Esprit*, complained about the state of the modern French novel. It is, he wrote, petrified either as individualistic self-satisfaction in the traditional form of a 'diary of private matters' ('journal intime') or as colossal tomes of historical novels; it is as if French novelists find it difficult to use the form of the novel to refract and confront contemporary public problems. The narcissistic confessional novel situates its protagonist in a social vacuum, and the historical novel is locked in a fixed historical process. In both cases the possibilities of the individual are reduced in relation to the surroundings.

This is not the case in modern Anglo-Saxon fiction, Olivier Mongin went on, especially not in the writings of 'immigrant writers', a term used by Mongin about Salman Rushdie, V.S. Naipaul, Hanif Kureishi and Kazuo Ishiguro. They all practise an uncertain tightrope walk between the tradition of their native countries and the English tradition of their choice. But the very consciousness of that choice is important, because it implies individuality as an experiment with socially determined roles or masks. With two different cultures as simultaneous points of reference, ideas and imagined fates can be played against each other in the space created between the two cultures. As formulated by Olivier Mongin: 'Whereas the French novelist tends to let her/himself be seduced by the illusion of the I or by the insurance policy of the historical tradition, the story as told by these novelists writing in English exists in a polemical nexus between their two cultures' (Mongin, 1992:2).[1]

Unlike the literary situation in France, I might add, the English novel of the last two decades has never wholeheartedly joined the confessional fashion. The exhibitionally private has been left largely for the European continent and the USA. Since its consolidation in the first half of the nineteenth century with Sir Walter Scott, the historical novel in England has developed very much into generic fiction. However, the realist novel in England has inclined steadfastly to the staging of life in terms of social comedy. Looking through his French glasses, Mongin would probably miss something deeply spiritual and sparklingly intellectual in the novels of those, like Margaret Drabble or Anita Brookner, who have carried on faithfully from Austen, Dickens, Trollope, Thackeray, Eliot and Bennett.

It is easy to agree with Olivier Mongin. 'Immigrant' writers such as those mentioned have indeed brought new life to the English novel. In the context of the English novel their work takes over a national predilection for comedy-of-manners realism, but at the same time puts that particular mode at the service of issues that transcend the smoking chimneys of the Midlands and the sophisticated tea-party problems of Hampstead. Reading them the reader looks out into an international arena and is asked to address existential, political and moral problems more ambitious and intriguing than readers of the contemporary English novel of the traditional mould are accustomed to. They have done no small service applying their grafting tools to a literary culture threatened by the admittedly refined but perhaps eventually barren inbreeding of insularity.

Olivier Mongin's critical observation, however, only covers a fraction of the modern literary situation in Britain. To begin with, 'immigrant' may indeed apply in practice, but Salman Rushdie, V.S. Naipaul, Hanif Kureishi and Kazuo Ishiguro are not immigrants in that strict sense of the word, since they, with different personal histories, are British Commonwealth citizens, and as such enjoy a particularly close relationship with Britain, if not necessarily a very cordial one. And, if Mongin had looked a little more carefully into the matter with which he is concerned, he would have discovered innovative voices among 'native' writers as well, for which a brief but suggestive list of names will make the point: Martin Amis, Julian Barnes, Ian McEwan, Angela Carter, Penelope Lively, Graham Swift. These are writers, who, along with those of Mongin's choice, have brought the late twentieth-century English novel out of its insularity and made it international. Not least because of the impact of imperial aftermath, British literature has seen a development into internationalisation complementary to the well-worn great tradition of the nation-tied and mainly social manners type of novel cultivated ever since Jane Austen.

The influx of 'immigrant' writers and the growing international orientation of 'native' writers during the last decades of the twentieth century have made it increasingly difficult to consider British literature in terms of 'national' and 'mainstream' in the traditional senses of the words. With English as the dominant *lingua franca* and with the former British Empire the widest-ranging ever, Great Britain is now at one and the same time a linguistic and cultural enclave with a 'narrow' national–state history and the 'exchange office' of an international linguistic and cultural situation rooted in imperial history and with far-reaching global effects.

Regionalism

Apart from vitalising the literatures emerging in the former colonies and offering readjustment of traditional readings of the former colonisers' literary canons, the regionalisation implicit in the notion of the post-colonial has had effects for the segmentation of national literary cultures as well. The replacement in the USA of the melting-pot ideology in favour of a new multicultural ('salad-bowl') awareness is quite symptomatic.[2] Also in Britain there was a markedly growing awareness towards the end of the twentieth century of the regional characteristics that make up the United Kingdom – England, Wales, Scotland and (Northern) Ireland – an awareness very much in concrete evidence in Antonia Byatt's selection of stories for *The Oxford Book of English Short Stories*, published in 1998, and considered from a theoretical perspective in Robert Crawford's *Devolving English Literature* (1992), followed by the same author's and colleagues' argument in *The Scottish Invention of English Literature* in 1998 that 'English literature' is really a Scottish construction.

In the series of Millennium Lectures commissioned by No. 10 Downing Street throughout 1999, British historian Linda Colley made the tension between devolution and centralisation in the UK the launching pad for her own suggestions for a sensible development of a 'multi-national, multi-cultural, infinitely diverse polity like Britain' (Colley, 1999:4). Recognising an identity crisis brought about by the loss of an Empire and a development towards national fragmentation, she recommends a British Citizen Nation for the

> three nations of Great Britain, together with the island of Ireland, ... too geographically adjacent, too small, and ... characterized over the centuries by too many complex and profound linkages, to go off on completely separate tangents in the future, or to be connected only by a loose, occasional Council of the Isles.
> (Colley 1999:3–4)

Whether or not Colley's Citizen Nation scenario is good for the British Isles is a political question not within the scope of my study, but it is noteworthy that the discussion about a national identity crisis is not only brought out in the open but apparently sanctioned by the highest political office. Colley's estimate of the situation acknowledges the need for the recognition of 'varieties of Englishness, as well as ... Irishness, Scottishness and Welshness' (Colley, 1999:7) in functional tandem with issues to do with ethnic minorities and women, whose problems, when it comes to questions of social equality, are structurally alike.[3]

Linda Colley's *Britons* (1992) is one of a range of histories written and published in the last two decades of the twentieth century to have problematised the sense of national identity and thus contributed to regional movements within Britain. Jeremy Paxman found himself on the bestseller lists with his anecdotal *The English: A Portrait of a People* in 1998. His curiosity spurred by radical major shifts in areas once considered of rock-bottom London-based stability – 'the end of Empire, the cracks opening in the so-called United Kingdom, the pressures for the English to plunge into Europe, and the uncontrollability of international business' (Paxman, 1998:x) – he set about distilling what is left of Englishness and, having probed into all the areas traditionally associated, positively or negatively, with the English, ended up with a compound of 'individualism, pragmatism, love of words and, above all, that glorious, fundamental cussedness' (ibid.:264). Rather than trying to side with adherents of 'English' or 'British', Norman Davies in his huge and methodologically daring *The Isles: A History* (1999) preferred to observe from outside and consider the 'isles' an inextricable complex in geographical and historical terms and to use national terms only when they apply to a specific situation:

> Having questioned the reigning conventions, I must endeavour to be accurate myself. I have been careful to show what is English and what is not, and only to use the British adjective in relation to the two periods where it is relevant – one ancient and one modern.
>
> (Davies, 1999:xli)

The tendency towards British regionalisation has made itself felt in approaches to and presentations of literature over the last decade of the twentieth century. The publication of the second volume of *The Oxford History of English Music* by John Caldwell in 1999 received a warm welcome by *Times Literary Supplement* reviewer David Matthews, who, however, began his review by taking the author to task concerning the difficulties involved when attempting to draw a line round specifically English music. After a roll call of composers left out or undeservedly included, Matthews regrets:

> Some of these questions would not have arisen, if 'British' had been substituted for 'English' in the title. I can anticipate

Caldwell's objections to that, though his chosen title might have had more validity, had he taken the concept of 'Englishness' more seriously than he does.

(Matthews, 1999:8)[4]

As Elizabeth Lowry observes in her *Times Literary Supplement* review of Byatt's 1998 collection of English short stories, the designation of 'English' has traditionally been taken to mean 'in English'. Byatt's choice of thirty-seven stories is made on the premise of English meaning strictly English:

> For a collection of *English* stories necessarily excludes Muriel Spark, Robert Louis Stevenson, Samuel Beckett, Frank O'Connor, Oscar Wilde, Patrick White, Katherine Mansfield, Janet Frame, O. Henry, Ernest Hemingway, Carson McCullers, Flannery O'Connor, Mark Twain and Edith Wharton, among others. And what does one do with naturalized or expatriate English writers who are not English by birth, like Doris Lessing, Joseph Conrad, Olive Schreiner, Kazuo Ishiguro and Henry James? Pity the poor editor, more or less obliged to welcome Somerset Maugham and sunset gin-and-tonics with open arms, while turning away James Joyce.
>
> (Lowry, 1998:23-4; original emphasis)

Byatt's idiosyncratically determined selection within the English domain is irrelevant for the present argument,[5] whereas it is precisely the grey-area cases regarding nationality which make impossible an attempt at maintaining a strictly national frontier as the condition of inclusion. Such a move forces the short story in English into a ridiculously limiting Procrustean bed.

The closest that Byatt comes to defining Englishness in a quantitative dimension is to describe her selection as 'writers with pure English national credentials' (1998a:xv), but with wise caution she refrains from venturing further into that slippery area. She is clearly much more at home with suggestive but vaguely generalising qualitative considerations, beginning with a negative definition: 'The English are what other English-speakers define themselves *against*' (ibid.), and going on to compile a list of alleged characteristics of the English short story pivoting on two qualities in particular: 'the persistent temptation to whimsy, and a kind of extravagance of what Henry James called "solidity of specification"' (1998a:xviii), the latter reformulated as the 'thinginess of things' (1998a:xix). As Byatt sees her task to be that of the observer rather than the analyst's, one will have to look elsewhere for a plausible explanation about the alleged English obsession with the 'thinginess of things'. The reader finds such a one in a brief article by Anthony Easthope in the British Council's December 1991 issue of *Literature Matters*. Easthope's line of reasoning is that the English national culture is empiricist. It has 'been dominated by the assumption that knowledge of the real is readily accessible to the experience of the unprejudiced observer' (Easthope, 1991:6). If this is indeed so, then we have a good explanation for the richness of Shakespeare's vocabulary – which Easthope estimates at about 80 000 words, to be set against the French playwright Racine with only 5000 words – with which to press the multiple phenomenal world into verbal shape. Easthope explains F.R. Leavis's dismissal of Shelley by the Romantic poet's abstract idealism, inviting a savage attack by Leavis 'on the very English grounds that in writing about the West Wind he does not know what the real world is like' (ibid.).[6]

The accumulated list of national characteristics found by Byatt in her perusal of numerous English short stories emerges from the following mosaic of quotations from her introduction:

> [About Bennett] . . . the mixed tones, precise observations, social shifts, and narrative surprises I was coming to see as English. (1998a:xvi–xvii)
> [About Forster, left out for precisely this reason] . . . the besetting English vices of archness and whimsy. (1998a:xvii)
> [About Trollope] . . . like many good English tales, it develops the comedy far beyond the climax the reader may expect . . . He is a person, not a type, though he is in a farce. This also I think of as English. (1998a:xix)
> [About Kipling] . . . draws unaffectedly and powerfully on the richness of earlier English literary writing. (1998a:xx) . . . after my reading, I felt that Kipling, with Hardy, and Graham Greene, was one of the true English masters of the form. (1998a:xxi)
> [About Saki] . . . equally characteristic, English voice, Saki's sharp,

remorseless tale of unredeemable human ferocity. It is the English dandy voice, at its best devastating, at less than its best silly or trivial. (1998a:xxi)
[About Chesterton] ... pleasing example of English whimsy ... combined with English religious mysticism ... and English in its gentleness. (1998a:xxii)
[About A.E. Coppard] ... in a practical English way ... petty English social priorities ... the English fondness for the little man and the importance of his life. (1998a:xxii)
[About P.G. Wodehouse] ... his genius is intimately involved in the range and depth of the possibilities of the English language. (1998a:xxiii)
[About Woolf and Lawrence] High modernism in English writing seems to be related both to a questioning of perception and to a desire to do away with the centre of self, or of social self. (1998a:xxiii)
[About Huxley] It is the teeth that make the story implacably comic, and yet it is also the teeth that provide the unpalatable pathos. Very English. (1998a:xxiv)
[About Malachi Whitaker] ... negotiates the minutiae of the English class-consciousness in a subtle and unexpected way. I like stories in which energy overcomes inhibitions. (1998a:xxiv)
[About V.S. Pritchett] ... the English way in which it makes the exploration of a part of the landscape, past and present, inextricably part of an exploration of the whole lives of the characters. (1998a:xxiv–xxv)
[About Evelyn Waugh] ... a splendidly heartless exploration of the English rural pieties, and English snobbism, by a satirist who certainly shared the pieties he was mocking. (1998a:xxv)
[About Graham Greene] What makes this tale English is again the mixed, ambivalent tone. (1998a:xxv)
[About Penelope Fitzgerald] ... sentences have a cool clarity that is part of a very modern English prose. (1998a:xxvii)
[About Rose Tremain] ... imagination reaches out in a new way into unknown places and experiences – not out of exoticism, but out of curiosity. (1998a:xxviii)
[About V.S. Naipaul and Kazuo Ishiguro] Both these writers use the English language perfectly, and with full knowledge of what has been written in it, to do something detached from

Englishness, looking *at* Englishness. (1998a:xxix; Byatt's emphasis)

[About subjects] There is English empiricism, English pragmatism, English starkness, English humour, English satire, English dandyism, English horror, and English whimsy. (1998a:xxix)

After this very inclusive list of writerly characteristics we hardly wonder when Byatt concludes that the 'English are hard to sum up' (1998a:xxx).

As a list of allegedly national characteristics, the list is interesting in so far as it seems to consolidate a range of national stereotypes. Byatt reads the stories obviously, but perhaps only subconsciously, prepared to find in them features that agree with a preconception of what Englishness is. More interesting, though, for the present purpose is the list – and indeed the whole publication venture – as symptomatic of a tendency to cultivate a notion of a common identity at a level more local than that of the whole of the UK.

Before the regional debate got really under way towards devolution, both John Fowles and Seamus Heaney had attempted to define particularly English qualities. Fowles's contribution, predating Heaney's by twelve years, pivots on the difference between English and British, the latter being an 'organizational convenience, a political advisability, a passport word' (Fowles, 1964:154) only. The quintessence of Englishness is a 'purging and often puritanical obsession with justice' (ibid.: 155). Justice, allegedly so quintessentially English, is associated with other virtues summed up thus:

> In philosophy it is our empiricism, our impatience with metaphysics, our taste for logical positivism rather than for castles in Spain. In law, our elaborate system of safeguards of the individual against state injustice.
>
> (Fowles, 1964:161)

Fowles associates England with greenness and the kind of instant justice meted out by the Robin Hood of mediaeval legend. So this 'green' Englishness is first and foremost an emotionally based attitude, a constant disinclination to side with those in power, crushing the individual in the process, suspect qualities attributed to red-white-and-blue Britain instead, described in these terms:

> What is the Red-white-and-blue Britain? The Britain of the Hanoverian dynasty and the Victorian and Edwardian ages; of the Empire; of the Wooden Walls, and the Thin Red Line; of 'Rule Britannia' and Elgar's marches; of John Bull; of Poona and the Somme; of the old flog-and-flag public-school system; of Newbolt, Kipling, and Rupert Brooke; of clubs, codes, and conformity; of an unchangeable status quo: of jingoism at home and arrogance abroad; of the paterfamilias; of caste, cant, and hypocrisy.
>
> (Fowles, 1964:156)

Against the despised British writers Fowles puts Norman Douglas, Robert Graves, Byron, D.H. Lawrence and Lawrence Durrell, voluntary Robin Hood exiles fleeing the 'double talk of the homeland' (ibid.:157), and adds to these Fielding, Smollett, Jane Austen, the Brontës, Lawrence (again!) and Forster, all of these metaphorically 'green' English writers.

Fowles does not have much patience with the 'Celts' who, with England, make up the UK. The Irish, the Welsh and the Scots get short shrift:

> The Scots, Welsh, and Irish are no more (or no less) English than the Australians and the Americans. There are in the United Kingdom the additional factors of geographical proximity and shared institutions; but that is all.
>
> (Fowles, 1964:156)

Distinguishing between an emigration – Fowles avoids the word 'colonialism' – based on an English urge devoted to the 'spreading and maintaining of our concept of justice' (ibid.:157) in contrast to the British wish to 'spread and maintain imperialistic and master-race ideals' (ibid.), Fowles makes a plea for an England, once stripped of global power as has been the case since World War Two, to set an example as a kind of umpire nation, able to see through the law, always looking for justice.

Seamus Heaney's Beckman Lecture, given at the University of

California, Berkeley, in May 1976, explores different kinds of Englishness in the poetry of Ted Hughes, Geoffrey Hill and Philip Larkin. Heaney says of the three poets that, despite their obvious difference in most respects,

> All of them return to an origin and bring something back, all three live off the hump of the English poetic achievement, all three, here and now, in England, imply a continuity with another England, there and then. All three are hoarders and shorers of what they take to be the real England. All three treat England as a region – or rather treat their region as England – in different and complementary ways.
> (Heaney, 1980:159)

Heaney attributes to each of the three a certain period in English history – to Hughes the bardic Anglo-Saxon, to Hill the scholastic Middle Ages, to Larkin clinical modernity – to which they relate for their specific kinds of Englishness. Borne by Heaney's propensity for writing mood-suggestive rather than fact-recording prose, his essay explores English echoes, drawing a double conclusion, one suggesting the reason for a heightened awareness of England, the other using Donald Davie's *The Shires* as additional evidence for pointing to an identity crisis and introversion caused by the first:

> The loss of imperial power, the failure of economic nerve, the diminished influence of Britain inside Europe, all this has led to a new sense of the shires, a new valuing of the native English experience.... English poets are being forced to explore not just the matter of England, but what is the matter with England.
> (Heaney, 1980:169)

If Byatt, Fowles and Heaney are essentialists trying to locate and define in positive terms what it takes to be English, Robert Crawford (1993), while sharing a desire to deconstruct the UK into its constituent parts, chooses a differential approach for the definition of his 'identifying poet'. Identity being a central modern obsession, there can be no sense of identity without an accompanying sense of difference, for which he signs on Bakhtin as his theoretical guide. At the intersection of two languages – three if we include Gaelic as well – Scotsmen have a culture-given advantage by being able to apply, indeed not being able to help applying, the differential view: 'They become double-voiced, acting out a dialogue between Scots and English' (ibid.:7). But the sense of local identity is not just a matter of geography, of interacting with significant others placed elsewhere, it is a dynamic in time as well:

> For regional and national identities are never fixed, but are fluid, part of an ongoing dialogic process whose every articulation is open to a different and transforming response. This means that there is no essential, unchanging Scotland, England, America, Australia, or New Zealand. Instead, there are Scotlands, Englands, Australias, Americas, New Zealands. For identity is dynamic, it alters; and the 'identifying poets' who come to be taken as spokespeople for these territories evolve for themselves voices which may often appear dynamically different from those of their local predecessors.
>
> (Crawford, 1993:13–14)

The identifying poet, for Crawford, is the poet with a strong sense of home, a sense which can only be honed by constantly contemplating the differential other in terms of time and place. It is indeed wholesome to be reminded of time as an identity parameter just as identity-determining as that of space. No doubt representations of England inherited from a pastoral tradition and cultivated as such in the Georgian poetry of the early twentieth century have persisted in minds both inside and outside England. The 'shires' image of England as invoked in, for instance, Edward Thomas's often quoted 1915 poem 'Adlestrop' is an image taken for granted as the ultimate justification of an English way of life worth dying for in Rupert Brooke's sonnet 'The Soldier' from 1914. Compare the final stanza of Thomas's well-known poem with the concluding verses of Brooke's even better-known, and, to some readers, infamous sonnet.

When Heaney cites Larkin's poem 'Going, Going' of 1972 to the effect that the poem is evidence of the poet's anxiety concerning apparently merciless and progressive industrial exploitation in England, he fails to notice that Larkin's discourse rings embarrassingly hollow because of its highly selective, cliché-ridden representations of an idyllic and socially harmonious England that probably never was. Larkin's display of nostalgia stands out for what it is when compared to Pat Barker's regionally English, historical novel trilogy that sets out to give the 'other' a chance of being heard. In a context of Edward Thomas, Rupert Brooke and Philip Larkin, this passage from *The Eye in the Door* (1993) from the trilogy containing also *Regeneration* (1991) and *The Ghost Road* (1995) is indeed a corrective:

> One of the ways in which he felt different from his brother officers, one of the many, was that *their* England was a pastoral place: fields, streams, wooded alleys, medieval churches surrounded by ancient elms. They couldn't grasp that for him, and for the vast majority of the men, the Front, with its mechanization, its reduction of the individual to a cog in a machine, its blasted landscape, was not a contrast with the life they'd known at home, in Birmingham, or Manchester or Glasgow or the Welsh pit villages, but a nightmarish culmination.
> (Barker, 1994:115–16)

As Crawford suggests, temporal adjustments to any notion of identity, as here regionally English, must necessarily be made. Taken to its logical conclusion, Crawford's differential intervention is, of course, just as tautological as its essentialist other, but as a reminder that identity is always a matter of give and take, Crawford's is a welcome contribution to what often seems to be a mere repetition of stereotypes of representation, even if proffered with the persuasive eloquence of a Byatt. While one hesitates to suspect as internationally oriented an author as Antonia Byatt of culturally radical Little Englanderism, the launching of an anthology of stories along strictly pre-union with Scotland and Ireland borderlines of course accommodates a separatist climate latently existing and politically enhanced with the Labour landslide election of 1997.

Robert Crawford's aim in his study, published in 1992, prior to his Bakhtin-promoting and theorising turn in his 1993 publication, is to argue in favour of distinctly regional differences within 'English' literature on the premise that if, deliberately or not, we totalize all the constituents of English Literature, and if, as both traditional literary history and post-structuralist criticism have done all too often, we ignore matters of local origin, then we perform an act of naïve cultural imperialism, acting as if books grew not out of particular conditions in Nottingham, Dublin, St Lucia, or Salem, Massachusetts, but out of the bland uniformity of airport departure lounges. The act of inscription is not a simple entry into the delocalized, pure medium of language; it is constantly, often deliberately, an act which speaks of its local origins, of points of departure never fully left behind.

(Crawford, 1992:7)

Crawford's two targets, both identified as 'English', are an 'Anglocentricity' as a 'phenomenon particularly located in the London–Oxbridge nexus of our own time, and, in earlier ages, in London as the seat of the Court, the place to which the eighteenth-century teachers of Rhetoric looked for their standards of language' (ibid.:13), and the fact that English literature is often used more of less synonymously with 'English-language writing' (ibid.:15).

Crawford chooses to focus on regionalism, with the 'region' as a segment recognisable by historical and cultural unity. What such small or vulnerable groups need

> is not simply a deconstruction of rhetorics of authority, but a construction or reconstruction of a 'usable past', an awareness of a cultural tradition which will allow them to preserve or develop a sense of their own distinctive identity, their constituting difference.
>
> (Crawford, 1992:5)

Taking cognisance of the fact that to Crawford the centre–margin dichotomy is not a static but a dynamic tension,[7] the project undertaken is not very different from the kind of study carried out by post-colonial and gender studies: on the re-examination of empirical data – literary texts – in a perspective that favours the traditionally marginal rather than the traditionally central, literature may yield messages different from the ones that we have become used to. Thus Crawford has attempted to remain alert to nuances of cultural politics embedded in most of the works discussed, nuances which set them apart from Anglocentric assumptions but which are ignored when these texts are read in an unexamined context of 'English Literature'. For some, my readings may appear eccentric, but this 'ec-centricity' is deliberate, a gesture designed to make us aware of issues too easily suppressed.

(Crawford, 1992:6)

Crawford's application of the post-colonial perspective to Scottish literature is symptomatic of the separatist trend reinforced by the possibility of the establishment of an independent North Sea oil-based economy, a separatist trend strong enough to be recognised politically as one of the planks in the platform giving access to No. 10 Downing Street in 1997. Crawford's well-argued attempt not only to define specifically Scottish literature but also to demonstrate the origin of the concept of 'English Literature' as a Scottish 'invention',[8] is clearly meant to legitimise in cultural terms a more generally political endeavour. However, at the same time as regions within Western nation states are claiming increasing attention, applying to Europe as well as the USA, and nations with former colonial status are building up national identities, the regions and emerging nations find themselves placed between an often very conscious effort aimed at recognising and lending status to the traditionally marginal, at the same time as these same margins are being forced into a global village of shared perspectives and values, a process greatly facilitated by the ubiquity of electronic media. Consequently, it becomes harder and harder for a region to remain regionalised. It is all right for Crawford to dig back into history and detect regional voices silenced or neutralised by a dominant political power, but – and Crawford admits that much – we have to do with a give-and-take system. Political and national hegemony being historical facts, there is no escaping them. They will have forced themselves on less strong communities, and a cultural dialectic will have begun at some point in time. In a world where regions have been left to themselves only because they show no signs of eschewing central dominance or are simply too weak to be interesting for the central power, regress into regional self-sufficiency may turn out to be a wish for a state that never was. The same goes for the situation at the end of the twentieth century regarding the question of an English, Welsh, Scottish or Irish literature in a perspective of 'English Literature', or for British – defined as English, Welsh, Scottish and Irish – literature in a perspective of the literature of other nations and/or regions. And vice versa. It is noteworthy that observers of the literary scene in Scotland and Wales record little, if any, political militancy in poetry, as with Douglas Dunn reviewing *Dream State: The New Scottish Poets:* 'actual politics appear to be seen by most of the poets in *Dream State* as an avoidable chunk of frustration' (1994:23) or with Roland Mathias attempting to assess the situation in contemporary Welsh poetry:

> perhaps the characteristic most widely shared among them is a greater degree of realism, of attention to society as it is, than was common to their elders. Any lament for the loss of Welshness is, inevitably, muted: instead there is an examination of the detritus, of the habits, new and old, of the evolving population, and an attempt at definition of the poet's own place in the continuing evolution.
>
> (Mathias, 1986:123)

The agenda for regionalism proposed by Crawford and – implicitly at least – by Byatt is an attempt to align cultural developments with political history, complicated further by the factor of language. In the case of Scotland there are Standard English, Scottish English and Gaelic. This makes for three overlapping linguistic, hence cultural, domains. This is perhaps more the rule than the exception regarding Europe as a whole: Italy and Germany until the late nineteenth century consisting of independent princely states sharing the same language but with considerable differences in terms of dialect, German also the language spoken in Austria and Switzerland, but again, like Scottish English, variations from the originally politically imposed High German. The case of Belgium, mentioned by Crawford in connection with the early efforts of Paul de Man's wartime deliberations on ethnic cultures, is special, in that one nation has two languages, and Switzerland has four. If Belgium is the example of a nation held together in spite of bilingualism, then Norway is the example of a nation trying very deliberately to develop a language that sets it apart from Danish, the language spoken by the former coloniser of Norway.[9] But, as a rule, the sense of a cultural identity follows language groupings.

If, as regards focus and methodology, studies of regionalist literature share a lot with post-colonial studies, indeed can be said to have been inspired by them, advocates of hegemony dynamics miss an important point about the present state of literature. Crawford is eager to avoid the 'bland uniformity of airport departure lounges', but the airport departure lounge is the symbol par excellence of much contemporary culture, in its negative aspect as the leveller of all national characteristics in favour of a carefully cultivated international atmosphere (although in practice you will find a great many national characteristics in international airport lounges), in its positive as the meeting place of people from all over the world. Travelling and literature have always belonged together; the writer's own travels and those of his protagonists form a category of desire of great importance as a literary energiser. In a concrete as well as in a metaphorical sense, travelling informs much modern fiction and poetry. To be in one place and to imagine another, or to be elsewhere observing foreign natural and cultural mores, to compare with, perhaps to long for, home are ubiquitous literary themes. What Crawford sees in the uniformity of the airport lounge is a contemporary literature characterised by postmodern restlessness and lack of any sense of belonging.

But on the other side of the coin there is the longing for new horizons and experiences and the refusal to be circumscribed by any one location. Modernist classic cases are Henry James, Ezra Pound, T.S. Eliot and, more recently, the migratory experience seems to have accelerated: American poet Denise Levertov was born in Ilford, Essex, and moved to the USA; poets Julie O'Callaghan and Anne Rouse were born and raised in the USA, but moved to Dublin and London, respectively; US poet Eva Salzman moved from the USA to Britain; Jane Duran was born in Cuba, brought up in the USA and Chile, and has been living in the UK for a long time; John Ash was born in Manchester and now lives in the USA, Fleur Adcock was born in New Zealand and now lives in London. Cosmopolitanism seems to be an inextricable part of poetic inspiration in the twentieth century, and the same applies to the fictional imagination.

It is right and proper that we should interest ourselves in literature in relation to the various power struggles obtaining between the sexes, the classes, the regions and the former colonies. Literature offers ample explicit as well as subtle evidence of the use and the abuse of political, social, cultural and sexual force. But we should also be aware of literature as a meeting place – a departure lounge – where a lot of different voices are heard and mix in ever new ways, without necessarily aligning themselves with any culturally dogmatic trends. It is certainly possible to read the novels of Kazuo Ishiguro in a post-colonial light – half-Japanese half-English Ishiguro came to Britain as a boy, was educated at the University of Kent and at the University of East Anglia, where he attended Malcolm Bradbury's creative-writing classes – but surely his is no simple case of the Empire writing back. Then there is Julian Barnes – British-born and educated – setting by preference his fiction abroad, mostly in France, and Martin Amis, Oxford-educated, fascinated by and writing by preference about the United States. Surely they, and many more writers of the travelling class, are not subjected easily to the binary-reductive methodologies of post-colonial or of regional studies.

In recognition of the precariousness of the dogma of polarisation in post-colonial and regional critical orthodoxy, I want to tilt the perspective away from colonised/region-responding-to-coloniser/metropolis to a consideration of what impacts a changing geopolitical situation, nationally, post-colonially and regionally aware, has had on the literary scene in Britain towards the end of the twentieth century.

Intercultural diversity

If cultural phenomena of the late twentieth century showed a marked tendency to make use of all sorts of available experiences and techniques, this only reflects not only a general change in demographics relating to Britain but a general shift in the way people in that part of the world look at the powers that be. In a project carried out by the *Observer* and Channel 4 in 1998 to name the contemporary power Establishment, the results – boiled down to national yielding to global and traditional power structures yielding to high exposure – were startling especially to those fond of traditional stereotypical representations of Britain. No doubt the result of a world shrunken by the media, Queen Elizabeth's giving way to the German Chancellor Gerhard Schröder, is a sign not so much of shifting loyalties as of a sense of international citizenship (*Observer*, 1998:1).

But the creative climate in the British Isles is of course not solely dependent on the impact of voices emerging from responses to a former Empire nation and generally increasing globalisation. Creative energies are released by sense of location and belonging within the isles themselves. A special case here is that of Ireland, whose literary bonds with the larger of the two islands are highly ambivalent. A degree of creative independence from the other British constituent areas is seen increasingly in Scotland and in Wales too, only to a more limited extent. As in Ireland, it is predicated on an indigenous Gaelic culture and language, but, it seems, also, and increasingly, on a growing general sense of the political and cultural constructedness of such notions as 'centre–periphery,' 'central–marginal' and so on, thus encouraging the cultivation of that which may have been assigned by convention to the 'boundaries'. But once the focus is on the 'province' it is impossible to retain a purely regional perspective. As the English north–south divide clearly demonstrates, a social perspective must accompany regional considerations, as must perspectives of ethnicity and gender.

When indeed 'marginality has become a productive space' (Wadham-Smith, 1999:108), that space is somewhere that allows both for the exploration of what against traditional backgrounds is seen as 'off-centre' and for the most individual of cultural mixes, constituted by geographical, social, cultural, ethnic and gender elements – quite apart from the circumstance that literature is hardly any longer generically 'pure' – and most rewardingly explored by keeping a keen eye on the determining forces of one or several of these in the case under consideration.

The present book is not intended as a general literary history of late twentieth-century fiction and poetry in Britain, but as elements of one possible literary history framed by perspective applied rather than chronological order and in recognition of the precariousness of a grand centre-assuming narrative. The great variety of literary voices making themselves heard, the transformation of literary Britain into an international airport lounge (however, anything but bland) and the lack of dominant aesthetic agendas, by some denounced as typically postmodern indifference, by others as a liberating and tolerant atmosphere of pluralism, calls for appreciation and assessment respecting this happy state of affairs. It therefore seems more to the point to write an account of some of the 'small' and decentred literary histories at present making up literary activities in Britain. A change of critical perspective in the direction of the complexities of an intercultural/transnational/transcultural scene is a much-needed complement to much current criticism that seems to prefer to think in terms of rather clear-cut national, social or gender dichotomies. This is not meant as an arrogant dismissal of post-colonial criticism, various kinds of materially oriented cultural studies, or of gender criticism. On the contrary, post-colonial criticism and its sparking of a critical interest in regionalism, and with sympathetic parallel developments in gender criticism and New Historicism, has offered valuable insights and, not least, which is important for the present purpose, served to problematise 'marginal' and 'central' in terms of political, economic, cultural, social and sexual power dynamics.

With chronology and mainstream perspective abandoned as methods of approach it might seem as if a methodological principle of complete randomness is introduced. Certainly there are alternatives to the foci of the individual chapters. But, arguably, the literary aftermath of Empire, the problem of English as language, the subject of gender and ethnicity, the internationalisation of fiction and the use of generic fiction for the construction of immigrant identities are areas that deserve critical attention. Given the restless and searching atmosphere of the 'airport lounge', the need to affirm individual identities is of the essence. The concentration of interest on 'compound voice', understood as the positioning and problematisation of enunciating textual subjects with multiple loyalties, is consequently a rewarding methodological platform when dealing with the specific foci.

Gradually, English and British have come to be seen as notions which are insufficient, perhaps even misleading, in relation to the contemporary literary scene. Post-colonial studies have shown the need for a more comprehensive approach, while on the other hand there has recently been a tendency by regionalists to move in the direction of smaller than nation state units. Doubtless there are minorities within Scotland, or Wales – not to speak of Ireland – to whom even these regions seem too large, and the future debate will be about regional demarcations. Outside the post-colonial and the regional we are facing a reality for which even the tag 'literature in English' may turn out to be too constraining, because English is increasingly a communicative medium detached from any specific national allegiance.

Modern literature written in or relating in some manner to Britain cannot and does not attempt to escape a past of Empire and colonisation. But the current situation is much, much more complex than a binary distinction between an indigenous English literature and emerging literatures in English would allow for. The modern writer, in or out of Britain, increasingly uses the whole world as her or his frame of reference, and refuses to be restricted by geographical, historical, generic, gender, social and market conventions and instead turns the permutations and combinations of all these into works of highly charged imaginative power. If the literary critic sometimes feels lost because his urge to categorise and generalise seems pedantic and beside the point in face of the impressive diversity of present-day literary activities, the reader can do worse than concentrate on the individual work, to sort out, unbiased by ready-made categories or trendy critical theory and practice, its very individual nature and the unique complex of premises on which it builds.

Britain is uniquely situated, in terms of history and geography, to be the catalyst for a rich offering of ingredients to change, by intercultural mergers, into a new and different intercultural literature. To provide the space and the facilities of the international airport departure lounge is a quite suitable literary future for a nation so responsible for the way the world is today.

2
Imperial Aftermath in British Post-World War Two Fiction

> Rather than leaving Britain without a role (as it was glibly supposed to have done), the loss of the Empire was probably deeply resented only by those members of the upper and middle classes who had once felt called to serve it as colonial governors, civil servants, district administrators, and law officers. Its gradual disappearance, together with that of its somewhat exclusive employment opportunities, was steadily compensated for by Britain's gain of a new cultural diversity following the immigration of a large body of workers, both professional and unskilled, from the Indian sub-continent and the West Indies.
>
> (Sanders, 1994:583–4)

With the demographic upheavals caused by globalisation, mass migration and a heightened sense of regionalism within the British Isles, the point of an indigenous or essentialist British literary legacy is increasingly lost to those not seeing themselves as heirs to that tradition. The result is that the British literary manner and morals tradition is being increasingly questioned as a model to be emulated. However, the process of questioning makes canonical British writers interesting not only in adversary roles, which may be actualised either as plainly oppositional literary statements or by insistence on post-colonial national independence, but also as foils against which alternative maps may be drawn. Thus, applying an aesthetics of absences, post-colonial criticism has become increasingly interested in the significance of the absent other in 'all-English/British' works as nonetheless present, but implicitly so as part of the political/social/economic premises on which literary universes are constructed.

The general post-structuralist shift in the critical climate away from a 'great works' approach to a view of literary works and the very concept of 'literature' itself as cultural constructs, which has been in process since the 1960s, has resulted in a shift of focus from the literary versus the non-literary to an interest in textual representation as such, with the 'literary' a cultural concept building upon certain cultural premises. This change of approach being in evidence all over the lit.-crit. map, it has also had an effect on the 'textuality' of Empire and colonialism. The first part of the title of Elleke Boehmer's *Empire Writing: An Anthology of Colonial Literature 1870–1918* (1998) signals clearly this change in focus, with the meaning of 'literature' in the latter part of the title being 'extended' by force of the former. It is indeed characteristically symptomatic of the 'discourse' approach that Boehmer does not find it rewarding or productive to enter into a discussion of literary and non-literary in either her 'Introduction' or her 'Note on the Anthology: Principles of Ordering and Selection'. Instead, the implicit opposition is between that which has seen print – writing/text/literature – and that which has not, and which cannot therefore be retained as articulated voice:

> A chief intention behind the anthology ... was to capture the multiplicity and proliferation of *writing* at the time of empire, and in particular to reflect responses from both within and without the British Empire's centres of power, and from mainstream and less well-known names. *Texts* were to cover a number of key areas of colonial perception, and would be drawn from a range of *genres*, primarily poems, novels, and short stories, but also the *related and supporting discourses* of essays, travel writing, published lectures, political pamphlets, economic analysis, memoirs, and a housekeeping manual. The 1870–1918 framework was broad enough to make it possible to find and embrace this kind of heterogeneity. The period included not only *literature* written in support of empire, or *texts* which give careful or coded voice to incipient doubts concerning the

imperial mission, but also, importantly, *writing* which speaks of the different reality of colonized and settler people, and of their emergent nationalist self-regard, though in many cases they continued to accept the fact of British world power.
(Boehme, 1998:xxxvii–xxxviii; emphasis added)

If Boehme adds to the traditionally literary spectrum a variety of sociological reflections – Dilke, Seeley, Froude and so on – or writings to do with the administration of Empire ranging from policy reports to trivial communications between Whitehall and officials abroad in public service, she also includes fiction popular in its day but largely forgotten by later generations. Whereas explicit issues of Empire do not play a prominent part in the by now canonical novels of Austen, Dickens, the Brontës, Thackeray, Eliot or Trollope, Empire is strongly present in the fiction catering to the contemporary audience longing for sensation and adventure, notably young readers. Explicit nineteenth-century literary interest in colonial possessions seems largely confined to the sensational romance variety of fiction written in accord with Charles Kingsley's gospel of 'muscular Christianity' and chiefly aimed at a juvenile audience, such as the work of E. Rider Haggard, G.A. Henty, R.M. Ballantyne, Captain Marryat, and Charles Kingsley himself. In their tales, Empire is an efficient and colourful backdrop for private and public enterprise overseas, colonial entrepreneurship and the general application of muscular Christianity. In the bulk of this line of fiction the right of the British to wield colonial power remains unquestioned, indeed is in most cases subject to praise.

Coinciding with an interest in literature as a system of cultural conventions not just coming into being as naturally as leaves on a tree but as a kind of deliberately contrived cultural product, writings reflecting on an awareness created in part at least by Empire and colonialism, post-colonial writings began to deconstruct what appeared as the naturally given from the 1960s. Jean Rhys in her *Wide Sargasso Sea* (1966) thus attempted an imaginative alternative exploration of the 'madness' of the woman in the attic so cursorily diagnosed and put away by Charlotte Brontë, whose sole reference to the British Empire was the *deus ex machina* inheritance from Jane Eyre's Madeira-based wine-trading uncle.

So did J.M. Coetzee in his *Foe* (1986), when he presented a gender- and ethnicity-focusing version of Daniel Defoe's *Robinson Crusoe* (1791).[1]

If we have seen an intensification during the last decades of the twentieth century of writings both against the British canon and the values it stands for by writers for national–historical reasons in understandable opposition to that canon, and as a foil for alternative imaginative explorations, there has, after the criticism voiced by E.M. Forster and George Orwell, been a significant post-World War Two development in 'indigenous' British writing to adapt to and come to terms with a post-colonial role.

Pragmatism in popular fiction

Mainstream fiction after World War Two remains expressive of the tight interweaving of the public and private safely ensconced within the coastline of Britain. We do not see much of the by now crumbling Empire in the writing of the 1950s realists. When William Golding in his *Lord of the Flies* (1954) responds to Robert M. Ballantyne's blueprint-for-colonialism, *The Coral Island* (1858) it is with a narrative not touching much on the social and political issues of the model. By then the successors to the Victorian adventure story had been transformed into alignment with the new global power balance, of which the British Empire did not count for much. At the same time we begin to see the beginnings of emerging literary voices from the Empire now being dismantled, eventually to be dubbed 'post-colonial literatures' or 'emerging literatures'. But squeezed in between the dominant canon of enhanced social realism of the 1950s and 1960s, formulaic mass-market fiction and emergent fiction in English from the former 'subaltern' cultures, there is a literary interest in the contemporary situation of the British role in the world to be seen in works of fiction popular in their day but now largely forgotten.

Although Doris Lessing's five-volume novel *Children of Violence*, comprising *Martha Quest* (1952), *A Proper Marriage* (1954), *A Ripple from the Storm* (1958), *Landlocked* (1965) and *The Four-Gated City* (1969), and Lawrence Durrell's four-volume novel *Alexandria Quartet* comprising *Justine* (1957), *Balthazar* (1958), *Mountolive* (1958) and

Clea (1960) are set in colonial surroundings, both works have clearly other central priorities than strictly imperial issues. The same is true of Nevil Shute's bestseller *Round the Bend* (1951), a story about an ecumenically inclined religious revival among aircraft maintenance personnel in the Middle and Far East. But while the reader of that novel may share the slightly puzzled attitude of the narrator Tom Cutter towards the strange religious goings-on on various aerodromes in deserts and jungles, the novel is interesting for the very pragmatic view of Empire aftermath offered by the narrator, who, not quite unlike Robinson Crusoe, carves out for himself a successful life overseas, furnished with the tools of his contemporary civilisation.

Although *Round the Bend* is hardly noteworthy by traditionally literary standards, it is a document of some significance when it comes to assessing attitudes towards Empire at the time when the retreat was sounded for all the world to hear. We learn very little about the actual political situation: the protagonist is interested first and foremost in his trade as a ground engineer of aircraft and, later, as pilot and air transport operator, just as his recollection of the recent war is mainly of hard work maintaining aircraft at home and in Egypt. The only reference to the plight of the Empire is found half-way through the book when the protagonist–narrator Tom Cutter realises that the Australians at Darwin will not let him land and be serviced there because he employs only low-wage Asiatic staff. Facing the unsurmountable obstacle of the colour bar, he tells his Sikh pilot: 'I'm very sorry about this. They've got this colour trouble on their minds here, and we've got the make the best of it' (Shute, 1968:198). The Sikh pilot responds by apologetically pointing to what is happening in his home country:

> 'My people do things as silly, or sillier than this', he said. It was just after the British had left India, and Pakistan and India were at each other's throats and mass deportations of pitiful refugees were taking place from both countries.
>
> (Shute, 1968:199)

But Tom Cutter refuses to see things from a political angle: 'It's economic,' I said. 'They know that we can undercut their rates because we employ Asiatics' (ibid.). The brief exchange of opinions is characteristic of Tom Cutter's attitude both in its summary treatment of events which make the headlines and in his pragmatic reaction. He is solely preoccupied with events which may affect his own situation in relation to the business he is setting up. He has seen an opportunity for his special skills in the combination of demand for transport required by the companies working the Near and Far East oil supplies and the possibility of hiring cheap labour for the operating and servicing of advanced technology. In other words, by cutting through all the taboos of race relations, the NCO type so familiar from the literature of Empire as stay and support has developed into a flexible entrepreneur measuring the world in terms of loss and gain, a businessman for whom race and class are only artificial barriers.

Tom Cutter does not hide his pragmatic attitude, rather he makes a point of displaying it by making numerous references to the economically rewarding combination of air transport expansion and cheap labour, added to which is an instinctive sense of diplomacy and politics, as in this scene, where he is persuading an English manufacturer of aircraft to give him credit: 'If I develop eastwards, then by using Asiatic pilots and ground engineers exclusively, I shall be using the people of the countries that I want to do business with. That's bound to make things easier' (ibid.:60). Where Tom Cutter finds his difficulties is back in Britain. But where black figures in annual accounts and good-looking budgets soon convince British manufacturers of aircraft of the soundness of Tom Cutter's project, it is less easy for the pragmatic pilot to persuade his own working-class people of the wisdom of his chosen path. To his parents' objection that he is employing niggers, he replies that his pilot is an Indian, an army-officer type at that (ibid.:62), and to a prospective fiancée raised on the Kiplingesque gospel of 'East being East and West being West and the twain never meeting' (ibid.:156), Tom Cutter can only answer: 'that sounds like bolony to me' (ibid.), which is also his answer to her assertion that the British will never understand the peoples of the East: 'I get on all right with most people... Asiatics are just the same as anybody else. I've not found them any more different to us than Spaniards, say, or Czechs' (ibid.).

Of much more practical importance, however, are the hindrances put in the way by British officialdom. When the British resident in the Gulf state which is the basis of Tom Cutter's company learns that the local sheik is going to offer Tom Cutter financing of the purchase of another aircraft, he invervenes, but only, in accordance with Shute's as ever well-developed sense of poetic justice, to realise his wrongness in the end. Tom Cutter is just as pragmatic when its comes to class as he is in questions of race. He got his 'education at the fitter's bench, not at a university' (ibid.:105) and never had any need to relate to fellow Englishmen of the governing classes. Only at one time does he give vent to a sense of frustration displaying his view of the social make-up of his country:

> Towards morning I gave up the idea of going to London to argue with the Foreign Office. They would only take the advice of their officials on the spot; I had no prestige, no influence or reputation that would weigh against these foolish people. I was just Tom Cutter, ex-ground engineer, who made too much money to please civil servants. If I had been Sir Thomas Cutter, Bart., deep in debt and divorced three times, I might have commanded some attention in official circles, but as just plain Tom Cutter I hadn't got a hope.
> (Shute, 1968:213)

So where Tom Cutter meets the resistance to his initiatives is in petrified British attitudes for which class makes all the difference – only easily overcome where financial gain is involved – and which certainly seems to live off inertia rather than contemporary reality.

It is always difficult to assess the extent to which the attitudes of a work of fiction reflects the current climate of opinion. If the received wisdom of academic criticism is right, this would be a characteristic of bestsellers, whereas 'serious' literature would be characteristic by going against the grain. Surely, Nevil Shute's *Round the Bend* communicates a view of the world left by the British Empire which is still there for a renewed attempt at financial exploitation, only this time by cooperation and not coercion. Shute shares with the British writers of realist literature of the 1950s – Angry Young Men, Movement and so on – a distrust of the Establishment, but he does not share in the hero-worship of the working class; nor does Tom Cutter, despite his financial motivation, have much in common with John Wain's social climber, and certainly not with Kingsley Amis's confused academic. In his novel, Shute subordinates all issues to the business interest. The story presents itself as one of five books – gospels – written to bear witness to the numinous powers of a half-Chinese half-English engineer. But even these powers are applied to the technological aspect of business, signifying a work ethic involving full emotional commitment.

Tom Cutter's thoroughly pragmatic attitude cuts through mistrust in both the local sheikdom and, eventually, in Whitehall, only to counter obstacles in the provincial working-class environment of his childhood and youth. Whether we may consider Tom Cutter a new-style Cecil Rhodes in pursuit of a different kind of Empire – as a literary type there is quite a lot of the muscular Christian in the aviator – or one who has genuinely solved the problem of alleged cultural irreconciliability voiced in E.M. Forster's *A Passage to India* by proposing free-market dynamics as the cure for uneasy racial relations, is not a point at issue here. What is remarkable, though, is Shute's refusal in this work of fiction to reaffirm the aporia endings of Forster's or Orwell's novels. In *Round the Bend*, the Empire is a matter of the past, only lingering on in a state of inertia in Whitehall and bourgeois Britain as irritants to the enterprising businessman–meritocrat. In a context of the sub-genre of the British novel of Empire, *Round the Bend* signals the reaching of a stage where the Empire matter has been moved into the background as a stage now left behind, cropping up now and then on a par with so many other difficulties impeding private and public progress.

C.H. Sisson's *An Asiatic Romance* (1953) qualifies for the genre designation of its title by its ingenious and fantastic plot relying on the playing of a practical joke: the report to a small party of British negotiators somewhere in Central Asia that England and most of Europe have been wiped out by nuclear war and their consequent fending for themselves in a small princely state where they are the victims of the inversion of traditional colonial power structure – only effective because among those involved there is not the slightest of doubt that information passed along the lines of official communications is always valid and dependable.[2] Insisting on carrying on in his accustomed Whitehall fashion, Sir Bertram Sligh, the senior civil servant in charge of a junior colleague, Dacres, and an NCO, nicknamed Curly, tries not only to placate the local ruler so as to save their lives, but he also attempts to continue advising him with a view to improving his state in the direction of Western civilisation.

The absurdity of the situation, whose full implications only dawn on those involved and the reader at a very late point, assumes Beckett-like proportions when we see the two administrators working strictly by the Whitehall book, not really capable of adapting to the situation. The allegorical implication of this romance makes it a benevolent but nonetheless quite pointed demonstration of Britain's post-World War Two status in the world. But if there is ridicule of the clichés of British colonialism – '"Let's take the least jungly of these fellows," Curly said to Dacres' (Sisson, 1953:17) – and criticism of the inertia of a government bureaucracy out of step with current affairs,[3] there is also a rather harsh exposition of the cruel mores of a tribal community in no way acceptable to Western standards. So the criticism goes both ways, with no heroes on either side.

Different as they may be in a great many respects, Shute's and Sisson's two novels nonetheless share an attitude to Empire as definitely a thing of the past, in both instances pouring heavy scorn on an administrative apparatus out of touch with a postimperial reality. But representations of the wish for a world-leading Britain die hard, as when C.P. Snow has his *alter ego*, Lewis Eliot, in *The Affair* (1960) report from a meeting in 1953 in Cambridge of leading British scientists and civil servants on the future of nuclear energy:

> It was a genuinely difficult situation. In principle, they were all ready for the Cavendish to take on some of the thermonuclear work. Luke told them, though one or two knew beforehand, the minimal facts about it. It was peaceful, he said, no one need have any moral qualms. In fact, the reverse. The only people who need have moral qualms were those who in any way obstructed it. For this, if it came off, would meet the

human race's need for energy for ever. *If this country got it first, it would stay as a major power for a couple of generations.*

(Snow, 1962:148; emphasis added)

If the national nuclear policy plays only a marginal thematic role in *The Affair*, it occupies the centre of the stage in Snow's *The New Men* (1954) and *Corridors of Power* (1964). And if we can rely on Snow to have represented accurately the political climate in Whitehall and Westminster, this would be clear evidence of a nation still very much committed by its parliamentarians to an imperial role. A similar wish for the glory of the past is one of the constitutive thematic elements of Ian Fleming's James Bond saga. Compare the following passage from *Moonraker* (1955):

'The way things are in the world at the moment it was decided that the sooner the Moonraker could give us an independent say in world affairs the better for us and', M shrugged his shoulders, 'quite possibly for the world.'

(Fleming, 1956:68)

Clearly, the seemingly generous but eventually treacherous patriot Hugo Drax was able to deceive the British government by appealing to their sense of post-war geopolitical frustration and fond compensatory chimeras. Whether Bond is assigned to fight the communists, as in the first couple of adventures or, later on, SPECTRE, a commercially inclined freebooting evil power, the explicit or implicit agenda is invariably the assertion of the British despite their diminished global role. Pressed by evil hankerers after world power on one side, Bond as an agent of Establishment inertia has to fight off not only competitors, notably the French and the Americans, on the other side, but also what he and his employers see as increasing domestic 'weakness'. Agent 007 voices his opinion briefly in *From Russia With Love* (1957): 'As for England, the trouble today is that carrots for all are the fashion. At home and abroad. We don't show teeth any more – only gums' (Fleming, 1959:142). But the broadside attack is put into the mouth of Tiger Tanaka, Bond's opposite number in Japan, in *You Only Live Twice* (1964):

You have not only lost a great Empire, you have seemed almost anxious to throw it away with both hands.... when you apparently sought to arrest this slide of impotence at Suez, you succeeded only in stage-managing one of the most pitiful bungles in the history of the world, if not the worst. Further, your governments have shown themselves successively incapable of ruling and have handed over effective control of the country to the trade unions, who appear to be dedicated to the principle of doing less and less work for more money. This feather-bedding, this shirking of an honest day's work, is sapping at ever-increasing speed the moral fibre of the British, a quality the world once so much admired. In its place we now see a vacuous, aimless horde of seekers-after-pleasure gambling at the pools and bingo, whining at the weather and the declining fortunes of the country, and wallowing nostalgically in gossip about the doings of the Royal Family and of your so-called aristocracy in the pages of the most debased newspapers in the world.

(Fleming, 1965:76–7)

With threats and competition abroad and slackness at home, James Bond is supposed both to save Britain – and the rest of the world – from actual threats by evil powers and to put the clock back to imperial time. Despite the change of tone generally and the shift of focus from the enemy abroad to the enemy within, the loss of British world power is one of the distinct generic marks of the secret agent novel after Fleming in British literature. A close reading of both John le Carré and Len Deighton reveals a deep concern for a nation that seems to have bungled a global responsibility and neither George Smiley nor Bernard Samson are willing to let go of such ingrained national virtues as a sense of decency, fair play, moderation or scepticism, even if such at times appear to be worn on the sleeve only by the national powers that be.[4]

Much of the fiction dealing with the British Empire in retreat in the two decades following World War Two, and with an immediate if not prolonged popular appeal, typically in novels by Nevil Shute, Nicholas Monsarrat, John Masters and Alec Waugh, present very sober images of Britons adjusting to the realities of a post-imperial world. As we have seen, Shute combines the energy and initiative of the adventurous Victorian hero with the pragmatism of the self-made entrepreneur making the most of his chance in professional fellowship with like-minded colleagues irrespective of ethnicity or religion, and in the process meeting more resistance from anachronistic Colonial Office red tape than from anyone else. In Monsarrat's *The Tribe That Lost Its Head* (1956) the scene is set for the return to an African protectorate of a British-educated chief designate, who will have to navigate among British colonial officers, fellow tribesmen bent on revolution and, in an impressively precise anticipation of late twentieth-century media culture, the manipulations of the ubiquitous press.

After the growing criticism of the British Empire in the literature of the 1920s and 1930s, in the 1950s and 1960s, when the retreat from Empire was no longer an issue with an uncertain outcome but a fact to be handled with as little general damage as possible, fiction concerned in one way or another with Empire and colonisation generally displays an attitude of remarkable sobriety and pragmatism, ranging from Shute's utilitarian approach to Monsarrat's and Sisson's timely reminders of the diversity and complexity of Empire in the context of a radically changed new world order.

Benefits of hindsight

If the fiction dealing in various ways with Empire through the two decades following World War Two takes the contemporary view, acknowledging the British retreat from global commitment in an imperial and colonial framework, the perspective is significantly altered in fiction – and film – of the next decades, from contemporaneity to one of retrospect and search for explanations of the phenomenon of Empire. But not only do we witness a change of chronological perspective, something happens to the status of Empire as literary 'matter' as well. Paul Scott, in a paper read to the Royal Society of Literature in 1968 and later, in somewhat revised form, read to audiences in India on his lecture tour in early 1972, claimed a double purpose in writing about India, most famously in his *Raj Quartet*. The main purpose of the paper was to give to the British public an idea of their interconnected relationship with the subcontinent, but about which the vast contemporary majority may be assumed to be ignorant:

> It is an ignorance that still persists, and, while it no longer has the same effect, one of the first fruits of ignorance is prejudice and so I am sorry that it does so. I should like to think that here and there in the books I write there are things which, at home, reduce the weight of ignorance, and consequently of prejudice.
> (Scott, 1986:121)

At the same time, though, the imperial matter is transformed into a symbolic force, which Scott acknowledges by answering the question why he, as a modern, serious writer, should have chosen the 'time-expired subject of the British Raj'. His answer goes: 'Because the last days of the British Raj are the metaphor I have presently chosen to illustrate my view of life' (ibid.:115). This indicates a transition of the fiction from an off-centre, generic novel about the Empire to a novel written in the central tradition – even in the sense of Leavis's 'great tradition' – of exploring moral relationships in terms of characters facing predicaments which will precipitate crises universal in nature however specific their origins.

Paul Scott's *Raj Quartet*, its four volumes written in the 1960s and early 1970s and published between 1966 and 1974, is set in India, the plot beginning precisely on 9 August 1942, the tetralogy ending on New Year's Eve 1947, but its coda *Staying On*, published in 1977, taking selected after-effects all the way up to 1972. J.G. Farrell's *Empire Trilogy*, published as *Troubles* (1969), *The Siege of Krishnapur* (1973) and *The Singapore Grip* (1978), singles out three periods and places in the history of the British Empire: Ireland on the brink of partial independence, British India facing Sepoy mutineers, and East Asia overrun by the Japanese during World War Two. Both sets of Empire-based novels are retrospective, bringing in a sense of distance, underscored in the case of Scott by a pervasive elegiac note which is not caused by regret for a lost Empire but rather out of pity for human relations, always difficult but all the more so under the strained circumstances of the British in near-independence India, whereas in the case of

Farrell a sustained undercurrent of sardonic humour lends the three tragicomical 'tableaux', temporally distant from each other and all of them distant from the time of their writing, a mood-determined implication of the eventual uselessness of human striving *sub specie aeternitatis*.

Both sets of novels deal with the theme of Empire, but as a complex situation prompting responses of course determined specifically by the nature of that situation, but also suggesting a certain quality of 'this could happen to anyone anywhere'. The opening of Scott's *The Jewel in the Crown* makes this aspect quite plain:

> This is the story of a rape, of the events that led up to it and followed it and of the place in which it happened. There are the action, the people, and the place; all of which are interrelated but in their totality incommunicable in isolation from the moral continuum of human affairs.
>
> (Scott, 1978:1)

The narrator then goes on to explain about the nature of the setting, the point which he also made clear in the passage from his paper quoted above:

> the affair that began on the evening of August 9th, 1942, in Mayapore, ended with the spectacle of two nations in violent opposition, not for the first time nor as yet for the last because they were still locked in an Imperial embrace of such long standing and subtlety it was no longer possible for them to know whether they hated or loved one another, or what it was that held them together and seemed to have confused the image of their separate destinies.
>
> (Scott, 1978:1)

It is perhaps not too much to claim that the *Raj Quartet* 'reduces' the imperial theme to a complex moral symbol which makes possible the acting out of a historically specific action, yet, in the last instance, with exemplary value.

In all three novels by Farrell the situations are the identical ones of threats to the integrity of Empire either by those ruled by Empire or, in the last volume, by those intent on creating an

Empire of their own. In all three cases, however, the very precariousness of running a good part of the world from Westminster and Whitehall and the terms dictated constitute the theme investigated with an attitude ranging from amused detachment to sardonic humour.

The all-important symbol in the three volumes of the trilogy being the state of siege, which is the very subject matter of the middle one, the British are presented in defensive situations. Like the case of Scott's epic of the last days of the British Raj, the narrative makes the most of the advantages of hindsight and constructs the past in terms of the novelist's Empire-sceptical present.

The Siege of Krishnapur (1973), which may be taken as representative of all three novels, has the structure of many a Victorian heroic romance about valiant deeds by those posted to remote places of the British Empire: against overwhelming odds, British-style civilisation wins through eventually. However, there are elements which mar this Empire routine in decisive ways. The toll taken in the form of casualties, most of them from various diseases, is considerable, a circumstance all the more aggravating because lives could have been saved if the ludicrous – by modern standards – advice of the staff physician had been ignored in favour of that offered by his less tradition-encumbered – Scottish(!) – colleague. Their disputes in the midst of misery and death are in themselves emblematic of the overall contemporary situation of Empire. Just as the ramparts are crumbling under the shelling from the mutineers and the Collector's residency is stripped of its contents (great care is taken by the narrator to describe the state-of-the-art collection of Victorian decorative objects) to furnish shot for the cannon, the self-esteem of the small community is crumbling. The Collector himself is hard pressed to reconsider his faith in the mission of the colonising powers. The Collector discusses the virtues of British civilisation with the newly arrived Fleury, who is a somewhat belated believer in the gospel of Romanticism, according to which '*All* civilisation is bad. It mars the noble and natural instincts of the heart. Civilisation is decadence!' (Farrell, 1973:171). The Collector has just been ceremoniously holding forth, when a sudden occurrence, nemesis-like, forces him to modify his opinion:

'Things are not yet perfect, of course', sighed the Collector. 'All the same, I should go so far as to say that in the long run a superior civilization such as ours is irresistible. By combining our advances in science and in morality we have so obviously found the best way of doing things. Truth cannot be resisted! Er, that's to say, not successfully', the Collector added as a round shot struck the corner of the roof and toppled one of the pillars of the verandah.

(Farrell, 1973:171)

After this point the Collector seems to be losing faith and on the brink of a more complex kind of understanding of 'civilisation' when in the nick of time a rescue detachment arrives in light-opera style and sets back the clock to the tune of the commanding officer's ridiculous cornucopia of patriotic clichés.

Scott and Farrell wrote their Empire cycles with the advantage of hindsight, glancing back at a geopolitical situation definitely over and done with in so far as colonial–expansionist policies are concerned. Whereas an elegiac note is detected here and there, we have to do with clinically conducted literary autopsies to learn about the cause of the death of Empire. If the diagnosis in the case of Farrell is lack of the will to, and perhaps the capability of, continuous adaptation on the part of the rulers to ever-changing political conditions, then in the case of Scott it is surely moral failure, a letting go in standards of behaviour failing to meet the ethical demands implicit in ruling.

If the accounts of Empire could be said to have been made up by Scott and Farrell, in a literary perspective their large-scale fictional retrospects also meant the end of the colonial novel as generic fiction, meaning a branch of fiction devoted to the theme of Empire. As we have seen, in the fiction of the 1950s and 1960s dealing with contemporary matters of Empire and colonisation, that is the dynamics and political reverberations of imperial retreat, issues of Empire and colonisation were already in the process of integration with other thematic issues, making such fiction, although to some extent generic, join the mainstream of the English novel of manners and morality. After Scott and Farrell, fiction did not eschew the theme of Empire, but either made it part of a larger whole if treated in a strictly British context, that is by British writers, or, as we shall see in Chapters 5 and 6, something which has contributed to the launching of a new kind of novel neutralising national boundaries in terms of geography and history.

A detached and analytical view from the 1990s

Towards the end of the twentieth century, with the Empire being definitely a thing of the past, with a very concrete aftermath of Empire in the form of massive immigration from all over the world into Britain, with globalisation at the top of the current agenda, and with Westminster-propelled but Whitehall-reluctant quasi-national status granted to the four regions of which the UK is made up, the tendency in fiction has been to re-evaluate the premises of former British ascendancy. Pat Barker has done so in relation to aspects of the social history of the World War One in her *Regeneration* trilogy (1991–5), Kazuo Ishiguro in relation to the dark chapter of British fascism in his *The Remains of the Day* (1989). An attempt at a sweeping glance from a Scottish vantage point was made by Allan Massie's *Shadows of Empire* in 1997.

Massie's novel tells the story of the break-up of an intellectual, upper-class English–Scottish family over a period of just over fifty years, beginning in the mid-1920s. In his ripe age the distinguished grand old man of British journalism Alec Allan reminisces on his life in family and world-political turbulence, with the decline of the role of the British reflected in the decline of his family. As the British Empire reached its culmination in the Victorian era, the foundation of the family fortune was made by Allan's great-grandfather, a Glasgow shipbuilder, only to diminish from then on. Allan's father led a life as politician and writer, not reaching the heights in either capacity but not doing badly either. When Allan receives the latest – and no longer very generous – royalty cheque for his father's *Corners of Foreign Fields*, a book celebrating the history of the British Empire, his memory is triggered. Perhaps the source for Allan's comment is the TV serial version of Scott's *Raj Quartet*, *The Jewel in the Crown*, with its substantial contribution to the heritage industry in British entertainment:

> The television success of *Corners* surprised many. I can't think why. It was just the sort of thing, half-true, half-trashy, bitter–sweet, nostalgic, sentimental, to be a popular success even in its third manifestation – book, film, serial on the telly. This last time round it fed a mood which was already established – regret for the days when Britannia ruled the waves, and the flag flew over a world-wide Empire – a mood which Mrs Thatcher may be said to incarnate.
>
> (Massie, 1997:1)

Nonetheless the preoccupation with the causes that led to the retreat from Empire is of central importance to the narrator. It need not have developed this way, and the narrative is devoted to seeking out the causes by placing Allan, as foreign correspondent of a British newspaper, in the midst of the world events that came to shape Britain's twentieth-century global role.

In a family gathering in 1934, when fascism is also a fact of domestic political life in Britain, Allan's father baits Toby, a young doctor and school friend of Allan's, about the situation in Scotland, where the quasi-fascist National Party is also gaining way slowly:

> 'Every Scot', [father] said, 'is, as dear old Rosebery put it, a Jacobite at heart, and a revived Scotland, within the Empire, would be a fine thing. I see Scotland as a self-governing Dominion within an Imperial Federation. Why shouldn't the Duke of York become Prince of Scotland and live at Hollyrood House? He has, after all, a fine Scottish wife.
>
> (Massie, 1997:82)

This tongue-in-cheek authorial anticipation of the devolutionary measures put into practice at the time of Massie's writing of the novel suggests a possibility of imperial future within a Commonwealth setting, not so different from what the aged narrator is witnessing, but this time within the European Community. Concerned with the political situation of Britain during the traumas of the two world wars and watching his three brothers' pursuit of different paths to create personal platforms with symbolically representative relations to the political past, present and future of Britain – one chooses to embrace fascism, one sets up private enterprise in the Far East, and one serves the British government in high civil service office but works, mole-like, for Soviet-style communism – Allan suggests a diagnosis of moral failure confronting those building up new Empires in the inter-war years and confronting the issues within the British Empire itself. The question pursued by Allan throughout Massie's novel is 'what caused the demoralisation of the Establishment' (ibid.:190) discernible as a 'disinclination to look reality in the face' (ibid.:191), a view put forward already in 1946 by an old French (!) professor of ethnology:

> 'You English', he pronounced with ancient malice, 'with your empiricism and your incapacity for abstract thought, do you suppose your Empire will endure? In twenty years it will have been swept away, for you have lost the will to govern and will sell it for American gold. And where will you be then? Will you be ready to become Europeans, or will you withdraw into dreams and mist?'
> (Massie, 1997:327)

And just a year afterwards, in 1947, there is Toby's eager effort to understand the apostasy of one of Allan's brothers to fascism. What he fell prey to was an *idea*, so alien to the English cultivation of the pragmatic. Perhaps the cause of the alleged demoralisation is to be found in the unwillingness to see anything else than *Realpolitik*, as Toby puts it, talking of his Scottish national background:

> We like to think of ourselves as hard-headed practical men, building the railways and bridges of Africa, and Asia and America, traders, manufacturers, and engineers, servants of the Empire and the rest – though that last one is a giveaway, for the Empire has been important as an Idea as much as a Thing.
> (Massie, 1997:348)

Massie's *Shadows of Empire* may be read as an anatomy of alleged British failure to face reality. But since dealing pragmatically with reality has been the British way, and that way having now led to ruin, the failure is really to be found in the lack of a larger framework in which to see the larger situation at any given time. Allan remembers when he realised the failure of Churchill to look to the Empire in any other way than partnership in the war effort against Germany.

In the perspective of the Empire theme Massie's novel is remarkable for the way it puts under scrutiny a political development, whose course into retreat from Empire and granting of national independence to former colonial regions has been taken as one of the never-questioned, 'grand narratives' of the twentieth century. The view aired by the elderly foreign correspondent implies, in terms of political reality, a revisionist perspective and, in terms of fiction, as the vehicle of discussion of that reality, an urge to elevate the English novel to a level that contradicts any accusation of parochialism.

I should not like to complete this chapter on imperial representations in literature without mentioning the rather peculiar retrospect of Empire offered by George Macdonald Fraser in his Flashman epic (1969–90) featuring an unashamedly chauvinistic and less than well-behaved British upper-class colonial cad, acting in various events crucial to the history of British India. Noteworthy is the way the Flashman stories reveal in full detail what E.M. Forster dared only hint at in his *A Passage to India*, that not all of those who extended and maintained the British Empire were of first-class human material. Although the Flashman novels are hardly written as seriously intended critiques of Empire, they indicate a growing irreverence for a past still considered sacrosanct by many. A more satisfactorily literary exercise in the revisionist vein is the novel *Ladysmith* by Giles Foden (1999). It is about the siege of the town of Ladysmith in South Africa during the Boer War, but seen from the perspective of those suffering the ordeals of a kind of warfare that did not distinguish, gentleman-like, between soldiers and civilians. Against the background of gory suffering, the young Churchill is made to run to and fro, cultivating his own political ambitions with no consideration of the atrocities on either side. With Fraser and Foden the debunking of imperial myths seems to have adopted a new and harsher tone.

As I shall argue in Chapters 5 and 6, significant developments in British fiction of the last couple of decades of the twentieth century can be shown to relate to the theme of Empire, either by integration in the British novel's traditionally moral domain, Leavis's 'great tradition', or by an urge to meet the world outside the home ground, by 'going international'. In both cases we have to do with developments growing out of the gradual integration of the Empire theme into the canon of twentieth-century British literature after its virtual absence, or at least marginalisation, from the nineteenth-century canon.

It is indeed hard, and perhaps there is after all no point in doing so, to distinguish between what may be construed as displacements or projections of a former imperial/colonial commitment and the globalisation to which not only Britain but also the rest of the world has been subject during the twentieth century, a development of course considerably enhanced by the revolution of communication and the media caused by vastly improved electronic facilities towards the end of the century. Nonetheless, British history and English language, having been so much more than a restricted national history and a regionally spoken language, have made 'Britain' and 'British' frames of reference at one and the same time, but not in the same way for all involved, readily accessible and desperately inescapable.

3
Verbal (Pre)Occupations

> There's always that point where
> the language flips
> into an unfamiliar taste;
> where words tumble over
> a cunning tripwire on the tongue;
> where the frame slips,
> the reception of an image
> not quite tuned, ghost-outlined,
> that signals, in their midst,
> an alien.
>
> (Imtiaz Dharker, 'Minority',
> in Astley, 1994:47)

In his 1992 survey, 'Poetry for the '90s', for *British Book News*, Peter Forbes reports that 'some see as a superleague' in British poetry since the 1960s the four Hs – Seamus Heaney, Ted Hughes, Toni Harrison and Geoffrey Hill – joined by Caribbean Derek Walcott and Australian Les Murray (1992:671). To name any selection of names a 'superleague' is, as evidenced by Forbes's cautious wording, hardly unproblematic after decades of canon debate. Even if we disregard this aspect, there is in any case a problem concerning the use of 'British' to designate the four Hs, since Heaney has deliberately chosen the Irish Republic rather than his native Northern Ireland as his place of residence.

Perhaps the metaphor from sports to be used in the case of contemporary poetry is not as misplaced as it first might seem.

British poetry since the 1960s has been thriving in a competitive system, from which explicit ranking may have been absent, but which has indeed shown the signs of such. In no other country are there so many poetry competitions, and in no other country do we see such deliberate efforts to market the 'product'. Even the cultivation of lists by the established publishing houses and the club-like structure of the impressive number of independent and very often extremely small poetry presses gives the impression of teams playing against each other. Also performance of poetry has a high priority in Britain, generally backed by a public or private sponsor. When we add the literary historian's craving for order and categorisation, the net result resembles the world of sports with its leagues, books of records, halls of fame, teams and general competitive spirit.

This is hardly a view which would be recognised, not to say welcomed, by many poets, since poets have traditionally been the most individual of writers. Nonetheless, the sponsorship by marketing groups – publishers, presses, journals dedicated to poetry, poetry book clubs, arts councils national and regional, and so on – combined with 'fan clubs', the best organised of which are the various branches of literary history and academic criticism, have drawn in the direction of canon-making rather than away from it. The result is that Forbes's survey, like so many others of the kind, is symptomatic of the wish both to set up teams and to market their games.

If, then, the four Hs plus Walcott and Murray are to be seen as the superleague of the latter half of the twentieth century, there must be some minor leagues, each with the hope of eventually winning the cup. Books of record are plentiful in the form of anthologies, and those in charge of the anthologies have been able to set the standards and determine the setting up of the games. This has been the case quite conspicuously with the group of poets establishing themselves both as leading poets and as 'brokers' of poetry by virtue of their offices as editors, commentators and so on. Craig Raine, Andrew Motion, James Fenton, Christopher Reid and Blake Morrison have surely made their marks as a distinctive 1970s and 1980s grouping, characterised by Forbes in his introduction to the *Poetry Review Special Issue* presenting (marketing!) their successors, the twenty-strong so-called

New Generation poets as strongly interlinked with 'each other and with a tradition [offering] basically, the Movement plus visual fireworks' (1994:4). Although not explicitly stated, the tradition referred to by Forbes in connection with Craig Raine and company could be said to be Auden rather than Eliot, with a strong admixture of the 'native' Englishness of Edward Thomas, looking back via Wordsworth to Neoclassical (elegiac) poetry. Surely, among the New Generation Poets traditional loyalties are very much present, but an international orientation is at the same time very discernible.

Language-reflected regionalism

In Seamus Heaney's 1976 Beckman Lecture at the University of California, discussed in Chapter 1, the poet distinguished between three kinds of Englishness represented by Ted Hughes, Geoffrey Hill and Philip Larkin. To the first he attributes the 'northern deposits, the pagan Anglo-Saxon and Norse elements' (1980:151), to the second the 'early Latin influence; his is to a certain extent a scholastic imagination founded on an England that we might describe as Anglo-Romanesque' (ibid.), and to the third the

> English language Frenchified and turned humanist by the Norman conquest and the Renaissance, made nimble, melodious and plangent by Chaucer and Spenser, and besomed clean of its inkhornisms and irrational magics by the eighteenth century.
> (Heaney 1980:151)

This seems to be a fair description of the linguistic reflections of cultural-epoch-derived kinds of Englishness characteristic of the three poets, but equally characteristic, however, is the relative lack of markedly regional specificity in their work. Rather, we have to do with vague and mythologised settings: Hughes's Yorkshire, which serves the purpose of being civilisation's other, Hill's King Offa country and other time warps with which to contrast with regret the modern world, and Larkin's ubiquitous suburbia, which is a state of mind, not any real location. Nor does the language employed by any of the three poets display regional attachments, but it reflects the contemporary state of linguistic standards. As such, the poetry of the three is representative of the general urge to 'purify the dialect of the tribe' in the direction of a linguistic lowest common denominator serving the purpose of maximum communicative capacity, not only in England proper, but in Great Britain as a whole and ultimately with a view to the global status of English.

Heaney claims an effort on the part of the three poets to confirm linguistically, and with long cultural echoes, an 'identity which is threatened' (ibid.) by the general tendency towards globalisation. But it is a confirmation, then, which in its almost metaphysical embracing of nationhood has done away with any concretely regional markers, at least in the 'standard English' employed in lexicon, syntax and orthography. The urge towards a uniform linguistic mode of expression, which is strictly English only by occasional referentiality but otherwise urban in origin and quite cosmopolitan in range, seems to have determined the development of poetic language over the centuries just as it has language registers for other uses. Strayings from this mainstream have been considered intentionally humorous, as in the Low Scots poetry of Robert Burns.[1] However, along with the effort on the part of Hughes, Hill and Larkin to catch the spirit of English, as Heaney would have them do, there has been a movement, increasingly making itself heard over the last few decades of the twentieth century, to re-establish linguistic ties with regions.

The linguistic reorientation and readjustment in the poetry written in Britain can be seen as a reaction against the centralism of which the uniform English of the canonical poets may be taken as just another expression. Given the relatively strong tradition in Ireland since the Irish Renaissance for keeping Irish (Gaelic) as a living language, it is not surprising that Irish poets, though bilingual, insist on writing in the traditional language of the island. This would perhaps not be interesting in relation to my topic here, since Ireland is an independent republic with inhabitants free to choose the language of their liking. But of course the century-old enforced relations with Britain and hence the *de facto* rule of English as the dominant language, with Gaelic more or less being kept alive by artificial aspiration (by local enthusiasts as well as EU decrees), make for a curious linguistic situation. Paul Muldoon's translations of Gaelic poems by Nuala Ní Dhomhnaill are evidence of a complex cultural situation which signals both a will to safeguard a threatened linguistic species and a need to communicate with a wider audience than the limited one of those – and not all Irish citizens do so – who understand and appreciate Gaelic. This would not be different from the situation of any other minority language in relations with a wider audience, but for the existence of the close cultural and linguistic relations between England and Ireland. When Dhomhnaill wants to eat her cake and have it, she thereby sends a political message no matter the actual contents of the specific poem. Printed in Gaelic original and English translation, her poems stand out with a double message not to be missed.

In the case of Gaelic versus English we have to do with two different languages, spoken in an area united by political and cultural history. But when we speak of regions, we have to do with dialects and sociolects which may be wide apart from each other, but in principle understood by all speakers of English. Low Scots may be considered such a dialect, since it differs in lexicon rather than in syntax or morphology from 'standard English'. Although regionalism has been gaining ground as a theme in British poetry of the last few decades of the twentieth century, linguistic representation seldom (with the few but very much attention-catching Gaelic/English poems as a notable exception) is found in a theme-supporting role. Scottish poets are adept shifters of linguistic register, as we see in the case of W.N. Herbert. In 'The King and Queen of Dumfriesshire' the orthography is standard English, whereas in his 'Riddle to my Wife in Brazil' the orthography is adapted to reflect Low Scots:

> Why is ut that we anely seem tae meet
> at a narra hoose wi nae windies
> an twa wee doors at either end?
>
> (Forbes 1994:108)

To write poetry in Low Scots may serve either to enhance an atmosphere of a certain local geniality or it may indicate a political point, carrying on where Hugh MacDiarmid left off.

But although British poetry has been showing an increasing awareness of the regional, the attachment is to be found in the signified rather than the signifier, as in the Welsh poetry by R.S. Thomas, or in Linda France's description of her family's moving south in 1962 when she was a child and her consequent difficulties of linguistic acclimatisation:

> To survive, I had no choice but to try
> To make my mouth echo back their fat *ain'ts*,
> . . .
> But discovered I'd also lost, mid-flight,
> My native accent I thought was bone.
>
> In its place was this anonymous voice,
> That sounds, to me, as if it belongs to
> Someone else
>
> ('North and South', in Astley, 1999:96)

Linda France's experience seems to have been made within England, but there is a parallel in Eavan Boland's poetic recording of going to England from Ireland in 1951:

> barely-gelled, a freckled six-year-old,
> overdressed and sick on the plane,
> when all of England to an Irish child
>
> was nothing more than what you'd lost and how:
> was the teacher in the London convent who
> when I produced 'I amn't' in the classroom
> turned and said – 'you're not in Ireland now'
>
> ('An Irish Childhood in England: 1951', in France, 1993:64)

Most contemporary poems dealing with the regional do so in terms of regional contrast, as we see in France's poem 'North and South'. Much of the poetry that concerns itself with the regional does so in terms of political and cultural hegemony, with England dominating Ireland, Wales and Scotland, and within England, with the south and the metropolitan area dominating the north. So the regional tends to make itself heard in themes of adversity or separation, but almost invariably adopting the common language, a paradox exposed by R.S. Thomas in his poem 'Reservoirs':

> Where can I go, then, from the smell
> Of decay, from the putrefying of a dead
> Nation?
>
> ('Reservoirs', in Astley, 1988:28)

Also in the Welsh poet Tony Curtis's elegiac satire 'Thoughts from the Holiday Inn' we are witnesses to the bitter realisation of local–cultural decay, though in this case globalisation rather than the English hegemony must bear the blame. Describing the anonymous nature of the international hotel, to be found in exact copies worldwide, the persona addresses the friend who is also the dedicatee of the poem:

> An in-house movie they choose and relay
> To each room in American and English – God forbid
> The native patois – *(These people down here, the Welsh – did*
> *You say – a language all their own – and ancient tongue? –*
> *King Arthur – well, I saw a movie when I was a kid, sung*
> *The songs all that summer – Danny Kaye – got it!)*
> John, what kind of progress is all this shit?
> They took the coal-miners and put 'em in a coal museum:
> And the people drove down, coughed up three quid ten
>   just to see 'em.
> Tourists one-nighting en route the Beacons, Bath or
> Ireland: 'Cardiff – what's that?' 'The airport . . . it's
> halfways there. I planned to break the trudge from
> Heathrow.'
>
> (Hulse, Kennedy and Morley, 1993:99)

If Thomas and Curtis express regret at having their regions run over by stronger national interests, there are also poetic voices finding fault with the place of their origin, as in Brendan Cleary's poem 'Sealink', when he cuts away any romantic notions to do with being Irish:

> There's nothing vaguely romantic to leave behind,
> just the graffiti sprawl of miserable Larne,
> ...
> & I wanted to escape the daggers behind language,
> the subtle testing our process at teenage discos.
>
> (Astley, 1999:54)

However, his English reception hardly makes him feel welcome after the passage away from the ignoble funnels and towers by Ballymumford, and one may indeed worry about the fate of the persona after this conclusive rejoinder in Cleary's poem 'Slouch'.

> They probe me: 'Mick, do you even belong in this country?'
> I won't slouch too early so I gleefully reply
>
> 'just as much as you belong in mine' ...
>
> (Astley, 1999:55)[2]

When the local dialect is transcribed, it sometimes has a certain antiquarian effect. With unmistakably Wordsworthian empathy, Katrina Porteous paints her portrait of the Northumberland fisherman, whose message to his interviewer is:

> ... 'Hinny, ye'll nivvor see –
> Ye divvin't tell them aa' ye kna
> Or all your stories in a day'
>
> ('Charlie Douglas', Astley, 1999:177)

This is a point already made in the mind of the interviewer watching the old fisherman at the tiller navigating by instinct:

> He's learnt their lineaments by heart
> And mapped the landscape beneath the sea.
> O, I was the blind man, not he
>
> ('Charlie Douglas', Astley 1999:176)

If this poem is not entirely successful, it may be due to the rather heavy didacticism voiced in these lines and to the impression left of ethnographer-doing-field-work. The fisherman's complaint against the trawler fleets playing havoc with the ecological balance in the area is lost to the interviewer who uses the man's bitterness only to cultivate a stage setting as the last of the Romantics.

The north–south divide which has been increasingly predominant with the gradual post-war closing of the mining and heavy industries in the north is a cultural barrier symptomatic, however, of social as well as regional differences. That there is such a coupling of the social and the regional is brought out by Tony Harrison with tremendous efficiency in his 1985 poetic Gray-echoing investigation of apparently pointless hooliganism in a Leeds churchyard, V. In the telling contrast between the educated man's analytical reflection, trendy vocabulary, and polished rhetoric, all implying the south and the metropolitan area on the one hand and the linguistic character of the projected interlocutor's utterings on the other, there is a world of difference:

> What is it that these crude words are revealing?
> What is it that this aggro act implies?
> Giving the dead their xenophobic feeling
> or just a *cri-de-coeur* because man dies?
>
> *So what's a* cri-de-coeur, *cunt? Can't you speak*
> *the language that yer mam spoke. Think of 'er!*
> *Can yer only get your tongue round fucking Greek?*
> *Go and fuck yerself with* cri-de-coeur!
>
> (Harrison, 1994:17)

The urban Leeds dialect is here obviously also a sociolect, used to paint a picture of a young man who, in the course of the poem's imagined conversation, turns out to be a chanceless and permanently unemployed person, whose surplus and unchannelable post-football match energy is let loose vandalising the gravestones. Getting eager to communicate with the interlocutor, the persona even slips into the dialect/sociolect himself, at least for a single line before he switches back into his preferred linguistic register:

'I've done my bits of mindless aggro too
not half a mile from where we're standing now.'
Yeah, ah bet yer wrote a poem, yer wanker you!
'No, shut yer gob a while. Ah'll tell yer' ow . . .'

(Ibid.: 20)

The cultural and social differences between educated/south and unprivileged/north is a leitmotif in Harrison's work, with dialect/sociolect transcription resorted to frequently in order to underline the contrast.

Alternative Englishes

Only two years separate Forbes's survey for the *British Book News* and his introduction to the special issue of *Poetry Review* launching the New Generation poets. But it is quite striking that the earlier essay attempts to categorise criss-cross-wise nationally and generically while displaying obvious difficulties applying 'British', 'English' and 'in English'. Attention has already been called to the inclusion of superleague Heaney as 'British', but 'Northern Irish poetry' (Forbes, 1992:673) gets separate treatment, while Scots poetry does not. 'From the Commonwealth' forms a section heading, and a brief list mentions poetry from Australia, New Zealand, India and the Caribbean published in England – place of publication here the criterion of inclusion – but curiously this section also includes 'leading black British poets' (ibid.), mentioning John Agard and Linton Kwesi Johnson, and going on to black British Glaswegian poet Jackie Kay, bringing in Carol Ann Duffy by way of comparison before going on to 'Asian poets living in Britain' (ibid.:674): Debjani Chatterjee, Sujata Bhatt and Tariq Latif.

The presentation of twenty younger poets in a single package as *the* new generation – between Bloodaxe Neil Astley's no less deliberately epoch-intending *Poetry with an Edge* in 1988 and his *New Blood* anthology in 1999 – has been judged by some to be much too much like the commercial hype marketing that we have got used to in the case of fiction. Be that as it may, the packaging criteria, resembling those of the Booker Prize for fiction with the exception of the last heat, eschewed the national/

regional as well as the generic. As described in the *Poetry Review* special issue, the idea was fostered by three publishers' editors (Bill Swainson, Christopher Reid and Robin Robertson) at the national Poetry Competition prizegiving event in January 1993. They felt that much poetic talent was about and deserving the wider recognition that a well-publicised campaign would give. A panel of judges would select from publishers' submission of 'collections by poets who would be under 40 at 30 April 1994 or who had been published for the first time since 1989 [and who] had to be UK citizens or normally resident in the UK and their work had to be written in the English language' (Forbes, 1994:53).

There seems to be no mention of selection or evaluation terms, apart from the implicit condition that the judges must agree on liking twenty collections of 'more than 32 pages with a spine' (ibid.). Taking stock of the twenty, Forbes initially observes that 'they don't entirely live up to the journalistic clichés of the new pluralism, regionalism, and the rise of the working class voice' (ibid.:4), but display an insistent individualism qualifying as true plurality. According to Forbes, the New Generation poets are postmodern in the sense that their poems are evidence that 'all cultures are now available to add to one's own inheritance' (ibid.:5). Apart from their undogmatic postmodernism (in some of them Paul Muldoon's more deliberately programmed postmodernist agendas have been a source of inspiration) they take their literary inspiration from abroad, many of them citing Elizabeth Bishop as their model, rather than from the English tradition, but when turning to that tradition it is Auden who towers in the landscape of the past. Forbes notes the absence of Afro-Caribbean poets and performance poets but rejoices in the fact that no less than seven Scots poets have found their way to the list, which is only slightly off gender balance with its eight female poets.

For four out of the twenty New Generation poets, however, the UK is not their native country. Michael Hofmann was born in Germany and came to England as a small child with his two German parents. David Dabydeen was born in Guyana and came to England to study. Michael Donaghy is of Irish stock and was born and educated in the USA before he moved to England at the age of thirty-one. Moniza Alvi was born in Lahore and moved to England as a child. In their poetry it is therefore often possible to discern the compound voice which is the result of an intercultural experience or a divided loyalty.

The forming of the New Generation poets group is, of course, an *ad hoc* initiative which only to some extent reflects the total contemporary scene of poetry in the UK. If we turn to Neil Astley's deservedly self-congratulatory celebration of two impressively active decades in poetry publishing, *New Blood*, published five years after the launching of the New Generation poets, the proportion of poets born or grown up outside Britain reflects that of the New Generation poets' twenty per cent – four out of twenty – by roughly the same percentage, ten out of a total of thirty-eight poets. We begin to see the corroboration of an unprecedented tendency in the poetic landscape in the UK.

The Australian poet John Kinsella opens the anthology. He is one of those included in the category of 'born or grew up outside Britain' (Astley, 1999:14), probably qualifying for this anthology by the fact noted in the note of presentation that now 'He lives in Cambridge' (ibid.:15). Kinsella must be said to place himself at one extreme of a line denoting a non-native relationship with Britain. He is Australian, a poet writing in English, choosing Britain for a time as his stamping ground, but not really one for whom the tag 'post-colonial' seems applicable. His is definitely not the voice of a writer of an emerging culture, probing his way for existential settlement. But for the sharing of a common language, Kinsella might have been any other foreigner coming to the UK, meeting a different culture on equal terms, rather like Henry James arriving in Britain a hundred years ago. Although this is not the case of all Australian writers (aboriginal writers being in a quite uniquely different situation) to all practical purposes and for a variety of reasons, economic, political and cultural, Australia, like Canada, has almost reached the degree of independent nationhood enjoyed by the USA, and which makes for global bisection whenever we talk of writing in English – just compare the terms of the Booker Prize, copyright domains and the distribution of writers in anthologies of writings in English on either side of the Atlantic, which seem to function on a basis of mutual exclusion.

However, at the other extreme we have poets like Moniza Alvi, who came to the UK as a small child from Lahore. Her poetry testifies quite openly to unease when it comes to the sense of national belonging, indeed it provides a considerable extent of her subject matter. Her cultural experience of transition is totally different from Kinsella's, and characteristic of that of tens of thousands sharing her Commonwealth citizen immigrant background. And again in her case, 'post-colonial' only partly covers her situation as assimilated UK citizen.

For some of the poets born or having grown up outside Britain an awareness of language is symptomatic. If they have used English as their first language, it will often have been a kind of English reflecting a history and cultural context different from the one(s) prevailing in Britain, so that it feels different from the varieties of English encountered on arrival. It is only natural for them to relate to language as a symbolic order, expressive of personal, existential conditions stressing untranslatability, ambiguity and divided loyalties. Whereas the Jamaican community in Britain seems to have established Caribbean English as the mode of expression for a lot of the dub poetry written and performed within well-defined cultural contexts, others have attempted to straddle British and non-British traditions by cultivating linguistic difference, sometimes between two languages, the Urdu and English of Moniza Alvi, or between two varieties of English, the Creole English and the 'standard English' of David Dabydeen. This group of poets uses language shifts and deliberate, linguistic clashes to probe into and clarify personal experience, but at the same time are perfectly well equipped to tackle subjects in 'standard English'.

Creolised militancy

In most cases the bilingualism practised by immigrants in the UK is unproblematic: English is spoken in all situations requiring communication outside the family or the immigrant grouping, whereas the language of the immigrants' origin is reserved for the purely private situation. The language of the immigrants' origins may be a language altogether different from standard English(es), or it may be some form of English having developed locally; it does not matter, for in either case a distinction between native and adopted language is keenly felt. If the immigrant is bent on integration, he or she is likely to embrace the adopted language and to observe an increasing distance from the original. But the wish and willingness to give up roots and to enter the melting-pot in order to find a place in the country of settlement may be countered by the lack of a corresponding wish and willingness among the hosts, resulting in an experience of a reception less than welcoming. The wish and willingness to integrate may also be more or less absent among immigrants, as seems to have been the case, not only in the UK, but also in the USA and in Western Europe in the last half of the twentieth century, with increasing population mobility in the process of becoming a permanent pattern on a global scale. With increasing numbers of immigrants it is both possible and perhaps more expedient to form groupings large enough to maintain the traditions and identity patterns of their places of origin, language being by far the most important.

The Black Caribbean community is the largest single ethnic grouping in Great Britain (according to the 1991 census; Storry and Childs, 1997: 244), originally immigrating in numbers to meet the labour demands of the accelerating British post-World War Two economy, and since forming a closely-knit community, mainly in London, where the Black Caribbeans make up 7.1 per cent of the Inner London population.[3] Jamaican Creole is the language medium of the reggae or dub poetry favoured by this grouping, which is spoken or sung/chanted and listened to rather than printed and read. In its versions aimed at international consumption, the usual commercially induced disarming in favour of the stereotypes of desire have neutralised its function as a genuine art form of both direct and subtle political and social criticism, not seldom ironic and humorous.

A distinctly aggressive tone marks the work of Linton Kwesi Johnson, underscored by the pounding rhythm that can be heard in his own recordings, but also fully present in the reading experience of the printed version. Johnson is familiar with the simple but efficient rhetorical devices of propaganda, as his celebrated 'Mekkin Histri' fully demonstrates. His goal here is to boost the morale of his fellow countrymen of the immigrant community, to make them feel that they are indeed a force in modern British history. Proving the refrain

> it is noh mistri
> wi mekkin histri
> it is noh mistri
> wi winnin victri
>
> (Hulse, Kennedy and
> Morley, 1993: 183–4)

by a will to success when opposing the police cordons in what in official reports would be termed riots, even to the point of implicit threatening (the burning down of houses), the representatives of government authority are individualised into types forming a political front – 'mistah govahment man . . . mistah police spokesman . . . mistah ritewing man' – identified simply as crooks and fascists. No doubt efficient at stirring a crowd of sympathetic listeners, the text is hardly the best point of departure for the cooperation needed not to make Inner-London Brixton into a permanent ethnic war zone.

Johnson's lyrics are usually transcribed into an orthographically faithful rendering of the performance phonetics. With no established standard orthography of Caribbean English, the space for individuality is considerable. A poet's attitudes to the immigrant-receiving culture are directly displayed in his choice of the length he will go to accommodate the demands of a standard English orthography. In 'Mekkin Histri' only a few concessions are made, as is also the case in a poem such as 'Inglan Is a Bitch' (ibid.:187–8). Here we have a bitter–humorous account of what must be said to be archetypal non-white Commonwealth immigrant experience. The choice of alternative orthography is in itself a demonstration of the wish to reflect a sense of political, social and cultural difference. Maintaining a linguistic identity of difference perhaps serves best to affirm attitudes and values within the peer group. The more the orthography deviates from the norm, the less accessible it is to those used to the norm, and its communicative value is proportional to the rate of deviation. So if lyrics like 'Mekkin Histri' and 'Inglan Is a Bitch' are linguistically aimed at the London-based Caribbean community itself, a poem like Johnson's 'Bass Culture' signals an effort to reach outside the closed ethnic community. The poem is part argument for, part demonstration of, the revolutionary attitude invested in reggae music. The historical argument is found in the introductory lines, in which the 'muzik of blood' is said to be

> black reared
> pain rooted
> heart geared
>
> (Hulse, Kennedy and Morley, 1993:185)

The energy gathered by this history of oppression is let loose in a 'frightful form [and] a righteous harm' (ibid.). In this poem the count of words written in standard English is considerably higher than in the two previously discussed, so – leaving out the possibility of the poet's idiosyncratic orthographic restlessness – we have a text signalling a wish for communication, although in this case what is communicated is a message no less bitter and angry than in other lyrics by Johnson.

Less militant than Linton Kwesi Johnson's reggae lyrics is the humorously articulated warning to the safekeepers of standard English in John Agard's 'Listen Mr Oxford Don'. Here the immigrant puts himself in the situation of a man on the run, with no other weapon than his power of 'mugging de Queen's English' (Allnutt, D'Aguiar, Edwards and Mottram, 1988:5). Resisting arrest

> I slashing suffix in self-defence
> I bashing future wit present tense
> and if necessary
> I making de Queen's English accessory to my offence
>
> (Allnutt, D'Aguiar, Edwards and Mottram, 1988:6)

What is being described in Agard's poem is a simple fact of linguistic life, the dynamic and current adopting by the standard language of words and phrases foreign to it if there is a need for them. The process is slow but inevitable. So the linguistic assertion of Agard's persona is a state of affairs central to the dialectics of language evolution and cultural shifts. The humorous response to the plight of the non-standard language-user is also to be found in Agard's 'Half-caste', in which the argument that phenomena are made up of opposite pairs is taken to deliberately ludicrous and absurd and therefore thought-provoking extremes, like

> when yu half-caste
> yu mean tchaikovsky
> sit down at dah piano
> and mix a black key
> wid a white key
> is a half-caste symphony
>
> (Allnutt, D'Aguiar, Edwards
> and Mottram, 1988:6–7)

Verbal play seems an especially tempting device to those for whom standard English is not the only given but one available register among two or more. That makes standard English in itself 'poetic' in Roman Jakobson's sense of the term, and so a subject of renewed – and renewing – linguistic attention. Agard handles this with gusto, as does Fred D'Aguiar, for instance in his punning 'Mama Dot Warns Against an Easter Rising' (Hulse, Kennedy and Morley, 1993:283), the rising here indicating the flying of a kite. There is, it goes without saying, a limit to the efficacy of this kind of language game, beyond which it turns into linguistic buffoonery and inevitably displays the poet in a way likely to be the opposite of his or her intention. However, most poets writing in orthographic representations of Creole/Caribbean English and connected by full- or part-time residence to Britain seem to prefer a middle way of modes of lyrical address less politically flamboyant than Linton Kwesi Johnson while often deploying humour to bring home their points. A special variety of this is to be found in women's creolised poetry, which will be treated in some detail in the following chapter, but the linguistic aspects of which should be noted under the heading of this chapter.

Both Jean Binta Breeze and Valerie Bloom, Jamaicans living in London, write poetry in which the orthography reflects only the most tenuous relations to any variety of standard English. In their first-person portrayals of Jamaican women in 'Riddym Ravings (The Mad Woman's Poem)' (Allnutt, D'Aguiar, Edwards and

Mottram, 1988:17–20) and 'Longsight Market' (ibid.:15–16) Breeze and Bloom deploy language as an essential part of their strategies aimed at showing the resistance and strength of women in the inferior positions of patient and (poor) customer, respectively. The uncompromising laying on of Creole serves the obvious purposes of identifying the two women in their contexts of national belonging and origin and of establishing contact with a linguistically well-defined audience segment. But, in addition, the humorous effect of the two women's volatile linguistic outpourings is somewhat modified by the realisation, which is the effect on the audience which may not be the primary one, but one also paradoxically implied by communicating poetry by performance, recording or printing, thus inviting outsiders in. To some, however, the insistence on purity of language in the two women's situation may leave an impression of the lack of space and opportunity that linguistic limitation, whether geographically or socially, invariably entails.

The merging of double linguistic loyalties

Using non-standard forms of English, as in the case of Linton Kwesi Johnson, who uses Creole for militant political purposes, is the exception rather than the rule in present-day British poetry. More characteristic, though, of the linguistic quandary of many of those who have another language than 'standard' English is a realisation of language as an identity mould restricting and liberating at the same time.

Lahore-born and London-resident Moniza Alvi writes poetry often featuring her awareness of a dual-cultural background, although poems like the celebrated 'I Would Like to be a Dot in a Painting by Miró' (France, 1993:31) or 'The Bed' (Dooley, 1997:19) place her in the company of cultivators of graceful, humorous verse such as Wendy Cope and Selima Hill. But Alvi often makes her cultural dualism the subject of poetry exploring the losses and gains resulting from leaving and adopting cultures.

A sense of unease and alienation emerges from 'Presents from My Aunts in Pakistan'. Receiving gifts in the form of traditional Pakistani clothes from her aunts back in Pakistan triggers the persona's memory of leaving the country of her birth to come to

England as a small child, followed by a vision of being back in Lahore, with her family, but 'of no fixed nationality' (Dooley, 1997:18). The poem uses her choice of clothing as an effective metaphor to express the sense of being culturally split: she tries on the salwar kameez sent by her aunts, but feels that she can

> never be as lovely as those clothes –
>
> I longed
> for denim and corduroy
>
> (Dooley, 1997:17)

Dressed in her Pakistani clothes,

> My costume clung to me
> and I was aflame,
> I couldn't rise up out of its fire,
> half-English.
>
> (Dooley, 1997:17)

Her sense of alienation and non-belonging is revealed by the word 'costume', normally used about clothes specifically national or ethnic or worn for play-acting. Contrasting the salwar kameez of Pakistan with the denim and corduroy, the standard US-derived youth uniform of the West, the persona calls attention to a cultural difference signified metonymically by habits of dressing. But the mechanism of signification is noteworthy. As signifiers, 'salwar kameez' and 'denim and corduroy' are parallel and presuppose immediate understanding by the reader. So, however foreign the designation 'salwar kameez' may sound, the use of it in this context presupposes the reader's familiarity with the designation in order to be able to appreciate the point of the poem. In other words, the poet, paradoxically as it were, takes for granted the reader's previous assimilation of a phrase in order to make it constitute a thematic contrast. So perhaps, after all, the declaration of 'no fixed nationality' has been subverted and invalidated from the very start of the poem by an apparent linguistic opposition being already dissolved by assimilation into English. The poet's sense of alienation and her double loyalties are enunciated from the already safe position of linguistic inclusion.

A need for safe positions *vis-à-vis* a sense of cultural non-belonging runs like a red thread through much of Alvi's poetry. In the exquisite little poem 'India' (France, 1993:32-3) the huge subcontinent is made manageable by being metaphorically transformed into the landscape of the palm of the hand. The same kind of bodily repossession of the otherwise far too vast and different is seen in 'The Sari' (ibid.:32), in which the distance and difference between India/Pakistan and England is made into a sari which wraps up the body of the speaker, being then her true country.

In 'Hindi Urdu Bol Chaal' (meaning a Hindi Urdu dialogue), language is again the issue, this time explicitly rather than implicitly as in 'Presents from My Aunts in Pakistan'. The writer is here a person 'borrowed from England' (Forbes, 1994:89) and as such not altogether familiar with the various languages of India and Pakistan: 'These languages could have been mine' (ibid.:88). In structuralist and semiotic fashion language is here widened into denoting systems of signification other than the purely verbal ones of Hindi and Urdu: 'there are so many – of costume,/of conduct and courtesy' (ibid.). The desire on the part of the writer is to make her way into the culture that could have been hers, but before which she now stands rapt in admiration but incomprehension, eager for language scraps which may allow her entry:

> At the market I'll ask *How much?*
>
> and wait for just one new word
> to settle like a stone
> at the bottom of a well.
>
> (Forbes, 1994:89)

Also in this poem the unease made into the thematic issue is stilled in the very act of formulating the poem in a language making expert use of facilities of expression in English which includes newly assimilated words like 'chapattis on the tava'. In a way the writer has already understood Hindi and Urdu, because what she is really after is not language itself as a complete, self-sustaining system of signifiers and signifieds, but language as a second-order system, a Barthesian myth, in which language as such constitutes the signifier, evocative of transverbal significance constituting complete cultures:

> It is not you I am meeting.
> It is a sound system travelling through countries, ascending and descending
>
> in ragas, drumbeats, clapping.
>
> (Forbes, 1994:89)

Facing verbal incomprehension by articulating the terms of comprehension is also a way of mastering the unknown or unfamiliar.

In comparison with Linton Kwesi Johnson's insistence on using language as a code to call for cohesion within the Britain-based Caribbean community, and with Moniza Alvi's adoption of standard English to couch her curiosity and longing for a culture of origin as impossible to regain as is the full mastery of its language, David Dabydeen's versatile shifting between Caribbean Creole and standard English combined with his firm sense of literary tradition produces a poetry which straddles two cultural experiences in terms of one another.

Dabydeen directly challenges contemporary British poetry in the opening lines of 'Coolie Odyssey (for Ma, d. 1985)':

> Now that peasantry is in vogue,
> Poetry bubbles from peat bogs,
> People strain for the old folk's fatal gobs
> Coughed up in grates North or North East
> 'Tween bouts of livin' dialect.
>
> (Allnutt, D'Aguiar, Edwards and Mottram, 1988:27)

Into this poetic universe consisting of a Seamus Heaney's poetic archaeology or a Toni Harrison's social awareness, it is 'time to hymn your own wreck' (ibid.). Hymning the wreck of a population brought to the West Indies from elsewhere first as slaves then cheap bonded labour, living a life of hardness, in turn making some of that population seek new possibilities in Britain, seems to be the driving force of Dabydeen's poetry. In retrospect sometimes personal sometimes collective, he suspends the hymn of the wreck between a time and place of origin and a present immigrants' existence in which

> In a winter of England's scorn
> we huddle together memories, hoard them from
> The opulence of our masters.
>
> (Allnutt, D'Aguiar, Edwards and Mottram, 1988:27)

When Dabydeen chooses to write in Caribbean Creole, it is often to present still pictures of local life back in former British Guyana, as in 'The Servants' Song' (Hulse, Kennedy and Morley, 1993:222), 'Nightmare' (Hulse, Kennedy and Morley, 1993:223), 'The Canecutters' Song' (ibid.: 224–5), 'Elegy' (ibid.:225) or 'Coolie Mother' (Allnutt D'Aguiar, Edwards and Mottram, 1988:31). When standard English is resorted to, it entails a shift of perspective not only to the present-day Britain of the immigrated and grown-up Dabydeen. It as if the adoption of the accepted structures and orthography triggers a sense of alienation that turns hymn into elegy. Sometimes this is a matter of purely personal relations, as in 'Catching Crabs', in which the grown persona, now 'writing poetry at Cambridge' (Hulse, Kennedy and Morley, 1993: 221), fears to face the vision of the long dead mother busy cooking in her kitchen because the sight of her will stir his emotions. The use of standard English in this almost Wordsworthian poem is interrupted only a few times, reflecting the cadences of Caribbean Creole, so much more effective when after telling how Ruby and the persona, the two boys catching crabs so long ago in Guyana, have gone to live in New York and Cambridge, respectively. The emotional effect is in no small degree due to the lapse into the language pattern of the persona's childhood language, as in 'Death long catch Ma' and 'I am afraid to walk through weed yard' (ibid.), leading up to the vision of

> Ma
> Working a ladle, slow-
> Limbed, crustacean-old, alone.
>
> (Hulse, Kennedy and
> Morley, 1993:221)

When Dabydeen speaks of the common experience, the language is stripped of any lapses into Creole. There can be almost mockery, not only in the degree of linguistic social correctness, but also, as in the example concluding 'Coolie Odyssey (for Ma, d. 1985)' that follows, in style teasingly reminiscent of high modernist poetry:

> We mark our memory in songs
> Fleshed in the emptiness of folk,
> Poems that scrape bowl and bone
> In English basements far from home,
> Or confess the lust of beasts
> In rare conceits
> To congregations of the educated
> Sipping wine, attentive between courses –
> See the applause fluttering from their white hands
> Like so many messy table napkins.
>
> (Allnutt, D'Aguiar, Edwards and Mottram, 1988:31)

Dabydeen has appropriated the tradition of English poetry and made it accommodate the experience and expressive needs of someone for whom that tradition is not just there for matter-of-course continuation but as an established system of values to be challenged since it leaves little room for voices alien to it. There is no escaping the fact that immigrant poets cultivating language variations which find only limited audiences in Britain – mostly the closed circuits of immigrant communities – will consolidate an outsider status, attracting only the passing attention usually bestowed on ethnographic curiosa. Although Dabydeen can write effectually in Creole, his contribution to creating space in British poetry with its Western legacy is, arguably, to be found in his new inflections of an already familiar poetic idiom, as demonstrated in his long poem 'Turner'.

Dabydeen's 'Turner' (published for the first time in its entirety in 1994), is a poem in irregular sections inspired by the poet's contemplation of J.M.W. Turner's painting 'Slavers throwing Overboard the Dead and Dying' exhibited at the Royal Academy in 1840. Acquired by Ruskin, admiring the bold use of colours and only attentive to its subject in a footnote, the painting illustrates the brutal commodification of Africans, who, when dying at sea, represented only insurance reclamations if lost to the sea.

In Dabydeen's poem the voice is that of the submerged head of a dead African in the foreground, addressing the body of a stillborn baby also tossed into the waves. Both the captain of the ship and the stillborn baby are named Turner in the wandering thoughts of the persona, who exists as disembodied voice only. In contrast to the voiceless Friday of J.M. Coetzee's alternative construction of the events of Defoe's *Robinson Crusoe* in his *Foe* (1986), this 'other' of colonising Western man shows an analytical grasp of the trade and labour conditions endemic to colonisation.

In the persona's universe the difference between the coloniser, personified as Turner the captain, and the Africans, expatriated by force to be sold as slaves, is one of 'logos' versus 'chaos', but here, as might be expected, in an oppositional pair in which the traditional valorisation is inversed, as is plain from this recollection of the persona's happy time with his family:

> And I squat with my two sisters, small as we are,
> I don't know exactly how much in age –
> Though since Turner's days I have learnt to count,
> weigh, measure, abstract, rationalise.
>
> (Dabydeen, 1994:2)

This enforced acquisition of learning is reflected in the verbal dexterity of the persona's thoughts, but is, basically, alien to his own cultural roots. So by his adoption of the English language, he has already appropriated a medium associated with the hostile logos of his exploiters. No wonder, then, that there is throughout the poem a central preoccupation with kinds of linguistic utterance to symbolise simultaneously the persona's being caught in a mode of expression alien to his experience and to highlight, in so far as the words of English will let him, that very situation of alienation.

In Dabydeen's fragmentary history of Western exploitation of native Africans, the mark of difference is the linguistic proficiency of men using language to exert control and mastery. In the climactic section XXIV of the poem it is described how Turner, here the captain of the slave ship, rapes the African boys, accompanying his physical dominance with teaching his victims set phrases in the Western use of language for the purpose of worshipping and redeeming the rapist:

> Each night
> Aboard ship he gave selflessly the nipple
> Of his tongue until we learnt to say profitably
> In his own own language, *we desire you, we love*
> *You, we forgive you*
>
> (Dabydeen, 1994:38)

Exhausted by repeated sexual assaults, the boys are made to appropriate Western metaphysics:

> and we repeated in trance the words
> that shuddered from him: *blessed, angelic,*
> *Sublime*; words that seemed to flow endlessly
> From him, filling our mouths and bellies
> Endlessly
>
> (Dabydeen, 1994:38)

The insufficiency of the logos of Western language to reflect the experience of the victims taken away is underscored by the repeated use of words like 'sob' (Dabydeen, 1994:1), 'laugh' (ibid.:4), 'screaming' (ibid.:8) and so on to describe the inarticulateness of the sufferers confronting the verbal cadences of Western logos. But the inarticulateness which Turner forces into verbal docility has its native African counterpart in another kind of language not, however, described as such. Rather than quoting the actual phrases of the speech of Manu, the tribe's wise old man, only the import of his speech is conveyed:

> One and the same pathway Manu prophesied,
> His voice lowered to a mysterious whisper
> As he told that time future was neither time past
> Nor time present, . . . he gave no instruction
> Except – and his voice gathered rage and unhappiness –
>
> (Dabydeen, 1994:33)

So Dabydeen's 'Turner' is not only a poem about colonial exploitation as a historical fact, but it is also a poem attempting to give an alternative kind of voice to those who in the ears of Westerners are barely articulate. This is a voice combining the sounds of immediate emotional response such as sobbing and laughter and, what is more, a voice capable of communicating what is needed to deal with the past, the present and the future. Within the universe of the poem Manu demonstrates this communicative capability to his audience, whereas the poetic persona, speaking the language of logos, can only convey the general import and sound cadences of the language overheard.

'Turner' is a linguistic construct which by its very nature cannot contain linguistically that which it sets out to redeem. The poetic speaker is one who speaks in wonderfully versatile linguistic inflections of that which is not his, but which has been forced on him, and who, because of this prison-house of language, can only witness from the position of the outsider that which was his.

Standard English and standards of English

Judging from poetry written and published over the last couple of decades of the twentieth century we can note a distinct awareness of regional and/or cultural belonging, at least among those poets who feel that their Britain is not the England taken for granted by many cultural spokesmen. This applies as well to poets with national awarenesses produced by their origins in the constitutive parts of Britain outside England – Scotland, Ireland, Wales – as it does to poets within England but feeling at odds with a tradition formed by the south and the metropolis, and as it does to poets having made use of the passport rights as citizens of the

British Commonwealth to immigrate. Not surprisingly, language is at the centre of concerns having to do with nationhood and regional belonging, and we see two tendencies at work explained by the dominance of a 'standard English' brought about partly by domination, partly by voluntary adoption.

One tendency is to emphasise multicultural Britain in poetry covering a wide range of themes and topics not traditionally associated with what most readers understand by British or, in this case perhaps more to the point, English poetry. The expansion takes us far wider than nation or region, but this aspect is certainly an important part of it. Poetry dealing with culture and experience other than what tradition or the assumption of a cultural centre dictates tends still to be written in an orthography complying with a given standard, and of which the spoken manifestation may vary, but does so within limits for which dialect and sociolect serves as a rather hazy criterion. So on the one hand we have poetry with a centrifugal dynamic to give voice to the national or regional other, while, on the other, it maintains a traditionally centripetal language standard. This is true of most of the poetry written by those poets who see themselves in perspectives of Britain's constituent parts, or within England.

The other tendency is one with its roots in the immigrant experience, notably cultivated by those of Caribbean or Indian backgrounds. For many of them it has been an act of defiance – civil linguistic disobedience – to insist on their varieties of English not only in performance but in print as representative orthography as well. Critical opinions on this practice are, as might be expected, divided. David Kennedy in his critical companion volume to the Bloodaxe anthology *The New Poetry* (1993), simply refrains from subjecting this poetic segment to critical discussion, as, he states:

> I have chosen not to write about Black British or Afro-Caribbean poetry not only because it seems inappropriate for a white critic to do so but because these poetries are still being theorised through perspective of language and difference.
>
> (Kennedy, 1996:8)

Sending a clear political signal of sympathy with immigrants with a non-privileged history, Kennedy's warning of hands-off is nonetheless of dubious value. As we have seen, a simple dichotomy like white versus black is of limited use in modern Britain where the ethnic intersects in great complexity with the regional, the social and the gendered. Quite apart from the patronising attitude of appropriation implicit in the white critic's decision that such a task is indeed inappropriate, the very communicative politics of poetry may be said to defy in principle such a deliberate containment. After all, poetry is written to be shared, and to put an embargo on certain segments of poetic output seems to amount to spiritual dictatorship. Nor is the reason for calling a critical moratorium by pointing to an on-going process of theorising valid. Literature does not stop and wait for the completion of its theory; why, then, should criticism? The complexity and continuity of poetic efforts is hardly to be expected to be brought to a kind of order, to stand still for the critic to gaze at leisure.[4]

A position opposite to that of Kennedy's is held in Gary Day's introduction to his and Brian Docherty's *British Poetry from the 1950s to the 1990s: Politics and Art* (1997). In what reads in many respects like a return to a Leavis-inspired literary–critical ideology of reading, Day argues that the virtue of the poetic effort is to create a sense of human togetherness:

> Literature aims to build a community, not Babel. It is a way of speaking to one another, in a peculiarly charged and formal manner, about the great issues of life: love, desire, passion, parenthood, ageing and death. That these are all class, culture and gender specific should not be regarded as a barrier to our understanding but a means of enriching it. No one can avoid an existential encounter with one or more of these issues and literature is a resource that helps us live them.
>
> (Day and Docherty, 1997:5)

On this premise Day sees the kind of attitude displayed by Kennedy in support of a splendid-isolation policy of specific groups as directly dangerous to the ends of poetic inventiveness as described above. Also the assumption that specific kinds of language should be held to be more suitable as expressions of specific kinds of experience, which cannot be expressed in 'Standard English', is invalid, since it assumes that 'one idiom is expressive while another is not' (ibid.:4). Day maintains that a view like that confuses the political with the artistic (a view, however, probably supported by Kennedy), with the result that 'political imperatives dull awareness of language as material to be worked, thereby rendering us insensitive to its protean possibilities' (ibid.:5).

The weakness of Day's line of argument is in the supposition that 'Standard English' offers at all times a pliable linguistic resource for experiences of a non-linguistic provenance. Accepting that view would mean taking away from a given culture its foremost means of expression, language, making that ancillary to something more important, with which 'Standard English' is nonetheless capable of dealing adequately.

If Kennedy succumbs to the absurd consequences of an attitude politically correct at the time when he wrote his study and thereby, unintentionally however, ghettoises linguistically marked poetry in English, then Day commits the error of extending the imperialist franchise of 'Standard English' as the master language. But neither extreme position seems to be called for. The interaction of cultural and personal experience in terms of poetic language(s) in Britain in the last couple of decades of the twentieth century has extended the space for linguistic interaction and made the whole of this new 'global English' larger as a linguistic resource than its contributing parts, including standard English as the supposedly purified dialect of the tribe.

4
Wholly Female, Partly Foreign

> standing without words
> but without need of them, being at home.
>
> (Jane Griffiths, 'Emigrants', in Astley, 1999:238)

The preceding chapter explored the meeting of cultures in the perspective of sense of belonging and in terms of language, showing how language is not only a medium of communication, but also, as a cultural fabrication inclined to inertia but capable of innovation, a forceful symbol of appropriation and change. Language is the barrier first met by the one attempting to straddle cultures, but at the same time the inevitable channel for any experience that wants communication. Language both mediates and forms experience, and to the extent that new kinds of experience settle as part of the common culture, language is invariably accommodating. But, of course, only up to a point. If the very structure of a given language, or even more radically, of language *as* cognitive structure, is claimed to be insufficient to give expression to experience different from the one that fostered the language, the barrier is indeed unsurmountable. In his poem 'Turner', David Dabydeen made the case for such a lack of common ground, as did J.M. Coetzee in his Robinson Crusoe make-over *Foe* (1986), but in most cases a more pragmatic attitude prevails, with the more moderate aim of creating space in English for a variety of experiences which, each in their way, require linguistic accommodation.

Although the radical measures of a Hélène Cixous and the *écriture féminine* to form a language allegedly better suited to reflect female experience have never found their way into English, there has, since Virginia Woolf at least, been a manifest awareness of the dialectics of (female) gender and language. One notes, however, that there seem to be two schools of thought among anthologisers and critics inclined or forced to concern themselves with this issue: it may either be dismissed as a fake issue or singled out as one of the most significant contemporary issues. In his *New Relations: the Refashioning of British Poetry 1980-94* (1996), critical companion volume to *The New Poetry* (1993) of which he was an editor, David Kennedy joins the former group:

> I have not devoted a separate chapter to women's poetry: to do so seems to me complicit with consigning women poets to a literary ghetto and with perpetuating conceptions of poetry by women as a kind of cultural sideshow.
>
> (Kennedy, 1996:8)

Sean O'Brien in his competitor volume *The Deregulated Muse: Essays on Contemporary British and Irish Poetry* (1998) seems to have been taken aback by the fact that most of the poets chosen for his critiques turned out to be male, and he hastens to regret in his preface the 'underrepresentation of women poets and of Black writing' (O'Brien, 1998:10). A chapter suitably entitled 'Redressing the Balance' about Fleur Adcock, Carol Rumens and Carol Ann Duffy places O'Brien in a position quite opposite to that of Kennedy. But O'Brien really sides with Kennedy when he returns to the matter later on in his preface and pays his somewhat heavy-handed tribute:

> poetry by women has come into clearer focus, both as poetry and in terms of attempts to redress excessively masculine accounts of literature and its history: Fleur Adcock, Carol Rumens and Carol Ann Duffy and several other poets of stature have shed a good deal of light while getting on with the poet's main task, writing poems.
>
> (O'Brien, 1998:11)

Judging by the attention given over the last couple of decades of the twentieth century to women's literature, of the present as well as of the past, there can be little doubt of the need on the part of writers, critics and anthologists to highlight the specifically female. Jane Dowson in her article 'Anthologies of Women's Poetry: Canon-Breakers; Canon-Makers', in *British Poetry from the 1950s to the 1990s: Politics and Art* (1997) introduced by the neo-Leavisite Gary Day, one of the two editors of the volume, offers this sensible and well-balanced view:

> The number of gender-specific anthologies suggests an emergence of poetry written and published by women and would support the impression of a new vitality in women's poetry; 'renaissance' is perhaps misleading in that it assumes a previous life, but there is a sense that women have at last successfully intervened into the privileged sphere of literary activity.
> (Day and Docherty, 1997:237)

In her introduction to the 'Quote Feminist Unquote Poetry' section of *the new british poetry* (sic!) (Allnutt, D'Aguiar, Edwards and Mottram, 1988) the editor expresses a certain reluctance to use the term 'feminist' as a tag by then too often associated with mere propaganda and used cynically by publishers to cash in on a trend. So Allnutt decided to 'let "feminist" slide into "woman", concentrating on the quality of the poetry' (ibid.:77). Quality to Allnutt is a question of making the language of the poem eminently capable of expressing some personally felt truth with language adequate to the task. In this declaration there is of course nothing new; it could be signed by all poets at all times. To get a glimpse of the implications of Allnutt's declaration it is necessary to consider the target of her resistance, which is the alleged preference on the part of males for such concepts as 'objective' and 'representative'. She quotes a line from Jeni Couzyn's poem 'The Message' to the effect that 'The message of the men is linear' (ibid.:78) which is not the way of literature written by women: 'The message of the women has never in the history of Western literature been permitted to grow into and out of itself in a coherent way' (ibid.:78).[1]

The attempt to track down a characteristic of women's poetry has been a favourite topic with subsequent compilers and editors of anthologies featuring poetry written by women. In Linda France's companion volume to Bloodaxe's gender-indifferent *The New Poetry* (Hulse, Kennedy and Morley, 1993) – and therefore by force of tradition underrepresenting women poets, in this case 17 out of a total of 55 poets[2] – *Sixty Women Poets* (1993) pays ample attention to the negative definition of what women's poetry is not like. By presenting her chosen poets alphabetically, France demonstrates an aversion to categorisation according to alleged male principles of linearity (France, 1993:14). Instead women are claimed to have an

> ability it seems almost physically to inhabit history and the passage of time, as much in the wider historical sense as in the way it is experienced in their own lives and those of their families, their parents' generations and their children's.
>
> (France, 1993:15)

If this seems still to contain an element of linearity, the point is made further on regarding the

> concept of non-linearity: life as repeating cycles, containing dark as well as light, bad and good, male and female. What is new here is that these opposing forces are seen as co-existing, part of the same whole; as if the duality has been exposed as yet another inherited out-worn tradition, used too frequently to divide rather than to unite.
>
> (France, 1993:16)

The leaving behind of a deliberately oppositional attitude in 'feminist' poetry succeeded by the comprehensive urgings of poetry by women reached a high point in Maura Dooley's *Making for Planet Alice: New Women Poets* (1997) when the awareness tentatively articulated by France in her introduction to the earlier volume has been consolidated

> thanks to the purposeful strides of women poets of the 1970s and 1980s, thanks to the rehabilitation of some lost poets of earlier decades . . ., thanks to the sheer slog of the women's

presses, the enlightened work of a few of the mainstream poetry presses (and the opportunist work of others), and, finally, thanks to a landslide of excellent and invigorating new poetry by women.

(Dooley, 1997:13)

Dooley sees her task as one of making up for whatever of worth may have gone unnoticed in the area of women's poetry of recent years. In this anthology we find, according to Dooley,

poets of the moment, inheritors, who seem to me to be responding to the shadowy closing years of this century with an energy, vigour, inventiveness and intelligence fit for the next.

(Dooley, 1997:14)

On this note of arrival of women poets sounded by Dooley, late twentieth-century women's poetry seems to be one of female intersubjectivity, deliberate lack of adherence to any effort towards compartmentalisation or categorisation, and a preference for trying on a variety of flexible linguistic responses to a reality considered multi-faceted and inclusive. This is a characterisation not very different from what the editors of *The New Poetry* anthology from Bloodaxe saw as the common denominator of the poetry collected for that volume: 'possessing at heart a new complexity in the available voices, syntax and language of poetry, and thus of its processes of perception' (Hulse, Kennedy and Morley, 1993:21), a characterisation not altered by Neil Astley in his introduction to the poets of the 1999 anthology *New Blood*:

They are highly individual writers who use a wide variety of forms and styles, choosing whichever is appropriate for each poem. This new pluralism is non-conformist: there are no groups or movements, no dominant influences, . . . These new poets don't imitate but learn from their poetic models.

(Astley, 1999:13)

Even if the climate of late twentieth-century British poetry is distinctly pluralist, with only a keen, postmodernist/poststructuralist, sense of the rhetorical determination of cognition to bind contemporary poets together, and even if the revolutionary 'feminist' has given way to the more pragmatic 'female', poetry has proved itself a rewarding way of exploring and mediating specific kinds of experience, of which the meeting of British culture with cultures of the former Empire is one, and of which women's situation is another. In some poems the two combine into a very pertinent thematics of foreign and female, the subject of this chapter. Contemporary British poetry has numerous examples of poems written by women who give voice to concerns to do with ethnicity and cultural differences. At the same time, however, such poems rarely focus exclusively on ethnic questions, but bring together a more comprehensive complex of problems to do with language, gender, family and class.

In what follows I have tried to focus on poetic statements at the intersection of female and foreign. I am quite aware that along both axes we have to do with relative rather than absolute sensitivities. Only in some cases can poetry written by women be said to be deliberately gendered, and 'foreign' is in most cases a misplaced tag, since women poets giving voice to experiences other than or clashing with what seems prevailing experience within a British universe represent a continuum ranging from alienation to integration. In like manner one would have to be careful with designations of nationality like English or British. By writing in English or in English-dominated Creole, the poets have chosen a frame of utterance which is extremely flexible and less and less to be associated solely with Britain, but with a culture complex dominated by the English-speaking countries and those who have adopted English as their linguistic means of global communication. In other words, it is not always easy, or indeed desirable, to try and determine a relationship solely with Britain, although the biography of the poet in question may indicate such a relationship.

Often a tension will be seen to arise between the place of origin, be that first- or further-generation, and, via English, Britain as such or as symbol of a Western way of life. Some of the poets considered below have the most tenuous of relationships with Britain in terms of national experience or passport holding. But the fact that they have chosen to be represented in anthologies which, despite casting their nets wide, emphasise a degree of relevance in a British context justifies their inclusion in this chapter. Indeed, judging by the poets represented in *The New Poetry* by Hulse, Kennedy and Morley (1993) and in *New Blood* by Astley (1999), more women than men displaying a 'compound voice' seem to have 'drifted around', so that 'migration' may actually be a term preferable to both 'emigration' and 'immigration'. For them the British context, at least in terms of anthologising and publication, must have been a deliberate choice, and as such inviting critical attention in the context of the present study.

Dealing with women's poetry at this moment in social and cultural history necessitates imposing a caveat on the part of the critic. Important on the agenda of women's writing, as a reflection of the larger issues in various women's movements, has been the doing away with any gendered 'givens'. This does not mean that all women's poetry shares the same agenda, nor does it mean that sharing it implies the deliberate eradication by the poetic imagination of any such verbal manifestations as support a conventional reflection. But it does mean that applying any preconceived attitudes to present-day poetry by women is an ill-advised critical procedure. Here more than anywhere else in contemporary literature it is rewarding to follow the advice that a poem must be judged in terms of its own features and implications, despite the exhortation from the more militant feminist quarters to apply ideological yardsticks first and last. Although this is the critical principle adhered to in what follows, the poems having been selected for the extent to which they elucidate the central theme of this study, the presence of a compound voice, of course arouses expectations of the way the compound voice in terms of a sense of belonging combines with other preoccupations, of family, of partner relationships, of conventional gender roles versus equal opportunities and so on have energised women's poetry in recent decades.

Essentialist constructions

The particular emphasis on gendered polarity sounded in Jeni Couzyn's 'The Message' (France, 1993:95), which may well stand as the reference standard in recent British poetry for gendered awareness, is also echoed in poems implicitly relating the British/Western in opposition to the culture of the poet's origin. Mimi Khalvati in her poem 'The Waiting House' (ibid.:187–8) describes what appears to be an ancient ritual in her country of origin according to which menstruating women go to a house to pass the time of their period. As self-contained statement the poem really needs no frame of reference outside the local paraphernalia described for the ritual to be carried out. But the poem, by its triumphant celebration of women's solidarity with each other and their special relationship with the earth, seems to invite comparison with the way that the British attitude to menstruation has been to hide away the phenomenon and to classify its role in other cultures as only ethnologically or anthropologically interesting. The implicit cultural diversity posited by the celebratory attitude of the poem is brought into the foreground when compared with the Irish poet Katie Donovan on the difference between actual female bleeding and the symbolic bleeding of Christ. In 'Underneath Our Skirts', a guest at a church wedding feels her period coming on while watching the ceremony progress. Caught between two 'holy' kinds of bleeding – Christ on the cross and the virgin bride on her nuptial bed – the speaker feels dirty and out of place, feeling that she has contaminated the double festivity of blood. But then the guest gathers strength and courage to assert her womanhood, since

> we, the original
> shedders of ourselves,
> leak the guilt of knowledge
> of the surfeit
> of our embarrassing fertility
> and power
>
> (Astley, 1999:121)

The assertion of female essentialism by women poets able explicitly or implicitly to compare different mores and concepts with those of Britain, either on its own or as the presentative of the West, comes out sometimes in direct sexual statement, as with Khalvati's poem on menstruation, but mostly, it seems, in more sublimated form as cultural accommodation.

Grace Nichols's 'Configurations' is a highly suggestive description of the various positions of love-making in terms of European maleness and non-European (African and/or Indian being indicated) femaleness, reversing humorously, but perhaps not without a certain sting, in the last verses the traditional power distribution:

> She delivers up the whole Indies again
> But this time her wide legs close in slowly
> Making a golden stool of the Empire
> of his head.
>
> (France, 1993:212)

In Sujata Bhatt's 'Shérdi' (France, 1993:59) the erotic overtones of sucking a sugar cane in Indian Sanosra has a phallic significance which is naturally brought to bear on the love act. But the poem demonstrates the impossibility of distinguishing between the sugarcane field with its nutritional yield and the love-making with its short-term pleasure and long-term yield.

The intercultural scene in Britain invites assertions of essentialist womanhood in combination with ethnicity, but most often, it seems, in contexts also offering perspectives of family, work and social issues. Carole Satyamurti and Mimi Khalvati are poets who have turned their awareness of the gendered universe to efficient use in poems drawing on a bicultural or multicultural experience, and in which the sexual/erotic is keenly felt as main energiser.

The dawning on the adolescent girl thinking in Carole Satyamurti's 'My First Cup of Coffee' of a life at the same time scaring and attractive beyond family and school is a very tender handling of this realisation. To begin with the girl attempts to emulate the sophisticated dressing and behaviour of adult women while enjoying coffee with her mother in the Kardomah. Her carefully prepared appearance for this first ordering of coffee, not orange juice, in a café, as a kind of social initiation rite, breaks down when she watches

Nicolette Hawkins
(best in the class at hockey, worst at French)
and a boy – kissing,
blouse straining, hands
where they shouldn't be: the grown-up thing.

(France, 1993:249)

And the girl realises that she would willingly exchange her civic accomplishments for a chance like that. In this faintly away-from-Britain setting, indicated by the term 'Kardomah', where an oppositional manners versus nature pattern seems to prevail, and in which manners equals female and nature male, the longing to cross the boundary and sacrifice manners for nature obeying her innermost urge, the girl realises the futility of imposed, culturally determined conventions. Satyamurti plays through the same theme in her ballad-like poem 'Sex Object', in which the very British-named protagonist Jenny Wilson has enjoyed the culturally tabooed attentions of a passing-by Romany clan member and now, after he has left, can afford to reflect that

these days
ideological unsoundness
is the most delicious sin there is.

(France, 1993:251)

Again here the distribution of values is made along a manners–nature distinction, whose violation is necessary for fulfilment, this time happily both realised and put into practice by Jenny. However, if the male is the agent in these two poems absolutely necessary for the woman to realise her potential, the situation is markedly different in Satyamurti's 'Fear of Corpus Christi: Warsaw'. The political–religious demonstration in what seems to be Solidarity Poland is completely made up by women and girls, with men only present as impassive, stylised imposers of power: 'soldiers with Modligiani faces' (France, 1993:250). This is a celebration of a political power of alternative methods from those of men, here at the level of very concrete subject matter.

More ambivalent are such poetic statements about womanhood in implicit contrast to maleness in poems such as Sujata Bhatt's 'What Is Worth Knowing?' (ibid.:60–61), Jean 'Binta' Breeze's 'For All Blue Notes' (ibid.:73) and 'I Poet' (ibid.:74–5). In the first of these poems different items of information are enumerated, loosely bound together by observations on 'facts' concerning Van Gogh's ear. The poem does not address directly any gendered issue, but suggests an untidy universe usually put into encyclopaedic order by an inventory compatible with Jeni Couzyn's suggestion that the 'message of men is linear'. Linearity breaks down under 'irrational' behaviour like Van Gogh's – cp. the 'men mutilating their roots in the race' (ibid.:95) of Couzyn's poem – and leaves room for reconstructing the world as the organic space of the female alternative of Couzyn's 'orchard'. The same kind of note is literally struck in Jean 'Binta' Breeze's 'For all Blue Notes'. The blue notes in jazz being the notes between B and B flat and E and E flat that the conventional half-note scale of classical Western music does not recognise, these are the notes that promise release from a strongly codified – male – existence, urging

>   simply letting go
>   remembering to forget
>   all that you think you know.
>
>   (France, 1993:73)

Breeze turns to Creole in 'I Poet' in which the persona records her turning into a writer, having been an avid reader. The turning point comes when the persona senses that she is being 'read' in the writings of others:

>   I sey, maybe
>   it was you readin me all de time.
>
>   (France, 1993:75)

Her realisation of her own continual construction is what is needed to make her the writer to suggest the reading, which is a project of an all-embracing nature dissolving any gendered or other barriers:

> an I tankful
> ...
> dat ah did read an love firs
> fah I know
> when I writin
> I poem
> is you
>
> (France, 1993:75)

The featuring of an awareness of female essentialism combined with the immigrant's experience of cultural distinctions and of the need for (re)socialisation gives to this variety of gender-conscious writing a certain urgency because of the double strain under which the poet may find herself. The reader may have expected the reinforcement of gendered alienation by the absence of any unquestioned, once and for all, cultural attachment. But, as we have seen in the examples above, the opposite seems to be the case. The immigrant's or the British-oriented cosmopolitan's perspective seems to be able to result in a heightened awareness of the, distinctly female, displacement from – or within – a British cultural and social context, liberating rather than restraining the poet in her poetic explorations of gender and self.

Language negotiations

If the message of men feeling trapped by the language barrier is linear, that is aggressive and often tinged with heavy irony, the similar predicament met with in women's poetry, extending the contrastive comparison in Jeni Couzyn's poem of linearity versus love, is one of desire for integration. In her poem 'River', Carol Ann Duffy describes how, at a turn of the river, perhaps demarcating a national frontier, the language changes into incomprehensibility, the woman seen beyond the turn speaking in an unknown language. There is a longing combined with a sense of frustration and loss in the poetic speaker's realisation of a possibility of communication which will never be actualised:

If you were really there what would you write on a postcard,
or on the sand, near where the river runs into the sea?

(Duffy, 1990:53)

Duffy, although not exemplary herself of the kind of cultural encounter which is the subject of this chapter, in this poem on existential consequences of linguistic difference nonetheless sounds a note shared in poems by women with very personal and concrete experience of the barrier, such as Warsaw-born and Britain-raised Maria Jastrzebska in her poem 'Bi-lingual'. But, just as in the case of the poem by Duffy, there is also here an ambiguity created by the tension between literal and symbolic meaning. Compare the fraught pause caused by the first line break in these central lines of the poem:

> If I told you I want you
> To press against these words
>
> (Allnutt, D'Aguiar, Edwards
> and Mottram, 1988:109)

The tone in this poem is one of a desperate urge for complete mutual understanding, concluding on a note of sad resignation when realising the impossibility of ever reaching it:

> There's a gap
> An enormous space
> ...
> I've paced up and down it
> It is the loneliest place I know
>
> (Allnutt, D'Aguiar, Edwards
> and Mottram 1988:109)

Possibly symbolically indicative of differences just as unbridgeable as linguistic barriers, the impossibility of successful communication – in love relations or indeed in any human relations – leaves the poetic speaker in undesired but inevitable isolation. Whether the point in Jastrzebska's poem is solely concerned with linguistic matters or there is a wider significance of which the linguistic aporia serves merely as a symbolic indicator, its very undecidability is evidence both of a facing up to simple communicative failure and of realising the symbolic significance of the Tower of Babel as an emblem of existential conditions when it comes to human interrelations.

Although totally different in context and aim, a similar ambiguity may be read into Lancashire-born and Dublin-resident Nuala Ní Dhomhnaill's 'The Language Issue', originally written in Gaelic and translated by Paul Muldoon. Of course the word 'issue' in a poem originally in Gaelic implies an agenda of bitter and prolonged political strife. The poem is about an undefined hope, which is placed

> on the water
> in this little boat
> of the language.
>
> (Hulse, Kennedy and
> Morley, 1993:171)

The boat is then launched into a river, where it may end up anywhere,

> in the lap, perhaps,
> of some Pharaoh's daughter.
>
> (Hulse, Kennedy and
> Morley, 1993:170)

In perspectives of both the Old Testament and the history of the language issue in Ireland, the poem hovers between the precedent of divine guidance and the contingency of mundane power relations. To see hope for a specific political outcome, here a positive future for the Gaelic language in Ireland, in the form of a child put Moses-like into a boat is perhaps not to express a very strong faith in the viability of the project. But in the context of the poem the language issue is made into part of a larger whole, centred on a myth of a child being miraculously saved and one day to receive great office and become a national leader, but also implying the desperation of a mother attempting a way out of a hopeless situation.

In her poem 'Hindi Urdu Bol Chaal' (meaning a dialogue between Hindi and Urdu) Moniza Alvi explores the differences between the major languages of India and Pakistan from the perspective of a listener absorbed in the vast cultural echoes that the languages imply. Fascinated by the history of Urdu

> borrowed from Sanskrit,
> Arabic and Persian
>
> (Forbes, 1994:89)

she encounters Pakistan through its language, it is a

> sound system travelling through
> countries, ascending and descending
>
> in ragas, drumbeats, clapping.
>
> (Forbes, 1994:89)

The persona, being 'borrowed from England' (ibid.), is searching for the 'kernel of language' (ibid.), that kernel which will be the key to all the cultural layers.

Compared with the aggressive and/or satirical attitudes to language by male immigrants as explored in the previous chapter, the language barrier examined by the poets in this section has an altogether different tone. Whereas in much dub poetry the project is cultural and political self-assertion, with linguistic reformation as the great lever, the tone in the poems just reviewed is hesitant and probing, accepting linguistic difference, displaying a hope to reach beyond language to some shared ground.

The eagerness to embrace the culture and traditions of her country of origin is a theme that runs through Moniza Alvi's poetry, but the eagerness is invariably countered by the impossibility of escaping her being 'borrowed from England'. In 'Hindi Urdu Bol Chaal' she has to elicit words of the desired language at the market by asking in English 'How much?', and in Alvi's poem 'The Wedding', a desire for a wedding in total harmony with local custom is marred by similar English borrowings, as when, on the guests opening their suitcases, 'England spilled out' (ibid.), and as when bride and groom leave after the ceremony:

> We travelled along roads with English names.
>
> (Forbes, 1994:89)

This sense of cultural difference, with the Pakistan of her childhood representing a lost attraction, stands out even more clearly in Alvi's poem 'Presents from My Aunts in Pakistan'.

Having received a packet of clothes from her aunts in Pakistan, the persona tries them on. Her adopted Englishness, however, prevents her from achieving the desired identification. The jarring notes are heard when the persona dressed in the new clothes realises that she is 'alien in the sitting-room' and finds herself longing for 'denim and corduroy' (Dooley, 1997:17). Sensing that

> My salwar kameez
> didn't impress the schoolfriend
>
> (Dooley, 1997:18)

and remarking that

> My aunts requested cardigans
> from Marks and Spencers
>
> (Dooley, 1997:18)

she falls into reverie, recalling briefly her sailing to England as a child and imagining her aunts busy wrapping the gifts now in her possession. The poem ends somewhat plaintively

> and I was there –
> of no fixed nationality,
> staring through fretwork
> at the Shalimar Gardens.
>
> (Dooley, 1997:18)

Alvi makes her recollection of the country of her childhood the absolutely desirable (her aunts longing for Marks and Spencers products, however, suggesting ironically its relativity), with England providing the backdrop of disillusionment, offering the drab rationality of the real against the imaginative flights of desire nourished by filtered recollection (after all, in 'Presents from My Aunts in Pakistan' the persona imagining herself staring at the Shalimar Gardens notes that 'there were beggars, sweeper-girls' (ibid.)). In 'The Laughing Moon' the persona recalls how on arrival

> Shakily England picked me up
> with her grey fingers.
> England had a cure for everything
> stuck between the bricks of houses.
>
> (Dooley, 1997:16)

But there is a third position between longing for the desirable but lost place of origin and the undesirable and very much present place of residence, a position described in Alvi's poem 'The Sari', in which the long piece of cloth is made figuratively to encompass all Pakistan and back to England where she is wrapped in it while being whispered to '*Your body is your country*' (France, 1993:32). Moniza Alvi's solution to the problem of her sense of estrangement, in so far as we may take her poem 'The Sari' as evidence for it, is to define belonging in terms of individuality.

Moniza Alvi can deploy the voice of the immigrant into Britain as well as the well-assimilated citizen. Some women poets, however, draw a picture of their culture of origin which goes against the 'liberated' Western view of things in general and the situation of the woman in particular.

Whereas a poet like Moniza Alvi in her poems about the immigrant experience responds to a sense of not belonging by resorting to an individualism for which home and abroad are equally irrelevant, there are poets who rejoice in their difference from Britishness, at the same time as they use this Britishness as a sounding board for a response which includes their sense of gender as well. This could be said to be the case in Grace Nichols's 'Abra-Cadabra' (France, 1993:212–13), in which a daughter is witness to her mother's efficient way of removing a foreign body from another daughter's nose. Before the successful application of pepper to provoke the sneezing that will emit the object, the daughter has made it clear by examples that the mother's knowledge of traditional remedies against trivial ailments surpasses that of any magician. Posed explicitly between magicians (male and 'native') and implicitly Western medicine (male and West/British), the inherited culture of the mother (female and 'native') holds its own. Another poem, 'Those Women', recalls a scene of women fishing. At one with nature

> in the brown voluptuous
> water of their own element
>
> (Hulse, Kennedy and
> Morley, 1993:155)

the fishing women present a picture of harmony and balance, which again here is in implicit contrast to a work situation where Britain has left its mark. A similar coupling of essence of womanhood in a decidedly non-British context with a basic (female?) occupation is also seen in Sujata Bhatt's 'Muliebrity', a brief poem describing the impact on the speaker of a girl gathering cow dung in Maninagar in India. The impact is so strong that the poet, routinely storing the image for future use, cannot make it merely instrumental but has to keep it as a unique display of womanhood, the 'muliebrity' of the title:

unwilling
to forget her or to explain to anyone the greatness
and the power glistening through her cheekbones
each time she found a particularly promising mound of dung.

(Hulse, Kennedy and Morley, 1993:242)

The implicit contrast to Britain – implicit in so far as any direct reference is left out but of course assumed by the use of English rather than the Creole supposedly spoken by the women in question – is fully worked out in Nichols's 'Tropical Death', in which a 'fat black woman' insists on looking forward to a 'brilliant tropical death' with all the traditional mourning. Not elaborating on the risk of the black lady dying far from the tropics, its opposition, its other, we find death occurring on a

> cold sojourn
> in some North Europe far
> forlorn
>
> (Hulse, Kennedy and
> Morley, 1993:155)

a place where, instead of the bawl that takes the lid off all pent-up feeling, the mourners are given Larkin-like to 'quiet tear wiping' and 'polite hearse withdrawal'. The Eurocentred and, in this case, Protestant-angled position of considering death an unpleasantness best sorted out in quiet is here altered in favour of a celebration of death so that it is turned into a celebration of life. But the enthusiasm displayed by the fat black woman may also have a less genuine aspect, as when the speaker in Nichols's poem 'Walking with My Brother in Georgetown' interprets the apparently carefree street life,

> Hibiscus blooming
> People grooving
>
> (Hulse, Kennedy and
> Morley, 1993:157)

as mere façade hiding a state of stagnation leading to the death of the community. Clearly the speaker, returned to her native country, is split between a wish to get home and belong with her roots and realising, in the more global/Western aspect of her experience, the impossibility of doing so, perhaps because the community of her origin has actually deteriorated, or perhaps because she is victim of the familiar delusions of nostalgia. The sense of double exile takes her to Sweden, where the poet Edith Södergran in 'My Northern-Sister' offers comfort by

heather and pine,
a taste of blue air,
the talking-memory of my own childhood trees.

(Hulse, Kennedy and Morley, 1993:158)

Resolving the dialectical tension of belonging to neither native nor adopted cultures by embracing Södergran in gendered solidarity is a possible synthesis, an intellectual and emotional dealing with a problem of alienation by sublimation, the sublimation perhaps signalled by the choice of 'standard English' as the channel of communication.

Between cultures

At the same time as Britain's demography is being altered in an intercultural direction, the consensus of undivided nationhood is being dissolved in favour of increasing regional awarenesses. This is, of course, a tendency which is not just visible in women's poetry, but characteristic of literature written in Britain generally. In women's poetry there seems, however, to be a rather seamless transition between the sense of 'inner' and 'outer' exile. Marion Lomax in her poem 'Kith' deals with the shifting historical situations of Northumberland, her native region, to which she is attracted, despite the region being a

foster-mother, telling me
she hasn't much to offer. I'll take
my chance: I don't believe her.

(Astley, 1999:37)

This being a poem about a sense of regional belonging, the poet in her note explains that her 'poems are concerned with divisions (emotional, physical, sexual and social)' (ibid.:36). Many poems by women on separation in terms of regional or national transition seem to point beyond a simple geographical dichotomy and its solution and into something much more complex and faceted, perhaps emblematic of an experience also in terms of gender and moment in history. A poem like Katrina Porteous's

'Charlie Douglas' about the lore of Northumberland fishermen vanishing in the wake of industrialised trawling, which reads like an almost mock-Wordsworthian exercise, is intended by its author to transcend the regional and vocational. Porteous sees fishing as a

> microcosm, embodying many themes... the continuity between the human and the natural worlds, and the importance of memory in shaping our present and future identity. So much in contemporary life breaks this continuity between past and future, individual and community, and estranges us from nature and ourselves.
>
> (Astley, 1999:174)

These poems of place, at first sight easily categorised as regionalist, on closer inspection and in the light of authorial elucidation qualify for inclusion in the orchard which is the female counterpoint to the uprooted – male – pines in Jeni Couzyn's universe.

Neither regional nor ethnic in the modern senses of the words is the Jewish community in Britain. Joanne Limburg in her 'Seder Night with My Ancestors' offers a fictive conversation along traditional ritualistic lines between her Jewish ancestor and the well-assimilated persona, whom they blame for lack of loyalty to the traditions of her people. To her self-defence of

> I say that all I want
> is to live my life

they retort that *'Without us you would have no life'* (ibid.:233). Indifferent in principle to gender, this poem's statement nonetheless shares the striving towards (female?) inclusiveness, a reaching out for community rather than the self-assertion on the part of the community as found, for instance, in several of the (male) Anglo-Caribbean poems examined in the previous chapter.

From another angle, but in a comparable situation with that of Joanne Limburg, we hear the voice of black, adopted-child Glaswegian Jackie Kay. In the wryly humorous 'In my country', the I is the subject of the casual attention of a woman encountered on the beach, apparently outside Glasgow. On the woman's asking where she comes from, she astonishes her enquirer with her matter-of-course: '"Here", I said, "Here. These parts"' (ibid.:76). Whereas in Limburg's poem the feeling of otherness has to do with the recognition of a cultural tradition apart from the mainstream British one existing without external evidence, Kay's poem plays on an obviously visible otherness, which turns out, paradoxically, to be insignificant in terms of belonging locally. Nonetheless, there is a longing for community in terms of genetic rather than social identity. Kay gives voice to this in her poem 'Pride', in which she meets a stranger on the train on its way out of Euston station. Himself an Ibo, he recognises similar features in the face of the poem's persona. He tells her about the Ibo culture with a look on his face:

> I've seen on a MacLachlan, a MacDonnell, a MacLeod, the most startling thing, pride
>
> (Astley, 1999:79)

and she imagines her own warm reception by her fellow Ibo as a kind of existential apotheosis. The difference between the night-train journey up through England towards Scotland in reality and the colourful circumstances of her 'genetic' community in her imagination is expressive of not only a longing for roots but a longing in terms of isolation – her lonely train journey interrupted for a brief time by the male Ibo – and community. Kay's long, dramatic poem *The Adoption Papers* is an exploration of her own – failing – sense of belonging, allowing both daughter, natural and adoptive mother their say.

Again here we encounter a situation which is not limited to the bare facts and the social difficulties met with by 'miscegenation' in a predominantly white society informed by middle-class values. Kay takes the issue far beyond such a predictable treatment and into contexts posited by the three women, including biology, gender construction, politics and class. The poem excels in moments of everyday, but nonetheless all-important, epiphanies, like the situation where the adoptive mother is subject to a visit by the social worker who is to report on the suitability of the home. The prospective adoptive mother has been at great pains to make her home look solidly respectable, having hidden all the signs of her radical political leanings: only a handful of world-peace badges have been left by oversight on involuntary display. Despairing when the visitor suddenly catches sight of them, she is ready to give up all hope, but quite unexpectedly finds sympathy, when her feared guest turns out to be quite human:

> I'm all for peace myself she says,
> and sits down for another cup of coffee
>
> (Astley, 1999:76)

The wish to belong in terms of organic community, with 'sisterhood' and family as first priorities, comes out clearly in the poetry of Mimi Khalvati. Her 'Rubaiyat' – an ancient Persian poetic form with a particular effect on minds familiar with the English literary tradition since Edward Fitzgerald's 'Omar Khayyam' rubaiyat – celebrates her grandmother's sense of beauty in what appears to be only waste. The grandmother's selection of the whitest deadhead from a pile on the ground and her presentation of it to the granddaughter makes her pine for a world 'that takes such care to tend what fades so soon' (Dooley, 1997:111). Iran-born but cosmopolitan and London-resident, Khalvati has a world of reference which encompasses Iran and Britain, and she finds her poetic fulfilment in the former. Her poem 'Amanuensis' is a celebration of the geometrical shapes of her Islamic background as the repository of her whole being lodged in a specific cultural tradition:

> From each trapezium,
> polygon, each small isosceles
>
> face, extract me, entwine me. Be my double
> helix! My Polestar! My Asterisks!
> Nestle in my silences. But spell me out
> and rhyme me in your lunes and arabesques.
>
> (France, 1993:186)

But, as we see in the 'Stone of Patience' (Dooley, 1997:112–13), there is an equally strong longing to free herself as an individual and, as we see in 'Blue Moon', it will happen in terms of an existential experience more general than nationality or ethnic belonging:

> My son needs higher ceilings; and my daughter
> sky for her own Blue Moon. You can't blame her.
> No woman wants to dance in her Mum's old room.
>
> (Dooley 1997:112)

Imtiaz Dharker is a Pakistani who grew up in Glasgow and now lives in India. Her poetry explores issues of religious fundamentalism, as in 'Purdah (I)', in which a young woman reflects on her new adulthood in purdah. It is as if her whole outlook changes by her hiding herself from the world, developing 'between the thighs, a sense of sin' (Astley, 1999:42). 'The name of God' approaches the fundamentalist issue from the angle of violence done in the name of God. Running away from the dangerously armed neighbourhood boys, the persona concludes that

> the name of god
> in my mouth
> had a taste I soon forgot.
>
> I think it was the taste
> of home.
>
> (Astley, 1999:46)

For Dharker the experience of belonging everywhere and nowhere has led to a personal realisation of outcastness as the ultimate, existential situation. This is what she deals with in 'Minority', a poem that begins with the declaration of the persona that she was born as a foreigner, communing on this fact only with herself until, meeting a stranger in the street, she realises that

> you know the face
> simplified to bone,
> look into its outcast eyes
> and recognise it as your own
>
> (Astley, 1999:47)

In her own comments on the subjects of her poetry, Dharker says:

> I enjoy the benefits of being an outcast in most societies I know. I don't want to have to define myself in terms of location or religion. In a world that seems to be splitting itself into narrower national and religious groups, sects, castes, subcastes, we can go on excluding others until we come down to a minority of one.
>
> (Astley, 1999:41)

Dharker might be said to draw the bleakest possible consequences from her sense of alienation, despite her protestations of enjoyment, and seems to offer an attitude only found rarely among poets writing on these subjects. But the realisation of her situation is reflected also by poets sharing her kind of citizen-of-no-country experience, although in the case of Jane Griffiths under less extreme circumstances. She has recorded her reactions to her family's moving abroad when she was eight. In her imaginative universe, alienation-released dreams have the nature of nightmarish threats in bird-like shapes ('Migration') returning overnight to their owners:

> whose waking
> each day was to a clogged grey
> dawn, whose night-time shadows
> had wings, scything steeply
> above their narrow beds
>
> (Astley, 1999:237)

Quite clearly, the poetry discussed above is evidence of concerns that take us beyond the purely national in terms of immigration or demographic aftermath of Empire. Coinciding in time with the rising awareness of the social and cultural construction of gender, the diaspora or migration experience blends with the gender experience, similarly structured as transition. The results are poetic statements in two dimensions, as it were, in which genderedness is inseparable from social and national issues. As the culture of origin always retains considerable power in the migrant's consciousness, no matter how attractive or necessary the adopted culture may be, there seems to be a parallel in terms of habitual and familiar positions of gender as against the various modes of questioning those positions. A recurring theme in the poetry of Imtiaz Dharker is the exploration of this schism. In her comments on the poem selected for the *New Blood* anthology, she writes:

> The image of purdah for me was on the dangerous edge of being almost seductive: the hidden body, the highlighted eyes, the suggestion of forbidden places. But of course it is also one of the instruments of power used to bring women to heel in the name of religion. (Astley, 1999:41)

We often find in the poetry of women migrants an unwillingness to succumb to simplistic solutions or announcements. In the case of Dharker here, the attraction of the familiar is less in the Islamic requirement of the purdah to satisfy religious commands than in the erotic resulting from this religious institution. That in itself is a complication of an issue which, as usually construed in non-Islamic cultures, is sexism disguised as religion. The refusal to give up totally, if for reasons perhaps not always primarily to do with an established culture of origins, on the offerings of the contexts of the personal past is characteristic of much of the poetry examined above. Strong impressions are made by poems that celebrate what I have called 'essential womanhood' in which the essential is made to stand out against the cultural background of the culture left behind by the poet and in which the very cultural distance may be said to enhance the poet's ability to concentrate. Also when it comes to language we see attitudes not quite as militant as those displayed by the poets discussed in the previous chapter, but rather such as allow for probings into the significance of linguistic loss and gain. All in all, judged by the texts selected for this chapter, the double bind of transitional gender and culture awareness forms a creative framework allowing for a more inclusive view than seems to be the case when the focus is solely on the migrant's experience of clashes with the receiving culture.

5
In the Great Tradition – but with a Difference

> One of the supreme debts one great writer can owe another is the realization of unlikeness (there is, of course, no significant unlikeness without the common concern – and the common seriousness of concern – with essential human issues).
>
> (Leavis, 1972:19)

Arguably the most significant feature of British poetry and fiction in the last couple of decades of the twentieth century is the enhanced presence of the 'other' in a variety of manifestations: in subject matter in terms of history, geography and gender, and in presentation in terms of problematised and problematising discourse modes. If indeed the tag of 'postmodernism' makes sense as a distinct category denoting the combination of epoch and approach in British literature, it must be in this particular sense of the literary highlighting of tensions or alternatives traditionally excluded or repressed.

To come up with one simple explanation why contemporary British poetry and fiction, by and large, is characterised by an effort to introduce the perspective of the 'other' is impossible, but several factors have contributed. The 'Empire-writes-back syndrome' has had considerable impact on the literary scene in the former hub of Empire, affecting both writers born and bred in Britain and ex- /post-colonial writers choosing Britain as home or at least as a *pied-à-terre*. The 'American connection', that is the increasing literary interaction across the Atlantic, in terms of both frames of reference and markets also plays a considerable role. The general questioning of historiography as an allegedly objective mode of writing has left its indelible traces on fiction in the form of a great variety of metafictional strategies, in the process also calling attention to the presence and function of structures familiar from fiction in texts posing as the very opposite of make-believe.[1]

The view of 'reality' as a verbal construction may, in English literature, be traced back to Lawrence Sterne and, to stretch a point, even to Chaucer, and is in evidence in the bud in the modernist works by Joyce, Woolf and Beckett. However, it was not until John Fowles's *The French Lieutenant's Woman* in 1969 demonstrated the potential of the mode in pedagogical clarity that postmodernist fiction can be said to exist as a dominant literary trend, with market success and general critical acclaim. Since then only comedy-of-manners genre-piece realism with roots in Trollope and Bennett and its present-day exponents in, say, Joanna Trollope and Rosamund Pilcher, and others of the AGA-saga school, has shown an interest in ignoring the lessons of the postmodernist relativist stance (commercially gratifying though it may be). Julian Barnes's playful *Flaubert's Parrot* (1984), Lawrence Norfolk's teasingly learned *Lemprière's Dictionary* (1991, and 1992 abbreviated version) and the huge *The Pope's Rhinoceros* (1996) are concert exercises in the art of handling various kinds of 'others' to do with literary conventions and history, as in the fictions of Christine Brooke-Rose and Jeanette Winterson. This predilection for metafictional experiment has certainly had its impact on British fiction generally, but perhaps in subtler ways than radical American and French textual remodelling would have led one to expect. The legacy of metafiction in British fiction is currently most prominent as a more or – (rarely) less concealed textual self-awareness, a certain discreetly writerly acknowledgment of loss of innocence regarding the ontological and epistemological status of the narrative. But also fiction of a more mainstream kind, and here Margaret Drabble would be an illustrative case in point, has been affected by this effort to put on textual display the presence of the textually 'other'.

If the presence of 'the other' in a variety of forms can be suggested as the thematic marker of much modern fiction and poetry, there have been other factors of significance for the shaping of the literature of the last few decades. In the early 1980s considerable interest in fiction was prompted by commercial boosting. Foreign takeovers of British publishing houses introduced American levels of author royalties, exciting public interest far beyond the common reader, as did the much-publicised literary prizes – with the Booker Prize in the lead, although in terms of prize money not the most generous – which made competition and ranking apply to literature as to sports (and universities). The reduced budgets of the Thatcher–Major years had, it is true, little effect on the dissemination of the kinds of literature relying on the market, but the unrest in artistic circles caused by the generally philistine inclinations of the powers-that-were seemed to find a rallying point in the mobilisation of extra energy to demonstrate the scope and value of art.

The Booker Prize recognises the existence of close ties within the English-speaking world, excluding only the first colony to secede from Empire, the USA. The reality of the British scene of fiction is that interculturalism is a characteristic that not only obtains regarding reading audience, with no strong barriers set up between anglophone nations when it comes to publishing and marketing, but also regarding subject matter and themes in the contemporary novel. A range of writers from countries associated with Britain through the former Empire have retained relations with the former imperial centre, some, such as V.S. Naipaul, settling as a young man in Britain, applying his perspective accordingly; others, such as Salman Rushdie, from a cosmopolitan position drawing on the Anglo-Indian relations of an Indian provenance. Others again, like Indian-born but Canada-residing Rohinton Mistry pointed their telescopes from voluntary exile at the problems of their home countries, whereas India-residing Vikram Seth finds it natural to range freely from location to location in his narratives, as is also the case of Michael Ondaatje, a citizen of Sri Lanka now living in Canada.

Alternatively, 'native' British novelists have increasingly chosen abroad as the locale of their narratives. Julian Barnes's love for France surfaced in his tour-de-force *Flaubert's Parrot* (1984), and the relations through time between England and France is the theme that binds together a number of stories told in different voices in his *Cross Channel* (1996). His *England, England* (1998) is a satirical fantasy on the potential development of the nation into an enormous theme park. Barnes has a special eye for the extraordinary perspective that forces the reader to revise ingrained ideas. Nicholas Shakespeare, in his *The Dancer Upstairs* (1995), has composed a haunting and brilliantly narrated tale set in Graham Greene-like Latin America, while Kazuo Ishiguro, equally at home as regards setting in Britain and Japan, removed his Kafkaesque *The Unconsoled* (1995) to some unidentified central European country, in which a Salvador Dali might have felt at home. And there is Bruce Chatwin's only work of regular fiction, *Utz* (1988) and John Berger's peasant trilogy *Into Their Labours* (1979–1990), both cutting any ties whatsoever with their authors' home countries.

In this chapter the focus is on works of fiction with their roots in the strong English tradition of the novel as an agent of moral enquiry – F.R. Leavis's 'great tradition' – in a centripetal move so to speak, but which, at the same time, exhibit an awareness of an 'other' related to Empire or its aftermath, though sometimes in terms of displacement. The next chapter will apply the opposite perspective and look at fiction which unfolds abroad, displaying the non-British as the 'other'. In either case we have to do with fiction that responds, if not always explicitly, to a situation brought about by a quite specific historical development, Britain first exploding into, then imploding from, Empire.

The Great Tradition as model

When in 1948 F.R. Leavis published his thoughts on 'greatness' in the English novel, the enthusiastic welcome bestowed on *The Great Tradition* as a revolutionary contribution to syllabus revision in the British academy largely overshadowed the conceptual premises on which the study built. Greatness, as defined by Leavis, is a question of the novelist recording 'an ideal civilized sensibility; a humanity capable of communicating by the finest shades of inflexion and implication' (1972:27). Presented as an absolute by Leavis, such a pronouncement is nonetheless deeply couched in and relative to a specific world view and existential stance. There seems to be an unbroken line from Matthew Arnold's 'high seriousness' and the ubiquitous Victorian ideal of 'earnestness' to Leavis's cultivation of greatness in terms of the integration of a strongly developed moral awareness into the construction of the fictional universe of the novel. Greatness in a novel being the display of a capability for 'a vital capacity for experience, a kind of reverent openness before life, and a marked moral intensity' (ibid.: 18), Leavis found it especially developed in the work of Jane Austen, George Eliot, Henry James, Joseph Conrad and D.H. Lawrence. Comparing these five novelists, it is indeed striking that only three can be said to be English in the narrow, regional sense of the term, as both Conrad and James were naturalised Englishmen. Giving a turn to Leavis's definition of novelistic greatness as the 'tradition to which what is great in English fiction belongs' (ibid.:16), we may therefore suggest that Englishness in Leavis's sense is the tradition which is the carrier of greatness defined as a special capacity for aesthetising moral preoccupations.

Greatness seen as civilised sensibility and moral intensity is then, in Leavis's view, the legacy of the English novel at its best, a legacy only English in the national sense by this nation's apparently particularly favourable cultural climate, the genesis and wider implications of which are left unexplored by Leavis in the context of *The Great Tradition*.[2] In the Leavisite perspective, there is, consequently, a specific domain for which the genre of the novel is particularly apt, a domain where the moral sensibility is acted out in terms of a state civilisation especially suitable and ripe for it.

If we accept with Leavis that the capacity for greatness in fiction has a special relationship with a central strain in the English novel tradition, we can see from his singling out of novelists worthy of the epithet that it may be an acquired virtue, something that can be learnt by those sensitive enough to what it takes to be great in this sense of the word. But if we divest Leavis's notion of its admittedly somewhat mystical aura and try to quantify what is presented as irreducible qualification, we may get a glimpse of characteristics of a novel tradition which is, perhaps, more tied up with the dynamics of a specifically national experience than Leavis would have us think, but which at the same time has proved a strong attraction for novelists only English by choice since Henry James and Joseph Conrad.

Leavis's notion of greatness in the novel finding its form as an 'organic principle determining, informing, and controlling into a vital whole' (Leavis, 1972:37) an 'ideal civilized sensibility' is a notion that gives priority to a kind of fiction dedicated to the exploration of themes and issues of a comprehensively existential nature and always anchored in a kind and at a level of society that recognises the need for the constant cultural processing and refining of responses to material circumstances, although the exact nature of these circumstances is only dealt with summarily by Leavis himself. His dismissal of both the Brontës, Dickens and Joyce as peripheral to the great tradition Leavis explains by their alleged lack of both a sufficiently serious existential concern and of a form of expression shaping such a concern into an organic whole.

It would be wrong to read Leavis as just the defender of the tradition of the English novel of manners, of which Jane Austen could be said to be the originator, Henry James the sophisticated modern transfomer, and such middle and late twentieth-century novelists as Barbara Pym and Anita Brookner the gifted epigones. The presence of George Eliot, Joseph Conrad and D.H. Lawrence on his short list of five to make up the great tradition of the English novel certainly falsifies such a view. But Leavis's notion of 'greatness' and 'seriousness' is critically productive if we combine what he assumes but seldom elaborates on, namely the rootedness of existential concerns in the given facts of culture in general, with both a well-developed sense of moral aim and purpose and an aesthetic awareness by which that aim and purpose may be rendered into a unified – 'vital' – fictional construct. In other words, a novel, to qualify for the tradition of greatness, should be one that by its aesthetic wholeness responds to a sense of cultural complexity experienced by the cultivated mind – the 'civilized sensibility' – interested in and capable of distilling the valuable from the contingencies of everyday life.

Just as we should acknowledge a change from Jane Austen to, more than a hundred years later, D.H. Lawrence, we should be careful not to look for epigones of the five novelists singled out by Leavis in our endeavour to update the list. What we should look out for is the kind of novelist interested in the moral implications of the larger perspectives of modern life, the kind of novelist capable of taking in the ethos or the spirit of her or his time, responding to it in full and with an aesthetic product, deeply satisfactory because it is discriminating rather than didactic, subversive rather than the follower of fashion.

If quite a lot of literature written in or relating to Britain over the last few decades of the twentieth century has taken for its theme political developments and social issues very much forming the general culture of the day, it would hardly be enough to be great or serious in Leavis's sense. Kingsley Amis and the other 'kitchen-sink' realists emerging in the 1950s respond too narrowly, in terms of the personal versus the social. This would probably also be true of the verdict on those working the theme of the angry and disillusioned young men of the 1950s into the broader scope of the state-of-Britain novel written by Margaret Drabble and A.S. Byatt. Those working in the wake of Beckett, Joyce, Calvino and Borges, such as John Fowles, Christine Brooke-Rose and Jeanette Winterson, would probably be dismissed as far too formalistic in their concerns, whereas a William Golding might possibly find a place in the great tradition.

But perhaps it would be wrong to look for the perfect novels fitting the description; perhaps it makes much more sense to pay attention to the word 'ideal' when Leavis talks about 'ideal civilized sensibility' and transform his requirements into a set of aims rather than fulfilments. In that perspective, we are looking for novelists trying to get the 'whole picture' or the 'full view' from a perspective decidedly moral in so far as their responses derive from a concern for the state of civilisation in terms of its genetic dynamics, in contrast not only to Leavis himself but also to Leavis's singled-out favourites (which perhaps explains his lack of further curiosity in that direction).

If we agree, at least for the sake of the argument, with Leavis that an especially important strand in the English novel is the one in which we find a profound interest in civilisation, that is in what it takes to be human in a given social context but raised above trivial day-to-day issues, combined with an aesthetic drive to make that into the central matter of fiction, we have a description which will include far more novels than those of the five novelists actually allowed by Leavis, though quite compatible all the same.

In his time, Leavis was concerned to free literary studies from the philological and antiquarian modes cultivated by the contemporary academy. It was important for him to point to novelists whose literary efforts were catalysts in a discussion ultimately concerned with the dynamics of human interaction, in that way an essential part of a current civilisation critique. After a long period of having been relegated to the limbo of elitists, there seemed, towards the end of the twentieth century, to be a growing understanding of Leavis as a critic situating the literary work in a larger cultural context. In a 'retraction' published in 1998, Terry Eagleton reconsiders the politically correct attitude of the 1970s to 1990s and traces the emergence of cultural studies as brought into being later in Birmingham to the Leavises, whose mode of approach contradicted their anti-popular culture aims:

> However grudgingly and selectively, his journal [*Scrutiny*] was an interdisciplinary organ from the outset, preoccupied with history, journalism, politics, music, anthropology, popular culture, and above all education. . . . Leavis's liberal humanism also meant a root-and-branch reform of the university: an end to *belle-lettristic* waffle and the examination system, an insistence on the cultural contexts of literary works, on the significance of criticism for wider social ends, a demand for intellectual seriousness and a scorn for amateur gentility.
> (Eagleton, 1998: 49–50)

If we transpose the Leavisite effort into a context almost three-quarters of a century later, when his ideas have certainly won through and when, paradoxically, he seems reduced to a merely idiosyncratic canon defender, we could say that Leavisite criticism would be not to single out novels in which civilisation critique is both means and end but to shift the attention from the fictional to the critical discourse with a view to applying a critical view privileging those elements in individual works of fiction which accommodate civilisation critique.

It is obvious that this reversal of the Leavisite perspective from the work of fiction to critical screening leaves us with a wide open field of texts not even closed by fictionality as such categorisation hardly makes any sense in this changed perspective. Since the novel is rooted in the representation of a reality assumed shared by writers and readers and devoted to problematising and discussing interlocking issues of that reality, all fiction, to different extents, displays elements relevant to this critical perspective.

The change of the Leavisite concern from the fictional object to the critical approach entails, in practical terms, the reading of texts as documents in a discussion centred on the nature and acquisition of specific kinds of culture. Clearly, for some texts such an approach will be only modestly rewarding, if the textual priorities are markedly different. However, it is my present claim that a critical approach that pays particular attention to the ways a given text negotiates civilisation critique will be extremely rewarding in the case of fictional texts emphasising thematic elements such as national and sub-national identity formation and cultural intersection. Such elements are to be found in the kind of fiction in which priority is given to the discussion of issues to do with the way people interact and the reflections that such interaction may result in: Leavis's 'ideal civilized sensibility; a humanity capable of communicating by the finest shades of inflexion and implication'. A.S. Byatt has proposed a distinction relevant here between kinds of contemporary fiction by suggesting another paradigm to complement, say, feminist paradigms and Marxist paradigms and postmodernist paradigms:

> My novelists are difficult to generalize about because they tell tales about different times and places, sometimes in different styles.... None of these novels are about the condition of England, or the class system, or the British Empire and its demise. They are also not novels about 'personal relationships' or motivation, or Freudian ambiguities, though they can be deeply moving about love and death and fate. They are interested in history and its relation to fable; they are interested in tricks of consciousness, dreams, illusions. The writers are taletellers. They are all, perhaps, fabulists in a European tradition. They have things in common with the Isak Dinesen of the Gothic Tales, with Calvino, Eco, the Dutch Noteboom, the Austrian Ransmayr, with Kundera and Nobokov.
>
> (Byatt, 1996:6)

In the strongly hybrid atmosphere of twentieth-century fiction the distinction between the 'natural' and the 'fantastic' is hardly one that the general reader would be aware of, but it should be said that what Byatt draws attention to, in the wake of Frye, Scholes and Lodge, is a distinction of some consequence in nineteenth-century fiction. Whereas it is indeed hard to define in one hundred per cent exclusive terms the kind of fiction that makes up Leavis's great tradition, since his selection is a symptom of the hybridisation also, we may, despite the pullings towards romance/fable in Conrad and James (and Lawrence to some extent), suggest that Leavis points to another kind of strain central to the English novel tradition, as here cautiously defined by Frye in 1957:

> When we start to think seriously about the novel, not as fiction, but as a form of fiction, we feel that its characteristics, whatever they are, are such as make, say, Defoe, Fielding, Austen, and James central in its tradition, and Borrow, Peacock, Melville, and Emily Bronte somewhat peripheral. This is not an estimate of merit: we may think *Moby Dick* 'greater' than *The Egoist* and yet feel that Meredith's book is closer to being a typical novel. Fielding's conception of the novel as a comic epic in prose seems fundamental to the tradition he did so much to establish. In novels that we think of as typical, like those of Jane Austen, plot and dialogue are closely linked to the conventions of the comedy of manners.... The novel tends to be extroverted and personal; its chief interest is in human character as it manifests itself in society.
>
> (Frye, 1971:304, 308)

Fiction, then, as novel/mock epic/comedy of manners rather than romance/fable/fabulation is the field where we can, tentatively at least, locate Leavis's great tradition. It is a kind of fiction within whose framework it has proved rewarding to position characters addressing problems with their provenance in social interaction. It is a kind of fiction in which society with its mores and restrictions is always very much present, even to the extent of assuming the formidable proportions of a co-actor, not infrequently in the role of antagonist.

Creating fictional universes within this framework at a time when British society is changing radically from monocultural to intercultural, that is, with the 'other' as a more and more visibly given in society, has meant bringing cultural differences and crossings into the foreground. This is to be seen as a dynamic within the fictional universes, for instance in the form of plot dynamics depending on differences of cultures, or in the relations of an author conscious of cultural difference towards his fictional universe.

In what follows I shall discuss five works of fiction – four novels and a short story – in various ways relating to Britain and from the last two decades of the twentieth century. They all respond to a Leavisite notion of 'great tradition' in their comedy-of-manners framework within which to explore an 'ideal civilized sensibility', but of course in contemporary contexts different from the contemporary contexts of Leavis's famous five. The five works of fiction selected here are discussed along a scale starting with a novel which to all appearances is 'indigenously' or 'natively' English, written by an Englishman, who has previously made regional Englishness the theme of a work of fiction. Graham Swift's Booker winner *Last Orders* (1996) is set in London's borough of Bermondsey, moving on into Kent, peopled with elderly south-of-the-river Londoners, whose sensibilities are sharpened by the death of a friend. In the process of carrying out his dying wish, they are forced into making up their personal, existential accounts. On this day of reckoning there is a certain realisation on the part of all involved of the difference between private and public, with feelings of estrangement towards markers of that history by which their private lives have been conditioned. History, especially in the form of World War Two, is the 'other' here.

Also pivoted on the historical as the other are the writings of the Japanese Kazuo Ishiguro, who came to Britain as a child, but was educated in a traditionally British way. His fictional speciality is to reveal private and public repressions of disturbing others. In the one of his four novels set in England, *The Remains of the Day* (1989), repression of a private kind symbolises repression on a national scale, a kind of other which it perhaps takes someone with his roots outside the British Isles to fully appreciate. In the case of Hanif Kureishi, a British citizen of Pakistani origins, the question of the other and with that the 'civilized sensibility' is one of ethnicity and cultural clashes basically, but much more complex as the ethnic divides into cultural polarities and gender gets into play as well.

If in Kureishi's *The Black Album* (1995) the protagonist is accurately aware of a choice between cultural contexts, the Chinese immigrants in Chinese–British Timothy Mo's *Sour Sweet* (1982) represent a community sealing itself up against their chosen cultural context, with the only very occasional appearance of their 'hosts' as anonymous and strangely behaving others. In Indian–British Salman Rushdie's 'Chekov and Zulu' (1994) the discussion moves on to a level where not only are cultural differences given verbal shape in the fictional text, but where textuality itself becomes a major player, in the form of an intriguing complex of intertexts, so that this text may be said to present the ultimate others in both multicultural and textual contexts.

History as other

Set in April – 2 April to be exact, of 1990[3] – and describing the car journey through Kent to Margate of a travelling party, there is seasonal and structural resemblance in *Last Orders* to Chaucer's *Canterbury Tales*, whereas the narrative mode with the party of four and a couple of close relatives confiding the (hi)stories of their lives reminds the reader of the way Virgina Woolf in *The Waves* attempted to present lives in terms of pure consciousness. The point of the pilgrims' journey in Chaucer's tale is to arrive in Canterbury Cathedral to worship at Becket's shrine. Their pilgrimage being devotional in nature, with secular stories to ease the slow progress from London south-eastwards, the travelling party of Swift's narrative have less than full faith in the common sense of the end of their journey – seeing their friend Jack's last wish of having his ashes poured into the sea from the pier in Margate put into practice – but nonetheless achieve some kind of modern-day redemption by being forced by the occasion to take stock of their lives.

The three friends, Vic the undertaker, Lenny the fruit-and-vegetable seller, Ray the insurance man and Vince, stepson of Jack and used-car dealer, are decided to carry out Jack's last wish, although they find it hard to see the sense in the act as such. As they close in on their destination, the weather in an impressive pathetic fallacy build-up deteriorates seriously, and in a torrent of rain they negotiate the slippery surface of what turns out to be a harbour wall, the jetty here being what a pier is elsewhere but now in any case lost some years ago to a storm, this misunderstanding underscoring the general sense of frustration and disappointed expectations shared by all involved. But when the ashes are about to be strewn, the rain eases and there is a stripe of light in the lead-grey sky and an elemental union is taking place as the earthly remains of Jack, together with the

> sky and the sea and the wind are all mixed up together... and the ash that I carried in my hands, which was the Jack who once walked around, is carried away by the wind, is whirled away by the wind, is whirled away by the wind till the ash becomes wind and the wind becomes Jack what we're made of.
>
> (Swift, 1999:294–5)

Jack's choice of last resting place is in lieu of actually retiring there with his wife Amy, Margate being where the two of them enjoyed a brief honeymoon just before the war.

Swift's mock modern-day pilgrimage is a story about possible fates of those young men and women who seem to have been frozen into eternal heroic icons in their army and navy uniforms and light and summery dresses. Their reminiscences take us back to a time considerably less heroic and much more muddled when it comes to motivation and acts of bravery. We are offered only the briefest of glimpses into the actualities of British war and immediately post-war history, a certain knowledge of which is taken for granted in order to appreciate such story elements as Vince's escaping early fatherhood and learning the butcher's trade by joining the army and going overseas to Aden, where his training as a mechanic seems to have overshadowed the political issues which go into the history books.

So *Last Orders* is a story of personal commitments, chances, frustrations and hopes in representatives of a population segment seldom given a voice in British fiction, which usually focuses on either the middle class or the working class. Swift's small-scale self-employed and lower-echelon office staff just getting by, have their roots in central, south-of-the-river London and a literal as well as abstract horizon formed by roofs rather than treetops. To them the topography is very much a matter of identifying places and routes in terms of transportation. Throughout their car journey a careful log is kept on the itinerary, so the reader is left with a firm impression of a city and a countryside in terms of a map rather than anything else.

Practically minded Londoners displaying 'ideal civilized sensibility' in a context where globalisation is seen only in brief glimpses and then to act as a foil to the moral stature of the dramatis personae, as when Vince suddenly finds himself realising that he has been pimping his daughter to the London-City businessman Hussein to secure a car sale. The sensibility is displayed time and time again in the way these people, not really used to delicacies of address or polished argument, act out their feelings accompanied by – and this is the central virtue of the narrative mode chosen by Swift – reflections that place these acts in perspectives of personal histories and take away any gaucheness which may have resulted from witnessing the act in isolation. Thus the former boxer Lenny's act of sudden physical aggression towards Vince is understood if not justified by the bitterness accumulated over Vince's jilting of Lenny's daughter Sally after making her pregnant.

In *Last Orders* the other is manifest in the form of World War Two, of Jack's and Amy's retarded daughter June, of the Hussein of foreign wealth and, more vaguely, as national history symbolised by Canterbury Cathedral.

All four old friends did war service: Jack, Ray and Lenny in the army and Vic in the navy, Jack and Ray in the same unit during the desert campaign in North Africa. Jack's stepson Vince also did military service for five years at the time of the British pulling out of Aden. So all of them were involved at 'grassroot' level in the making of modern British history, but all of them came back only to find themselves frustrated by the discrepancy between the nature of their personal efforts for king and country and the way society seemed to ignore them on returning. Memories of war keep cropping up as flashes of memory either to do with military routine or the playing down of anything amounting to heroic action: sand and exhaustion in the case of Ray and Lenny, sea burials in the case of Vic, and motor maintenance in the case of Vince. When Vic suggests they make a detour to see the navy war memorial at Chatham, which none of them have ever dreamt of seeing although it was erected as a tribute to men of their kind, the others are incredulous and somewhat self-conscious. Facing the memorial the three old veterans each draw the same kind of existential conclusion, of which the memorial, and the wars that it stands for, are in the last instance only symbols. Vic the undertaker muses:

> But I know about the dead, I know about dead people, and I know that the sea is all around us anyway. Even on land we're all at sea, even on this hill high above Chatham where I can read the names. All in our berths going to our deaths.
> (Swift, 1999:125)

Ray puts his many years as a 'lucky' racing better into his response:

> But it's hard to have an attitude where there aren't no odds given and you can't see no larger mathematics. All you can tell by looking down the lists, and it don't matter that they're set in bronze on a white wall on top of a hill with an obelisk stuck in front of them an' all, is that a man is just a name. Which means something to him it attaches to, and to anyone who deals, same way, in the span of a human life, but it don't mean a monkey's beyond that. It don't mean a monkey's to things that live longer, like armies and navies and insurance houses and the Horserace Totalisator Board, it all goes on when you're gone and you don't make a blip. There's only one sensible attitude to take, looking at the lists, there's only one word of wisdom, like when Micky Dennis and Bill Kennedy copped it: 'It aint me, it wasn't me, it aint ever going to be me.' And there's only one lesson to be drawn, it's as cheery as it's not cheery, and that's that it aint living you're doing, they call it living, it's surviving.
> (Swift, 1999:127–8)

And there is Lenny along the same lines:

> It's a question of duty. There's a soldier's duty, a sailor's duty. Heligoland. Jutland. But if you ask me, that aint duty so much as orders. Doing your duty in the ordinary course of life is another thing, it's harder. It's like Ray always said that Jack was a fine soldier, Jack should've got a medal, but when it came to being back in Civvy Street, he didn't know nothing better, like most of us, than to stick like glue to what he knew, like there was an order sent down from High Command that he couldn't ever be nothing else but a butcher.
>
> (Swift, 1999:132)

Active service, once the inescapable reality of their lives in stark contrast to whatever they were doing at the time, has become a kind of existential exception, only leaving a lesson of disillusionment to be stoically responded to.

Graham Swift writes from the core of England and Britain in this fiction about the modest but sadly shattered dreams of loyal British citizens and the harsh realities of post-war and post-imperial Britain. Although this is more generally a novel about the vanity of human wishes, the five men suffer from a common failure to feel themselves part of a consensus culture. The new money in the shape of Hussein, for whose condescending and after all not very munificent custom Vince suddenly realises with self-disgust that he has compromised himself and his daughter, is a reminder of the way intercultural Britain is constituted. But a much more forceful impression of the sense of an 'other' is left by the burial party paying their visit to the monument to dead navy servicemen at Chatham. Set up to commemorate the ultimate sacrifice for King and Country, a sacrifice not demanded of the four older men although they were at constant risk during the war, they approach it as tourists, with only Vic for a moment responding to it in different terms. With World War Two having long ago in Britain assumed the shape, status and function of a myth in extension of the home-front propaganda offered during the war, the discrepancy between the realities of war, as experienced by the four men, and its subsequent representations, among which of course a war memorial is one of the more conventional items, has widened to become indeed unbridgeable. As the destination of this updated Chaucerian pilgrimage is not of the grandeur its name seems to signify, notions and expectations have to be revalued to fit in with a world that has overtaken the men and left them as anachronisms, just as the ending of the novel reads like the pathetic anachronism of fiction belonging to an age given to unity and consensus.

A.S. Byatt in her introduction to *The Oxford Book of English Short Stories* notes about V.S. Naipaul and Kazuo Ishiguro:

> Both these writers use the English language perfectly, and with full knowledge of what has been written in it, to do something detached from Englishness, looking *at* Englishness.
>
> (Byatt, 1998a:xxix; original emphasis)

Ishiguro and Naipaul may indeed raise eyebrows at the hint of patronising attitude in the first sentence of this statement, but it is certainly true of both writers that they cultivate detachment in terms of nationality as a vantage point for approaching Britishness – in their cases Englishness is certainly too narrow a frame of reference – from intercultural angles. For Naipaul his 'triple citizenship' as British, West Indian and Indian has given him the possibility of cultivating several detachments *vis-à-vis* cultures of origin and of adoption, whereas for Ishiguro his coming to Britain in 1960 as a six-year-old child and going through a traditional British education must have given him only the vaguest sense of country of origin against the actuality of the adopted country. But then, perhaps, Leavis's 'ideal civilized sensibility' is the privilege of the writer for whom the double vision of immigrant and native in relation to Britain is not a question of perfect balance between the two, but of having the former outweighed by the latter, leaving the naturalised immigrant with just enough sense of foreignness to experience the adopted country like a doctor treating a dear relative with love and clinical distance simultaneously. Henry James and Joseph Conrad share this double vision of the naturalised foreigner with Naipaul and Ishiguro, whereas of course the same can hardly be said of Jane Austen, George Eliot and D.H. Lawrence. Yet it may be argued that a similar kind of detachment is at work in these writers, for whom there was a distance between actual and desired situations: for Jane Austen the social distance between parsonage and gentry, for George Eliot the imposed distance of the female writer forced to market her writings under a man's name, and for Lawrence the distance between what he saw as a petrified civilisation only to be redeemed by a greater physical awareness.

Kazuo Ishiguro's *A Pale View of Hills* shares its narrative structure with *An Artist of the Floating World* (1986) and *The Remains of the Day* (1989) whereas the structure is somewhat different in *The Unconsoled* (1995), with a return to a (semi-)realistic universe in *When We Were Orphans* (2000). Characteristic of the first three novels is a narrative technique comparable to Browning's in the monologues: a partly deliberate partly unconscious repression of central events and elements in the narrator's life, the gaps however making the reader gradually aware of the true state of things. Detachment, distance and repression thus become aspects of the same phenomenon: the reluctance to come to terms with an unpleasant, perhaps even mentally destructive, reality.

In *A Pale View of Hills* and *An Artist of the Floating World* we overhear Japanese people reflecting on their lives, only hinting at the events which have determined their present circumstances. In *A Pale View of Hills* there seems to be a traumatic event lurking in the past of what appears to be a perfectly assimilated and well-balanced person. Once the reader begins to piece together the past of the women living in the aftermath of the nuclear bombings of Hiroshima and Nagasaki, there appears as image of a narrator desperately holding on to normality by refusing to face certain events back there; allowing them access would mean instantaneous mental breakdown.

In *An Artist of the Floating World* the situation is somewhat different, since here we have to do with a narrator, who has deliberately chosen to distance himself from his past as an artist contributing to the Japanese war effort by making war propaganda, a past now frowned upon and blocking his post-war career. The narrator remains unconvinced of his war crimes, but allows them to dwindle into the background by letting everyday trivialities possess him totally.

The Remains of the Day follows this pattern, only this time transposed into the 1950s – July 1956 – when Stevens, a butler 'inherited' by the new American owner of a distinguished English country house, combines business with pleasure when he sets out on a motor journey to call on a former housekeeper to persuade her to rejoin the service staff. As he motors through a countryscape fulfilling all the stereotypical expectations of 'olde Englande', he muses on his past, taking pride in his professional behaviour throughout a lifetime of service to Lord Darlington. As his complacent thoughts proceed, the reader is made aware of a man with a pathologically stunted emotional life, always determined to carry on in his duties without regarding any larger or alternative contexts.

Ishiguro's novel is a brilliantly exercised portrait of a person driven to emotional destruction by an overwhelming sense of duty, a sense which surely has origins which psychoanalysis would reveal. But the novel is more than the drawing of a complex portrait. It is a subtle indictment of certain political activities in pre-war Britain for which the butler's emotional tunnel vision becomes a metaphor.

If it is possible to talk about repressed national memories, then the sympathy for the Nazi cause in prewar Britain in the British Union of Fascists led by Sir Oswald Mosley is one such case. The fictional Lord Darlington in Ishiguro's novel has secret meetings with German officials and British sympathisers while the butler and his staff are expected to be part of the furniture. So they become 'partners in crime' by their silence and lack of initiative.

In terms of discourse a postmodernist tour de force, *The Remains of the Day* explodes two well-entrenched British myths at the same time: the validity of the stiff upper lip and the image of all the nation united to fight the Nazis. It offers a fictional glimpse into a part of the past excluded from the notion of a Britain united in concerted war effort against Nazism. Using the figure of the loyal butler, a phenomenon greatly amplified in literature, Ishiguro uses one myth-related construct to reveal the cracks of another. But in this hall of mythical mirrors one begins to wonder if the novel is not indeed, in allegorical fashion, a more general indictment of a post-war Britain, like the butler, refusing to get new bearings in a new world – the old castle now owned by an American businessman – and happily ignoring the lessons of the past. The novel qualifies, in the light of such a reading, as a text engaging with issues familiar from post-colonial writings, but definitely in terms of morals, not of the social or political.

The 'other' in multicultural London

Part *Bildungsroman* (of the *Künstlerroman* variety), part civilisation critique (from an ethnic and multicultural perspective), Hanif Kureishi's *The Black Album* presents a London Pakistani youth's attempt to come to terms with a double cultural context. In comparison with the maze-like London of Timothy Mo's *Sour Sweet* (discussed below) the metropolis in Kureishi's novel is an emphatically postmodern market-place offering all sorts of existential panaceas for a culturally bewildered youth. With the youth having halfheartedly given his Islamic fundamentalist brethren the benefit of the doubt, while at the same time cultivating a sexual relationship with his older and liberally experienced college professor, the story ends on a rather exhausted note, promising no fulfilment, only the (picaresque) possibility of more of the same:

> He didn't have to think about anything. They looked across at one another as if to say, what new adventure is this?
> 'Until it stops being fun', she said.
> 'Until then', he said.
>
> (Kureishi, 1995:276)

'Being fun' is indeed the principle that seems to energise life for young AD 1989 Londoners, except for those fired by a holy mission, and to whom Shahid experimentally gives his tentative and temporary sympathy. Split between a fundamentalist and strict religious culture for which the end justifies any means, however violent, and a hedonist culture, of which also Shahid's own non-religious family is part, only further exploration of potential titillating stimulation – 'fun' – seems to be the way forward, an existential situation a paradigm shift away from Lawrence's Paul Morel setting out to actualise the potential he has found in himself, or Joyce's Stephen Dedalus turning his back on Ireland to follow an artistic vocation.

Shahid's existential uncertainty is the instrument which allows Kureishi to probe into a society in cultural transition. Shahid's bookish background is the safe Western canon, and at that considerably broader than that of the average first-year college student:

> Shahid had picked up Joad, Laski and Popper, and studies of Freud, along with fiction by Maupassant, Henry Miller, and the Russians. He had also gone to the library almost every day; desultory reading was his greatest pleasure, with interruptions for pop records. He had moved from book to book as on stepping stones, both for fun and out of fear of being with people who had knowledge which might exclude him.
>
> (Kureishi, 1995:20)

At a loss to answer his fundamentalist mentor-to-be Chad's traditionally utilitarian query why he keeps reading when the reality of the world is more than enough to deal with, his mental response is along Leavisite lines:

> He looked ardently at the books piled on the desk. Open one and out would soar, as if trapped within, once-upon-a-times, open-sesames, marriages like those of Swann and Odette or Levin and Kitty, even Sheherazade and King Shariya. The most fantastic characters, Raskolnikov, Joseph K., Boule De Suif, Ali Baba, made of ink but living always, were entrapped in the profoundest dilemmas of living. How would he begin to answer Chad?
>
> (Kureishi, 1995:20)

If he is attracted by the literary representations of the 'profoundest dilemmas of living', Shahid's own picaresque vagaries in London in search of some existential absolute are indeed of exactly this kind, only shifted in pace and emphases, that is in kind but not degree, from the literary examinations of Leavis's Great Five. The 'ideal civilized sensibility' at work when Austen, Eliot, James, Conrad and Lawrence act out their fictional dramas is not a question of staying within a monocultural context. Rather – and for this the 'immigrants' are particularly well situated – we have to do with sensibility sharpened by a personally acquired sense of cultural fault lines, hinged on class and on what James called the International Theme, both of which imply representations of identities formed by exposure to the 'other' in a number of manifestations signalling the challenge of standards accepted by custom. Kureishi has his protagonist Shahid testing the temptation and possibilities of fundamentalist religion in the political cauldron-climate of 1989, with the new world order taking shape at the same time as the regressive blow of the fatwah against Salman Rushdie – a sub-theme of the novel – stirs up violent feelings on both sides and not only draws the line more markedly between followers of Islam and infidels but also opens up deep rifts in Islamic communities abroad as well as in Britain.

Only one of Timothy Mo's novels is set completely in Britain: *Sour Sweet* (1982). In a successful writing career Mo has made the most of his half-Chinese lineage and Hong Kong childhood to use the eurocentrically-defined Far East as the theatre for his fiction, in which cultural clashes and ethnic hybridity form the overall theme.

Londoners of 'native stock' only appear as extras in *Sour Sweet*. They are the customers served by Hong Kong emigrated Chen, his wife Lily and sister-in-law Mui in their successful south London take-away diner (and the lorry drivers whose additional appetites Mui finds it remunerative to satisfy), and the occasional policeman and social worker. In this novel of Chinese Triad-gangsters operating in Britain within a closed community usually 'sold' to the British public and tourists as picturesque Soho in central London and Chinatowns in the larger cities, the reader is forced to have a look at London and Britain through the eyes of the immigrant eager to become part of the adopted culture but for a whole range of reasons stuck in his old:

> The Chens had been living in the UK for four years, which was long enough to have lost their place in the society from which they had emigrated but not long enough to feel comfortable in the new.
>
> (Mo, 1997:1)

In this particular story it is the son's traditional duty towards his father which makes Chen turn to his own people to raise money, in the process having to 'regress' to what he originally wanted to get away from. It is this 'flaw' that makes for his tragic fate. But otherwise life proves kind to the small family, with Lily understanding much more than she lets on, navigating with increasing ease and familiarity in the foreign surroundings.

Reversing the perspective of London presumed well known to (Western) readers and reducing the 'natives' to extras is a narrative device of great effect for the purpose of highlighting by alienation. This is not the London as financial or trade centre, not the Big Ben cum Houses of Parliament and red double-decker buses of millions of postcards. In *Sour Sweet* the metropolis is a contourless maze, in which as an immigrant not too sure of your status or rights you can get safely lost. The description of Chen's daily commuting from their NW9 flat, which he and his family have occupied for three-and-a-half years, to his job in a Soho restaurant off Gerard Street is that of someone stealing his way in:

> At the end of the row was a passage with a double bend, so that what seemed to strangers like a blind alley was in reality a concealed entrance, constructed on the same principle as a crude lobster trap. A sharp right turn after passing an iron bollard took the knowledgeable or intrepid into a gloomy canyon formed by the blind backs of two forty-feet high Georgian terraces. Rubbish filled the alley. At night rats scrabbled in the piles of rotting vegetable leaves and soggy cardboard boxes. There was a muffled silence in the enclosure. At the other end another series of baffles led, quite suddenly, into the brightness and sound of Leicester Square. This was Chen's habitual shortcut to the Underground station.
>
> (Mo, 1997:26–7)

When the need arises to get away from the Soho-located Triad gangsters, the solution is to find another maze in London south of the river. Again, the neighbourhood is a place to get – productively – lost in. Lily succeeds in losing a police car in pursuit when licenceless – too expensive with all those taxes and so on! – and drives round London in their newly acquired old car.

If London is a contourless maze, a place of hiding places, the 'natives' are only cursorily observed and their manners and ways wondered at. An old man with running eyes is dismissed by Lily as looking 'like one of the old colonial types' (Mo, 1997:160), and it is quite telling that the only 'real Englishman' with whom the

132 Intercultural Voices in Contemporary British Literature

Chen family communicates is their new South London neighbour, the Greek garage-owner Mr Constantinides, who is seen by Mui thus: 'You couldn't very well get a more flesh and blood specimen, redder and hairier, than the present example of an Englishman' (ibid.:104). The family's observations on the English are few. They respond with the kind of generalisation with which Westerners traditionally approach Africans and Asians: 'Lily found it difficult except in certain obvious cases to distinguish between those bland, roseate occidental faces. They all looked the same to her' (ibid.:137). They find the English behaving in mysterious ways (about Mr Constantinides: 'Their ways are odd' (ibid.:114)) and they find the workers whom they serve slightly threatening: 'The English were peppery, often manufacturing pretexts for anger when none reasonably existed: a stare held too long, failure to meet their round eye at all' (ibid.:83) and the 'surly and impassive English who came her way' (ibid.:94). The English seem to prefer easy comfort most of all, a softness of life which disgusts the Chens and which Chen himself is decided to oppose by keeping fit. Generalised prejudice also seems to thrive this side of the ethnic barrier, as when Mui ponders, 'For all their good qualities the English had a tendency to go on appearances rather than more fundamental judgments' (ibid.:152). The stereotypical Western anticipation of corruption in non-WASPish parts of the world is countered nicely by Lily's precaution of putting a banknote in her empty driving licence plastic folder – as events later prove, a wise arrangement. The way the English care for their elderly people – or rather do not care – is a constant source of wonder and scorn: 'nothing less than shameful neglect, a national disgrace' (ibid.:86), the opposite ironically leading to Chen's death.

So the tables of prejudice are turned on the English, the reader contributing much more by way of implicit context in the perusal of this novel than may be immediately realised. Compared with Kureishi's *The Black Album* there is a significant difference in the way that 'ideal civilized sensibility' is applied to subject matter, a difference explained partly by the difference in temporal setting of the two works of fiction – Mo's in the early 1960s and Kureishi's in the late 1980s – partly by the kind of trouble in which the immigrant Chen gets himself involved because of strong cultural ties with his cultural origin and in which the second-generation, Kent-raised, middle-class Shahid finds himself by setting out in search of 'ways in which he could belong' (Kureishi 1995:16). Shahid is increasingly bewildered not only by acknowledging his status as a member of an ethnic minority in Britain, but also by the contradictory signals from his own people, some of whom strive to assimilate, some of whom with contempt towards the British now take on the '"brown man's burden"' (ibid.:6) in purely secular matters, and some of whom are determined to fight for a religiously founded state. But in both novels there is an equally keen awareness of the nature of the forces which their protagonists are up against.

Salman Rushdie's 'Chekov and Zulu' from *East, West* (1994) is a showpiece of ostentatious intertextuality, with explicit borrowings from *Star Trek* terminology and political-thriller plotting in the story of 'Chekov' the shrewd diplomat and his close friend 'Zulu', the intellectually somewhat less endowed security officer. As they are both in London at the time of the assassination of Prime Minister Indira Gandhi, a plan is hatched to infiltrate the Sikh community in London to see if the murderous trail leads to or from London.

Chekov, a dapper thirty-three-year-old Indian career diplomat, is ambiguous in his attitude to Britain, able to engage the linguistic registers of Indian English and English English – in addition to his proficient command of Hollywood-originated *Star Trek* lingo, the preferred mode of communication between the two friends. Although he is adept at mimicking the mores of his host country, there is no doubt about his national loyalty.

When Rajiv Gandhi is assassinated in May 1991 in southern India, Chekov is present and close to the Prime Minister (Zulu having long ago set up successful shop in Bombay as a private-security entrepreneur). In the scene where time has stopped at the moment of the Tamil woman firing her gun, Chekov (a fellow victim?) has time to reflect:

'These Tamil revolutionists are not England-returned', he noted. 'So, finally, we have learned to produce the goods at home and no longer need to import. Bang goes that old dinner-party standby; so to speak.'

(Rushdie, 1994:170)

A superficial reading of the story would leave the reader to interpret the story as the realisation that only now – with 'home-grown' political activists – has India gained full independence. However, the story is much more subtly about the construction of identities and the expression of emotions, all in terms of the culturally given. For this purpose, stereotypes of the other are continually debunked, with the *Star Trek* intertext functioning as both emotional safety valve and blatantly constructed foil.

Roles are shifted and values rapidly renegotiated in the introductory scene, cut and pasted location-wise from so many secret-agent yarns, with Chekov and Zulu sitting on a bench in Embarkment Gardens. When Chekov suddenly exclaims, 'Crooks,' Zulu is ready for immediate pursuit, but Chekov intended the colonial British as a whole. When Chekov, despite admitting admiration for the British ('I see the remnant of greatness and I don't mind telling you that I am impressed' (ibid.:155)) concludes that his own home 'has been plundered by burglars' (ibid.), Zulu again understands this quite literally by offering his opinion that the thieves are probably no longer in the neighbourhood. Chekov goes on to lecture Zulu rather pompously on colonial exploitation, with so many Indian treasures now on display in Britain. Again Zulu takes the air out of Chekov's balloon by pointing at a tramp asleep on the next bench, asking if he too is part of a colonial conspiracy to exploit the colonised. When Chekov assumes the part of the overbearing teacher holding forth in a neo-Marxist manner of analysis showing how the British working class were exploited and exploiters at the same time, Zulu is ready to contribute instant deconstruction by stubbornly sticking to the concrete: '"But a beggarman is not in the working class," objected Zulu, reasonably. "Surely this fellow at least is not our oppressor"' (ibid.:156).

This kind of debunking takes place repeatedly in the story, significantly in the telephone conversation between Zulu and his wife when he wants to pass a message for help in coded *Star Trek* language to Chekov and during which the life-and-death import is nearly missed in the wife's reluctance to be persuaded by this childish language. Also at a dinner party held by Chekov an on-the-spur rhetorical effort by Chekov on the British education of the big Indian statesmen is eventually drowned by the banal observations of his – true-to-stereotype – 'septuagenarian Very Big Businessman's improbably young and attractive wife' (ibid.:164–5).

Rushdie has Chekov facing death in the sci.-fi. English of *Star Trek*, not in his immaculate, diplomatic English, nor in the English adapted to Indian languages which he uses in conversation with Zulu and Zulu's wife. But again, in the conclusive scene, the Hollywood idiom is shifted from signifier to signified. Chekov and Zulu used this kind of language when at school:

> Lots of us tried the names on for size but only two of them stuck; probably because they seemed to go together, and the two of us got on pretty well, even though he was younger. A lovely boy. So just like Laurel and Hardy we were Chekov and Zulu.
>
> (Rushdie, 1994:165)

'Chekov and Zulu' reflects the concern in Rushdie's massive *oeuvre* to consider and reconsider received wisdom, with linguistic flexibility the ultimate symbol of the evasiveness of fixed and permanent values. Time and again, in this story and in the rest of Rushdie's work, the play of floating signifiers reveals lack of trust in any ultimate and stable signified state, except the longing for genuine attachments and the inescapability of death.

Rushdie's short story may be read as an exploration of existential fundamentals in terms of the givens of culture, of which language is both means and symbol. As an example of a piece of fiction expressing an 'ideal civilized sensibility' in a contemporary – post-colonial and globalised – context, 'Chekov and Zulu' must be said to live up to Leavis's idea of greatness.

It is, of course, highly doubtful whether the writers discussed above or others who have chosen an English 'format' for their fiction have done so in relation to an articulated notion of an 'ideal civilized sensibility'. Characteristic of Leavis's five novelists eminently representative of the great tradition in English fiction is the concern for the moral aspects of the specific time and social environment in which their characters find themselves. Jane Austen, George Eliot, Henry James, Joseph Conrad and D.H. Lawrence may all be said to be novelists exploring themes of transition, responding each of them to upheavals in their communities in terms of moral consequences. Furthermore, characteristic of Leavis's five is their various kinds and degrees of outsider status, least, perhaps, in the case of Austen, and most in the case of Conrad. Still, Austen's personal situation made her an onlooker rather than a participant in the social games she described. A.S. Byatt's observation with reference to V.S. Naipaul and Kazuo Ishiguro to the point that their distance is what enables them to 'do something detached from Englishness, looking *at* Englishness' (1998:xxix) could be said to apply generally. Distance itself, however, does not do the trick. For instance, Vikram Seth's *An Equal Music* (1999), written by an Indian author, set in Vienna and London, with a cast of English men and women only, and with no trace whatsoever of the author's national roots, is not, however subtle in its use of music and brilliant in its narrative control, the kind of story that I have discussed above. In that respect it lacks the interventionist drive, so to speak, into the civilisation in which it is set, for which some kind of distance, either of the author's own situation (Ishiguro, Kureishi, Mo, Rushdie) or as displacement of authorial situation, as integrated into the fabric of the novel as theme of alienation (Swift). Nor is it a feature of the very popular comedy of manners type of fiction represented by Nick Hornby, which views society and morals from the position of the insider, lacking the perspective of distance, whether authorial or displaced as an element in the narrative universe.

If Leavis's notion of 'ideal civilized sensibility' must be somewhat reoriented in the light of British history since the mid-twentieth century, its demand for the awareness in the narrative discourse of moral implication of social situation is still relevant as one of the ways to cope with a present curving away from a consensus view of the past and coming to terms with a radically changing demographic, political and cultural reality.

6
Global Villagers

It is only by remaining dynamic, by evolving, that a culture or a literary tradition continues to live. It is its loopholes, its openness to the 'other' or 'others' which allows it to review and develop itself. In literature and in poetry it is those writers who look abroad who are often its most valuable territorial voices.

(Crawford, 1993:13)

If, as I argued in the previous chapter, there has been a tendency for writers of fiction privileged with the outsiders' point of view in relation to Britain to embrace the conventions of the 'great tradition' with its focus on character and morals with a 'technique' honed on 'ideal civilized sensibility', there has been a symmetrical tendency for writers privileged with the insiders' point of view to look abroad, sometimes accompanied by a temporal shift of setting as well.

The subjection of foreign mores to an English or British sensibility is characteristic of the peculiar generic mix of fiction (formal aspects) and travel account in the very personal travelogue. This hybrid genre has been cultivated since commercial possibilities were seen in emulating the cultivated – and rich! – male adolescent's Grand Tour of Europe. Tobias Smollett's *Travels Through France and Italy* (1766), mocked and improved on by Laurence Sterne in his *A Sentimental Journey* (1768), may be said to be prototypes of a genre, which, at the time of the height of Empire and growing scientific curiosity during the nineteenth century, branched into learned reporting aimed at the London Royal Society, as, for instance, in Sir Richard Burton's work, or degenerated into sensational journalism aimed at the British newspaper-reading public, or became specialised guidebook writing useful for British customers at Cooks.

The travelogue having ceded to the information-packed Baedeker type of guidebook since the mid-nineteenth century, the travelogue as a kind of *catalogue raisonné* of a very personal experience of being abroad has had a renaissance in the late twentieth century in the hands of such different writers as Jan Morris and Bruce Chatwin. As a reaction to the mass tourism developing exponentially in the latter half of the twentieth century, the individualism of the youth culture-conscious backpacker enlightened and at the same time disgusted by the public appropriation of global matters symbolised by a CNN kind and scale of coverage could only be met by a degree of intimacy when it came to the relation of travel experience corresponding to the reactive individualism.

As observed in Chapter 2, British fiction set abroad in the centuries of Empire has, in the main, been of the sensational kind aimed at a young audience and portraying the British adventurer–colonist as a pioneer settler, scientific researcher or missionary, sometimes all three at one time. Only as the sun begins to set on Empire do we see novelists applying the conventions of the 'great tradition' to dealing – and then critically – with Empire, whereas the response to the radically new situation in terms of the fiction directed at a mass audience took a very pragmatic view of the situation from the 1950s, or, in the form of the secret-agent thriller, sought to compensate fictionally for a reality lacking in national grandeur.

However, the Grand Tour travelogues of the eighteenth century, the sensational 'colonial' fiction of the nineteenth century, the critical 'great-tradition' fiction of the early twentieth century, and the pragmatically oriented mid-twentieth-century mass-market fiction, have all, however much the action may be set somewhere in the (former) colonies, had Britain as the central point of reference. The Enlightenment era travelogues are notes that constantly compare with conditions at home, the nineteenth-century colonising hero abroad (and his late twentieth-century successor the SIS or MI6 agent on his assignment for queen and country) is constantly aware of his white (English)man's burden, and a diminished Britain is the backdrop of both critically and pragmatically minded dramatis personae in early and middle twentieth-century British fiction set abroad.

There are writers, of course, on whom these neat categories fit only with a high toleration margin. In the cases of Somerset Maugham, Graham Greene and Lawrence Durrell we have very idiosyncratic motivations for settings abroad, not least instigated by the personal histories of the three writers as voluntary exiles from a Britain which confined them too much. Nonetheless, in them, despite the striking absence of any particular position on Empire at a time when such a position must be said to have been almost mandatory, the awareness of the Englishman abroad looms large.

The kind of fiction selected for attention in this chapter is fiction written by British writers who have preferred a setting abroad, combined sometimes with a temporal 'displacement' as well, for stories or novels in which Britain is either absent or, if present, not directly linked with the (former) Empire of (post)colonialism, but serving as a personal link to put the experience abroad into some kind of perspective. When a novelist chooses a setting for his narrative other than her or his native ground, it may be for all kinds of reason, ranging from personal attraction to a foreign place to the adoption of obviously symbolic overtones or conventional values attached to a given locale, the difference between the latter two being often hard to appreciate. Putting an individual or a group on a desert island obviously enhances the elucidation and test of character and power of endurance, but since Daniel Defoe the locale has become a literary topos, with compelling intertextual linkages in addition to those of immediate consequence from the symbolic overtones. The thematic significance of William Golding's *The Lord of the Flies* (1954), for instance, is readily appreciable without recourse to literary antecedents, but as both existential statement and literary artefact it has its place along with other desert island stories.

Of less unambiguous symbolic functionability in relation to British writers is the Mediterranean. Chosen as a place of permanent or temporary residence by British poets and novelists since the early nineteenth century, the sunnier climate and 'exotic' cultures of the area have been made to signify existential values alternative to those at home in Britain. To E.M. Forster Greece (in 'The Road from Colonus', 1911) and Italy (*Where Angels Fear to Tread*, 1905; *A Room with a View*, 1908) meant a liberating challenge to what he saw as a British life style building on the repression of feelings and lack of interhuman contacts. Also D.H. Lawrence (notably in his poetry) and Lawrence Durrell (in both *The Alexandria Quartet*, 1957–60 and the *Avignon Quintet*, 1974–85) looked to the Mediterranean as the literary catalyst of emotions stifled in a British context. But the Mediterranean, *in casu* Venice, also in some cases has come to represent the demonic, as we see in both Ian McEwan's *The Comfort of Strangers* (1981) and Jeanette Winterson's *The Passion* (1987) both in this respect pointing back to Thomas Mann's obsession-probing novella *Der Tod in Venedig* (1912).

In a number of instances British writers' setting of fictional narratives away from Britain serves the purpose, described by A.S. Byatt in the previous chapter, of creating a wider space for fabulation, sometimes enhanced by a temporal 'displacement' as well. If this choice of locale is meant to create a sounding board for romance, adventure and the fantastic, authentic local colour is here of less importance than projections of the imagination's 'pathetic fallacy'. But it is hard to distinguish it from the kind of fiction in which, as Byatt says about Rose Tremain, her 'imagination (like that of many other younger English writers) reaches out in a new way into unknown places and experiences – not out of exoticism, but out of curiosity' (1998:xxviii).

Rather than pursue this line of distinction between 'exoticism' and 'curiosity' in relation to the foreign, which is hardly anyway a genuine contrast, I shall look at ways in which the other of the foreign has been constructed in selected British fiction of the last decades of the twentieth century, a period during which 'globalisation' has become a household word. The focal point will be the degree of presence of what may be put admittedly somewhat inadequately as a British consciousness or awareness in the texts under consideration.

The relationship between home and abroad in a context of writing has often been taken to be one of 'inspiration by contrast', as is basically the message of Robert Crawford:

Ashbery in France or in the nineteenth century, Murray in Scotland or in Australia's Aboriginal culture, MacDiarmid in Salonika, Marseilles or London – these are but a few instances of identifying poets who develop an identity with and for their own culture through a fructifying engagement with another culture and literature.

(Crawford, 1993:13)

Opposed to this view, which sees the local or the regional as potentially enhanced by exposition to the other, we find a view which despairs of the lack of potential existential or cultural rapport. In his 1999 Booker-winning novel *Disgrace*, South African writer J.M. Coetzee has his narrator David Lurie meditate in his self-imposed rural exile on the person and situation of the neighbouring native farmer:

> What appeals to him in Petrus is his face, his face and his hands. If there is such a thing as honest toil, then Petrus bears its marks. A man of patience, energy, resilience. A peasant, a *paysan*, a man of the country. A plotter and schemer and no doubt a liar too, like peasants everywhere. Honest toil and honest cunning.
>
> (Coetzee, 1999:117)

David Lurie is curious about Petrus's story of his life, but is not certain that the medium suffices:

> He would not mind hearing Petrus's story one day. But preferably not reduced to English. More and more he is convinced that English is an unfit medium for the truth of South Africa. Stretches of English code whole sentences long have thickened, lost their articulations, their articulateness, their articulatedness. Like a dinosaur expiring and settling in the mud, the language has stiffened. Pressed into the mould of English, Petrus's story would come out arthritic, bygone.
>
> (Coetzee, 1999:117)

In Crawford's argument, abroad serves as that against which the 'identifying poet' may measure his or her ultimate attachment to his or her origin. In the work of identifying poets, then, the absent abroad looms large by implication, just as to Toni Morrison the black presence is everywhere in American writing, also when not specifically there (see Chapter 8). This presence by absence is beyond the concern of this chapter, although acknowledged as an important parameter in all texts emerging from contexts of tension or repression. What concerns me here is something much less speculative and theoretical, namely the significance of settings abroad both as a general literary trend of late twentieth-century British literature and its actualisation in individual works.

The fiction under consideration here is not in the category of the absent abroad under scrutiny in Crawford's study, nor is it of the kind indicated by Coetzee's narrator, who can see no possible redemption of one culture in another language. Rather, it is in between. Set abroad in relation to its British author, this kind of text negotiates the foreign in terms of the homely, and vice versa. In contrast to Crawford's perspective, in which the other is present by its very absence, either this kind of fiction balances the foreign and the British, as in Ian McEwan's *The Comfort of Strangers* (1981), Julian Barnes's *Flaubert's Parrot* (1984) and *Cross Channel* (1996), Martin Amis's *Money* (1984) and Maureen Duffy's *Illuminations* (1991), or the foreign seems to have liberated itself completely of any distinctly British other, severing its national origin in order to apply itself to whatever has prompted the interest or commitment of its author, evidently facilitated by the *lingua franca* status of the English language, but not caused by English cultural hegemony, as we see in D.M. Thomas's *The White Hotel* (1981), Bruce Chatwin's *Utz* (1988), John Berger's *Into Their Labours* trilogy (1979–90), Martin Amis's *Time's Arrow, or The Nature of the Offence* (1991) and *Night Train* (1997) and Nicholas Shakespeare's *The Dancer Upstairs* (1995).

If we place this kind of 'global' fiction at a point equidistant from the positions represented by Crawford and Coetzee's narrator, and reorient in relation to the kind of Great Tradition fiction under consideration in the previous chapter, we see that two tendencies reveal themselves: one coming in from abroad, as it were, assuming forms and concerns central to a British tradition, and one, radiating out from a British centre, more or less separating itself from its origin, to embrace concerns which, however local they may be – Budapest in Chatwin's *Utz*, the French Alps in Berger's *Into Their Labours* and so on – constitute a global option in relation to their authors' British nationality. It should be emphasised that we are dealing with tendencies only, and that, when talking of writers' origins, backgrounds and interests, we are on highly individual ground, subject to risky generalisation. To problematise the thesis we may point, for instance, to Timothy Mo, in the previous chapter taken as a representative of the immigrant voice. In his *An Insular Possession* (1986) we have a story wholly set – and artfully mock-authenticated – in Macao and Hong Kong during the Opium Wars. Here the link to the West/Britain is established by the British and American merchant/colonisers. With no links whatsoever to the country which he has described through the eyes of the immigrant in *Sour Sweet*, the action of *A Redundancy of Courage* (1991) is set in East Timor with one of the local Chinese as the protagonist, telling his story eventually from another exile in South America.

Or we could consider Kazuo Ishiguro's *An Artist of the Floating World* (1986), which is set in Japan and peopled with Japanese only. In his *The Unconsoled* (1995) the setting is in some mythically Kafkaesque/Borgesque central European city, in which a pianist has arrived to give a concert, only to be increasingly swallowed up by apparently quite absurd incidents. But in a sense, this very versatility underscores the tendency in some literary quarters, and to critical as well as popular acclaim, to consider the world their playing ground, refusing to be tied down by any givens in relation to nationality. That this is not just a matter of these two writers having immigrant backgrounds is illustrated by reference, for instance, to Russia-oriented D.M. Thomas, one of whose first novels, *Birthstone* (1980), is set completely in Cornwall.

The tendency to take on the world as subject for fiction, rather than remaining at home, is doubtlessly a phenomenon following hard on the heels of mass communications and media shrinking the world and making it generally accessible. So it would apply to literature anywhere. But no doubt the tendency has been enhanced within a British post-imperial context, in which the ground has been especially well prepared for the global perspective, open to 'natives' and 'immigrants' alike, just as any 'native' literary tradition by its enforcedly ideal status has become, paradoxically it may even be said, public to an extent not paralleled elsewhere.

Contrasts and supplements

In his two 'French' novels Julian Barnes is not primarily concerned with any comparative studies of national identities. Rather, the comparative, or the contrastive, is part of a major project to do with the nature of narrative as a cognitive tool, especially regarding the relationship between past and present. All the same, nationality does play a role in so far as the action is pivoted on plying across the Channel, which is also a shift between states of mind often associated with 'national character'.

For both narratives story-telling provides structure and substance. When the origin-seeking narrator of *Flaubert's Parrot* is eventually confronted by the postmodernist lesson of the ultimate reality of the simulacrum, he has been warming up to this lesson all along. This explains his lack of astonishment and dismay on learning that there is no such thing as the one and only original of Flaubert's story 'Un coeur simple', but there is an endless supply of parrots available, so that there will be enough shrines for visitors to worship at for a long time to come.

In *Flaubert's Parrot* a devoted amateur of Flaubert, Dr Braithwaite, while researching Flaubert in France, reveals glimpses of his own personal history of a middle-class professional's conventional life, which seems to have been led according to the accepted social code of maintaining a smooth façade towards the public. Behind the façade, however, his wife Ellen harboured a despair, prompting her to live a secret life of her own from the age of fifty. Any attempt on the part of the observing husband to communicate, understand or help proved futile, the futility due to the radical difference between life and narrative:

> Ellen. My wife: someone I feel I understand less well than a foreign writer dead for a hundred years. Is this an aberration, or is it normal? Books say: she did this because. Life says: she did this. Books are where things are explained to you; life is where things aren't. I'm not surprised some people prefer books. Books make sense of life. The only problem is that the lives they make sense of are other people's lives, never your own.
> (Barnes, 1985:168)

Approaching Flaubert in all the possible ways employed by literary criticism, the teaching of literature and so on, Dr Braithwaite attempts to make sense of Flaubert, or rather, to explore the kinds of frame within which we usually make sense of literature, and, by extension, of modes of verbal discourse as the reservoir of a now always in the process of becoming the past.

In this Chinese-box system of discourses – Flaubert in relation to his fiction, Flaubert and his fiction in relation to Dr Braithwaite, Dr Braithwaite's life including Flaubert and marriage in relation to Barnes's novel, Barnes's novel in relation to actual reader – in which each more inclusive context provides an explanation of the less inclusive, any definitive meaning is doomed to be elusive.[1] At this point, and with reference to the concern of this chapter, it is relevant to inquire if this postmodernist *tour-de-force* of Derridean trace-hunting could not have been set in an English context, with, say, Trollope or Thackeray as the chosen object. The inquiry may be swept aside by just asserting that Barnes, as indeed his available biographical data display, has a penchant for France and French literature, and that a writer of fiction naturally makes use of what is within his personal sphere of interest. But then again, this penchant has its origin in a fascination with a kind of otherness which in a number of ways constitutes alternatives or challenges to the way of life obviously functioning as a hindrance to Dr Braithwaite's self-assigned objective of exploring the conditions on which understanding of the other – his wife Ellen – is possible, making didactic use of a blatantly different figure, the persona complex of a writer in his life-style so different from stereotypical notions of Britishness.

Barnes's choice of Flaubert's Normandy as an effectively contrastive backdrop for cognitive exploration in terms of the verbal discourse of (necessarily historicising) narrative is a writerly strategy repeated, but with some difference, in *Cross Channel*. During a train ride in 2015 from London to Paris, an elderly writer, in the last narrative of ten, muses on the topics which, on his returning home, are to become the stories preceding this last one. Considering the imaginative writer's trade, he decides that no act of memory is able to capture the exact nature of the past. Thinking of his grandfather when passing a cemetery of World

War One, the writer is affirmed in his certainty that, unlike Proust's protestation to the contrary, reconstruction is impossible: 'No act of will could recreate that putteed and perhaps mustachioed figure of 1915. He was gone beyond memory, and no plump little French cake dipped in tea would release those distant truths' (Barnes, 1996:206). Comparing the actualities with what-might-have-beens encountered during the train ride – the former constituting the données elaborated into the fictions made up of the latter – he arrives at the conclusion that such 'distant truths' may only be 'sought by a different technique . . . meant to thrive on knowing and not knowing, on the fruitful misprision, the partial discovery and the resonant fragment' (ibid.). In this underplayed reformulation of an essential point from Aristotle's poetics – that the probable will have a truer ring than the possible – and with discreet echoes from both Brooks and Bloom on the creative process, is the elderly writer's artistic credo. Like the wrong conclusions about persons met on the train, the past will play tricks on you. To his surprise and disappointment the writer once had to realise that his grandfather, 'that putteed and perhaps mustachioed figure of 1915', did not refrain from telling about the atrocities of trench warfare because of emotional trauma or heroic reticence, but because he served far away from the front line. His Great War had simply been uninteresting, not worth talking about.

Rather than despairing at the impossibility of ever achieving any historically accurate truth – 'You made the local connection but you missed the overall structure' (ibid.:204–5) – the elderly writer eventually takes comfort in thinking of himself as a

> gatherer and sifter of memories: his memories, history's memories? Also, a grafter of memories, passing them on to other people. It was not an ignoble way of passing your life. He rambled to himself, and no doubt to others; he trundled, like an old iron-wheeled *alembic* creaking from village to village and distilling local tastes.
>
> (Barnes, 1996:210)

In this case the local seems to be constituted by the writer's personal attachment to France, where he went to teach as a young graduate, but with France looming as the great other to Britain in European history. The narratives in the collection framed by the elderly writer's cross-Channel journey are all centred on Anglo-French meetings up through history, some of them in hostile terms, some of them under more friendly circumstances, but all of them arranged in such a way as to make for fateful and life-determining encounters of consequence to those involved. The local (in time as well as in space) is where connections are made and the bricks of history moulded into shape. Not themselves attempting any bid on 'overall structure', they respect chronological progression and they portray the creation of new kinds of local significance resulting from local meetings. So perhaps, after all, that is where the overall structure displays itself, in the realisation that the overall is the accumulation of the local, and that the formation of the local is a question of a never-ceasing dialectic of encounters.

Contrasting and comparing life on either side of the Channel in *Flaubert's Parrot* and in *Cross Channel*, in terms of individuality and detached parts of an overall history, the nature of whose 'pastness' is problematised throughout, Barnes makes use of a history of mixed national feelings from the Battle of Hastings to the European currency debate. English, and later, British literature has availed itself of this particular cultural interface, notably in Shakespeare's history plays, the debt of Restoration Comedy to the French stage, the significance of the French Revolution for the English romantics and, in like measure, the significance of French Symbolist poetry and poetics for British (or rather Anglo-American) Modernism. Since the days of High Modernism, however, France has hardly figured in British literature, either explicitly or implicitly. By counterposing France with Britain, Barnes opens up a wealth of historical echoes, from political, via cultural to specifically literary history. Moreover, he uses the transgressive move to create a platform for displaying a heightened awareness of textuality as the highly questionable but only available repository of historical cognition. No doubt the introduction of the French other enhances the writer's – and in turn the reader's – sense of the boundaries of writing by forcibly exposing the familiar to the unfamiliar. In *Flaubert's Parrot* and in *Cross Channel* the use of a well-established binational relationship might be said to serve the ultimately literary purpose of being the chief metaphor of textual striving for supremacy when it comes to meaning and truth, turning out, however, as unstable and shifty as the state of now rivalry, now cooperation across the Channel.

Cutting the cord altogether

An increasing amount of contemporary literature is 'rootless' in a perspective of national origin. Since the German publishing firm Tauchnitz began buying rights to print and distribute literature written in English throughout continental Europe,[2] the availability of literature in English, most of it written by British, Irish and American authors, has been an essential part of a global book culture. But the lead on the marketplace of literature in English may also be measured in terms of translations into other languages. A glance at bestseller lists round the world reveals this fact immediately. The power of 'global English', particularly as 'Americanisation', is as evident here as it is in film, life-style industries and trademark exports. The literary current also, but to a much lesser extent, runs the other way, of course here always in English translations: Italian Umberto Eco, Norwegian Jostein Gaarder and Danish Peter Høeg being striking examples from Italy, Norway and Denmark, respectively.

Literature selling in cultures different from those of its origin may be assumed to do so either because it has a 'universal' appeal or because it is enjoyed by readers appreciating whatever amount it may possess of 'local colour'. In practice it is impossible to separate the two. To take the example of Peter Høeg's *Smilla's Sense of Snow* (1992), the locale is partly Copenhagen, partly the innards of a ship bound for Greenland. To non-Danish readers the Copenhagen setting provides an 'exotic', local-colour element, whereas the ecological thematic orientation in combination with the multicultural implications of the murder case and the multicultural-cum-gendered status of the half-Inuit half-Danish protagonist has an appeal beyond the merely national, chiming in with contemporary world trends.

When we begin to dissect the film version of *Smilla's Sense of Snow* in relation to the novel on which it was based, we begin to understand the dynamics of what happens when a local cultural product is translated into a product shaped for an international audience. The film version strikes many Danish movie-goers as strangely defamiliarising, partly the result of the foreign language spoken – English – in familiar surroundings, partly because cultural clichés are resorted to in order to make clear essential elements of signification in such a way that they make sense beyond the local limitations. To signal clearly the daughter Smilla's disenchantment with her well-off medical specialist father in terms of social difference – the father pursuing the conventional pleasures of the rich, the daughter declining the same – there is a scene in the kind of club-like restaurants which have become set pieces in film located in all big cities of the world, probably all modelled on London's Pall Mall clubs. Both language spoken and clubby atmosphere to indicate wealth and imply overtones of social Darwinism and lack of community feeling are elements in a film language created to enhance export value for which the local may be effective as an exotic backdrop to an action depending on easily recognisable situations signalling values and from which the plot may receive its next twist.

Surely such 'translations' are more obvious to one belonging to a culture for which transformation of language is necessary if a book is to succeed internationally or if a film is produced from it intended for the international market. But a similar situation is to be found also with regard to English-speaking cultures, because the principle is identical: appeal beyond the national depends on the adoption of elements of signification which have gained international currency, a currency directly proportional to the energy that goes into the distribution process.

In the field of generic fiction – whodunits, thrillers, romance, science fiction and so on – a situation of international availability has been the case for a long time. Plot models and atmospheres are 'shareware' and are used by writers all over the world, irrespective of places of origin. When Philip Kerr names his three novels about a sleuth in Nazi Germany the *Berlin Noir Trilogy* (1989–91), the atmosphere is switched on immediately. Eco thrillers have proved highly exportable, and so have sentimental hard-luck stories since Erich Segal's *Love Story* (1970), with Robert James Waller's *The Bridges of Madison County* (1992) as a striking example from the 1990s.

Whereas generic fiction has long been in the internationally public domain, and its free-for-all status recognised by writers and readers alike (British-type formal detective stories are turned out in great number also by non-British writers, in demand for a world audience craving British mysteries) the tendency for non-generic fiction writers to cut their national ties and set their fiction in places away from home is a development gaining speed towards the end of the twentieth century and part of a postmodernist cultural climate from which it gets much of its rationale, first and foremost in the celebration of the liberated signifier.

The tendency is not, of course, limited to a British context, but an international phenomenon. In Canada, Sri Lanka-emigrated Michael Ondaatje wrote a pre-World War Two Sahara romance in his *The English Patient* (1992). In the USA, cultural critic Susan Sontag wrote an innuendo-saturated and intertextually rich narrative about Lord Hamilton in Naples (*The Volcano Lover: A Romance*, 1992), to name but two novels praised by readers and critics as highly original works.

Whereas it is the privilege of any writer to roam freely in his own imagination and set his or her fiction accordingly, there is often a strong reason for doing so, quite apart from considerations to do with the routine dynamics of much generic fiction, and quite apart from any personal preferences for settings abroad. In Martin Amis's *Night Train* the tables are turned on the private eye whodunit to make it into a quite extraordinary existential exploration, the point of which is no less than a truly universal concern. In the same writer's *Time's Arrow* the temporal and spatial line inclines backwards from late twentieth-century USA to the Holocaust-ridden Third Reich. Bruce Chatwin's *Utz* shares the Holocaust concern with Amis's *Time's Arrow*, but from the perspective of the victim. In D.M. Thomas's *The White Hotel*, the Holocaust also figures prominently, but here linked uncannily with an investigation into basic primordial urges accommodated in a Freudian universe. In John Berger's 'green' trilogy *Into Their Labours*, the scene is set in the French Alps, but with this region clearly symbolising a peasant world in opposition to an industrialised city world. All these works set out to explore issues which might be said to apply to the generally human condition. It is striking that considerations of composition are reflected as prominent narrative devices, with an enforced simplicity in the cases of Berger and Chatwin, genre parody in Amis's *Night Train* and deliberately anti-realistic strategies in Amis's *Time's Arrow* and Thomas's *The White Hotel*.

Set in the French Alps, John Berger's *Into Their Labours* trilogy, *Pig Earth* (1979), *Once in Europa* (1989) and *Lilac and Flag* (1990), echoes Oliver Goldsmith's 1770 poem 'The Deserted Village', likewise an elegy on the abandonment of rural life for the attractions of the city. Berger's variations on the pastoral theme continues a genre dating back to Greek antiquity. Setting the love life of workmen and women in a rural environment, the pastoral gives literary shape to dreams of work as play and to erotics as a game of no consequences and requiring no long-lasting commitment. Berger reworks this central European literary tradition into a present-day pastoral elegy, in the last volume tracing the exodus of two young peasants into the corrupting city, concluding with a vision which may be interpreted as a wish-fulfilment dream.

The pastoral was always an idealisation of life, expressing a wish for the simple and a rapport with benevolent nature. Living on as a topos in literature, the awareness of its opposite, symbolised by the 'dissolute city' in which Michael's son in William Wordsworth's poem *Michael* (1800) destroys all future hope for the old shepherd, and anticipated by implication in Goldsmith's poem, has lent to the post-Romantic use of the pastoral an inevitable irony. So when Berger sets about to use it, it has already been invested with its own opposite, the reality of modernity. This explains why these stories of peasant life in an unkind nature contain their own negation, their doom. Staying on requires a deliberate shutting out of all that is outside, with enforced simplicity and naivity the necessary conditions of life. There is always the possibility of escape to the better material conditions of city life, but, as *Lilac and Flag* demonstrates, for those who leave the dream may be all they eventually end up with, since what the city stands for is as destructive as that which they left.

Berger's trilogy is about people in an industrial age caught between the devil and the deep blue sea of equally impossible traditionally rural and modern city lives, redeemed only by the doubtful recourse to dream and wish-fulfilment. The author's sympathy, though, is with the mountain peasants, whose doomed way of life and whose half-realised sense that this is the case, pervade the narratives and give them a sadness all the more poignant because the reader is aware of the lack of any remedy.

Berger's concern in his *Into Their Labours* trilogy is for a way of life threatened beyond any possibility of restoring. Elegy is the key in which the pastoral of modernity must be played, and the tragic foredoomedness is highlighted in a spare prose without any interference from a narrator endowed with divine powers or, in the case of *Lilac and Flag*, the old woman narrator telling the story of the two young lovers as if it were a well-known myth already. This is a series of narratives which could have been set anywhere in the world where an old peasant tradition is openly at odds with modern life, depending on city-based industry and commerce. Written in English and published in a British context (Granta/Penguin), the setting of the story in a locale foreign to such a context but still quite close in geographical terms to the author's own country makes characters and events stand out as phenomena familiar and unfamiliar at the same time. No doubt setting the narratives in some distant part of Britain would have tipped the scales towards empathy enhanced by language and well-known surroundings and made difficult the distance required to appreciate the didactically exemplary purpose so obviously an essential reason for the writing of the narratives.

Being a student of Russian language and culture explains D.M. Thomas's choice of Russia as the setting of his second work of fiction, *The Flute-Player* (1979) and his sequence of improvisation novels, and the Kiev/Babi Yar culmination passage of his breakthrough novel from 1981, *The White Hotel*. Applying the notion of desire, as described by Freud, to the atrocities of the Holocaust proved too much for many readers, while others found the author's gift for stylistic imitation of Freud and the seamless transition from fiction to the documentary of an eye-witness report of the mass killings in the Babi Yar gorge a violation of the norms allowed for fiction.[3]

Be that as it may, *The White Hotel* is another example of a work of fiction by a British author set away from the author's own country. As in the case of Berger's trilogy, Thomas's concern is with forces which transcend the national, only in this case we have to do, not with demographically conditioned ethics, but with a fictional counterpart to the development of seeing Freudian psychoanalysis as a cure for symptoms to Freudian psychoanalysis as a symptom of a 'disease' couched in the same modernity which is the aim of the attack by Berger.

Thomas appropriates Freud as interpreted and developed by Foucault and Lacan and also challenges traditional notions of textuality in perspective of 'ownership'. Freud's case histories being increasingly read as stories has shifted them into the fictional domain. Perhaps nowhere else has the postmodern paradigm shift from 'positivist objectivity' to 'textual subjectivity' been so demonstrably clear as in the change of perspective to do with Freud's work. To engage with this, as Thomas does, is to accept the postmodernist textuality position and at the same time to indicate ways in which we, in the scientific atmosphere of the twentieth century, have misread reality by relying on language as a sufficient means of handling that reality, while all the time language has constituted the reality for us. When Thomas makes Lisa Erdman's mysterious pains, diagnosed as hysteria symptoms by Freud on her first consultation, the proleptic signs of her later death by machine gunning in Babi Yar, the point is to demonstrate the metaphorical nature of Freudian efforts of positivist explanation, the metaphorical dimension underlined by the several repetitions in different modes of identical events in the narrative, and the eventual positioning of Freud himself among the patients arriving in Israel following upon the one ineradicable event of the Holocaust.

Whereas Thomas attempts to link poetically, as it were, the textuality of Freudian psychoanalysis to the fact of the Holocaust – the epigraph taken from W.B. Yeats's 'Meditations in time of Civil War' and the 'Author's Note' are clearly indicative of such a link – Martin Amis's approach to the Nazi genocide is an endeavour to understand, as the extended title *The Nature of the Offence*, a quotation from Primo Levi, suggests, the nature of the offence. The nature of the offence, Amis suggests, is unique in its combination of the atavistic and the modern. Nazi Germany built a *Reichsautobahn* in the traditional German style of logistic efficiency, right into the very centre of the primitive, reptilian brain.

The usual procedure for the exploration of phenomena is to relate effects to causes, and the effect of the Holocaust is then caused by the combination of primitive xenophobia and need for scapegoats and the means to deploy an efficient apparatus for dealing with it. Although more precisely and poignantly diagnosed here than most writers have been able to, the Holocaust remains too monstrous for literary accommodation or enters the path of sentimentalisation. Keeping the public aware of the monstrosity requires constant defamiliarisation, as just another realistic novel only serves to trivialise it. Amis's solution is to turn things on their head: he proceeds in inverse direction by temporal regression. In this way the cause–effect relationship is eliminated, and each regressive step backwards in time takes the life of the narrator from retirement and death in the USA through his time as a KZ doctor all the way back to his conception.

The fact of the Holocaust caused many contemporary continental European writers to consider silence as the only proper response, since no words seem sufficient to deal with what Nazi Germany did to the Jews and other scapegoat groups. The Holocaust has always loomed larger in the literatures of the countries whose populations were directly affected by the genocide. In British literature there has been no tradition of relating to this in any way other than sporadic, quite individual writings. Perhaps not very surprisingly, literature in England in the years after the war concentrated on issues to do with the local rather than that which was beyond the nation's borders. In the few cases that British literature concerned itself with issues beyond the parochial, they had to do with an imperial perspective rather than what had been happening right on the nation's doorstep.

If *Time's Arrow* is about the problem of addressing the nature of the Holocaust offence specifically and the relations between primitive urges and ways of satisfying them by rational means more generally, it parallels D.M. Thomas's attempt to make sense of the self-understanding of as disparate Western cultural phenomena as hysteria and Holocaust within some common context. The two works of fiction are as much about the articulation of power as they are about the specific subject of the Holocaust; indeed one may go so far as to suggest that they are essentially essays in Western civilisation critique, attaching symbolic value first and foremost to the Holocaust, although the evocation in both texts of the atrocities certainly is forceful.

Extending the perspective from the West to the world, Martin Amis in his *Night Train* uses the well-tried form of the whodunit to address the problem of existential meaning. Harking back in aim and ambition to Samuel Beckett, this novel exploits a form of fiction for which rationality and causality are integrated elements. An open-ended whodunit is a contradiction in terms, but open-endedness is the very point of this investigation of a suicide leaving too many traces inviting motivation to be credible. Only the red herrings are not there in order to be eliminated and the one and only motive expected to emerge briefly before the reader turns the last page never appears. The red herrings are teasers arranged by the suicide to provoke the investigator – and the reader – to question the very notion of false and true and to accept the right of an individual just to opt out, not to take on the slings and arrows of outrageous fortune, not because existence proves too much, but as a gesture ultimately to be seen as confirming meaninglessness in an indifferent universe.

Globalised fiction

The fact that English is the mother tongue in so many countries ensures a wider audience for literature in that language than that of any other language. To a certain extent this linguistic interrelationship has resulted in a sharing of literary traditions by writers not by birth part of them, as argued in the previous chapter about the adoption of the manner of the 'Great Tradition' as a set of specific emphases and interests. The ease of access to a variety of national literatures enjoyed by the English-speaking countries has been increasingly widened to encompass literatures in other languages by swift translation, either as part of deliberate marketing strategies by publishing companies increasingly multinational, or as the result of efforts by individual enthusiasts eager to spread the knowledge of authors with whom they have come into contact through mastery of languages foreign to English.

For a very long time there has been a special relationship between the literatures of Britain and of the USA. It was not until the post-World War Two period that US literary historians made an effort to sever threads with the English literary tradition and to call for the recognition of a tradition genuinely American and not just the budding of a very late branch added to an English/British stem.[4] No observer of national literary scenes today would be in the least doubt that the contemporary profiles in English and American fiction are very different from one another. It would indeed be hard to imagine a Don DeLillo or a Tom Wolfe generating their fictions from a British context, nor would it be easy to repatriate a Margaret Drabble or an Anita Brookner within an American one. In both cases we have to do with authors so concerned with issues belonging to facts and traditions of their respective cultures that the difference amounts to one between, say, German and French fiction. And the same applies to the difference between, say, Indian authors writing in English like Anita Desai or Arundhati Roy or Canadians like Robertson Davies or Margaret Atwood compared with both English/British and American fiction, or compared among themselves. There is probably a solid marketing interest in keeping up traditional or otherwise defined national characteristics in literature in order to satisfy American 'consumers' eager to read a 'typically' English/British novel or vice versa. Of course there has always been a big craving for exotica served up as fiction, a craving many so-called emergent literatures are profiting from. But still the English language must be said to be the great leveller also when it comes to cultural dissemination in the form of literature.

Arguably, the area in which national literary characteristics have been in the process of deletion for a long time is generic or formula fiction. It is one of the long-standing points of dispute whether Edgar Allan Poe or Sir Arthur Conan Doyle is the originator of the detective story. Be that as it may, the present situation in the field of detective fiction and related sub-genres is one of interchangeability. The English murder-in-the-vicarage variety enjoys global appeal, and emulators of Agatha Christie in English-speaking and non-English-speaking countries alike are legion. So are emulators of originally Los Angeles-situated private fighters of urban evil. We find hard-boiled whodunits reconstructing cityscapes all over the world in the Los Angeles mould. Feminism-inspired detectives, private or in public service, have popped up everywhere on the world map without, it seems, any particular national provenance, although American writers like Sara Paretsky and Sue Grafton provide most of the elements adopted by others. So generic fiction offers formulas free for all, although also here the principle of exportable national emphasis prevails to a great extent. The development of the secret agent novel by British writers in the Cold War period by Ian Fleming, John le Carré and Len Deighton has had imitators, but part of the appeal of that particular branch on the generic tree obviously is with the peculiarly British atmosphere encountered in the famous three. Quite the opposite in national terms when it comes to the procedural variety of the whodunit: although Erle Stanley Gardner has his imitators everywhere, the success of the genre in the USA, and its appeal to readers outside the country, has to do with the central role played by the law and the courts in American society.

But also when it comes to general fiction, that is non-generic fiction, a tendency towards looking beyond the regional or the national is clearly discernible. In this respect British fiction divides into the kind of fiction which lets go of the author's national ties altogether, and fiction which is still firmly set within a British context but in which the 'foreign connection' is of integral importance to the plot. The two kinds are not, like so much else in literature, to be separated into two watertight compartments, but overlapping and complementary. Nor are they sudden appearances towards the end of the twentieth century. Since Daniel Defoe had Moll Flanders transported to New England, Charlotte Brontë reversed the fortunes of Jane Eyre by a legacy generated by colonial trade and Charles Dickens spirited Mr Peggotty, Em'ly, Mrs Gummidge and Mr Micawber away to Australia to prosper, the Empire has provided deus-ex-machina relief for distressed fictional characters. But then the Empire has functioned as the frame of reference to the exclusion of other localities foreign to the sphere of British influence. It is this particular aspect which changed in the aftermath of Empire, when the resource of imperial possessions no longer provided the author with an extension of the – partly at least – familiar. The Egypt of Lawrence Durrell's *Alexandria Quartet* is less a British protectorate than the necessary setting for the author's mystical leanings towards gnosticism, and the desert island of William Golding's *Lord of the Flies* is an existential microcosm and not the potential colony of either Daniel Defoe's *Robinson Crusoe* or Robert Ballantyne's *Coral Island*, the model of Golding's parable.

When Bruce Chatwin traversed Australia and wrote of his journey in *The Song Lines*, the focus was no longer on the continent in its former imperial relations, but on the possibility of repossessing something lost by getting in touch with primaeval energies. Chatwin's only novel, *Utz*, wholly set in Hungary, removes all ties whatever with the author's country and its past relations in this story of the 'poetics' of collecting. This story of love for fine things and the need for sacrifice is fittingly set in a country whose occupation by the Nazi Germans, whose belief in the expendability of the lives of non-Arian peoples triggered a situation of instantaneous fatal risk in the occupied countries, for which there was no parallel in Britain.

The complete severance of threads with the British writer's home culture is, however, of rare occurrence in comparison with the kind of story where we find the foreign setting retaining a tie with Britain. In Nicholas Shakespeare's *The Dancer Upstairs* (1995), the link is the British journalist Dyer, who gets to know the story of how the regime in a Latin American state succeeded in capturing a guerrilla leader. The politics are all local, although most of Latin America is indicated, and the tenuous thread back to England is all in Dyer's job as foreign correspondent of a major London newspaper and the local presence of his aunt Vivien, formerly of the Royal Ballet but long ago married to a Latin American diplomat and busy running a national ballet corps and various charities besides. Thus framed with a tenuous link to Britain, a story of a local security officer's hunt for the guerrilla leader commences.

In Shakespeare's fiction, the narrator's British background works first and foremost to secure a situation that enhances the credibility of the story, to make it connect with the British reader's own frame of reference. In another story about far-away guerrillas, Timothy Mo's *The Redundancy of Courage* (1991), not even such a tenuous link is offered. In that story about the guerrilla activities of a member of the Chinese community of East Timor pressed into the guerrilla forces in the mountains and becoming their mine expert, the only link with a British frame of reference is knowledge of the author's nationality – in the case of half-Chinese Mo ambiguous – and, perhaps, the faint quality of the novel as a stylistic exercise of making up a Somerset Maugham kind of plot and presenting it in the manner of Joseph Conrad and Graham Greene mixed. But this kind of fiction, absolutely detached from Britain, although Mo's mixed background may explain his interest in Chinese settlements abroad, is comparatively rare in comparison with the kind of fiction that, although set abroad like Nicholas Shakespeare's *The Dancer Upstairs*, retains a link with the author's place of origin. Maureen Duffy's *Illuminations* (1991) and Rose Tremain's *Music and Silence* (1999) are two novels in which the setting abroad has definite significance for the thematic concerns of the novels.

Tremain's novel is set at the late-Renaissance court of the Danish King Christian IV. It presents the king as a man suffering from financial worries, which threaten to jeopardise his rule and, on the personal front, from a love life lacking both spiritually and physically. In this unenviable situation his appreciation of music is his sole comfort, especially the lute music played by a newly arrived English musician, a musician that he will have to pawn to his nephew, the English King Charles I, as security for a substantial loan. The English lute-player and Charles I are at opposite ends of the social scale, and the English king is represented as a sovereign very much aware of his superiority to his uncle, the Danish king. Their meeting point is the musician, with whom Christian builds a relationship based on mutual regard and a common interest in and understanding of the power of music. The dreaming and distant King Charles, however, appearing as a negative foil in terms of function in the historical fiction, is interested in removing the musician from the Danish court to weaken the Danish king and thus reducing the political potential of Denmark at a time of severe power struggles in Europe.

The choice of late-Renaissance Denmark in Tremain's historical novel was probably due to the author's fascination with the Danish king's complex character: his enormous energy in public affairs, of which so many buildings remain hard evidence, combined with the private person's vulnerability and sensitivity. The novel paints a picture of Europe in the early seventeenth century which has not England or France at the centre, but a comparatively poor North European kingdom, in relation to which England is attributed a new role. At the level of power, personified in Charles I, cavalier disdain and splendid isolation seem to rule. But at the level of artistic sensitivity and spiritual insight, personified in the lute-player, there is an opening up towards continental Europe. The lute-player joins King Christian's royal band of mixed nationalities as the most natural thing. He notes the variety of national playing styles and praises the general sound effect as unity in variety. He appreciates the king's confidence and holds it in great respect, since it cuts the king down to human size. He falls in love with and decides to marry one of the 'almost-Queen' Kirsten Munk's maids. All in all, the lute-player's function in the novel may be said to be to explore the foreign and to find it inviting, trusting and inspiring. Against this, the short glimpse of the lonely King Charles in his Whitehall Palace is one of austerity and barrenness.

Continental Europe functions in a similar eye-opener way in Maureen Duffy's novel, *Illuminations*. Hetty Dearden is a university academic who has taken early retirement. As her last duty she is going to Germany to give a lecture on British relations with the EEC, entitled 'Towards an Idea of Europe: Origins and Expectations', to stand in for a colleague prevented by a child's illness. Preparing her paper she stumbles over an account from the early Middle Ages of the English nun Tetta going deep into Germany to find out about the fate of her aunt missing for ten years, and also to take up the position of abbess of a local nunnery. The account shows the fate of a woman ready to go out into the world, winning power and prestige but, not least, self-awareness and self-confidence. The fate of Hetty Dearden turns out in a similar pattern: going to Germany makes her reconsider her life, and she ends up by acknowledging her attraction to a young German woman who is involved in political activism.

Illuminations is mainly a novel in the tradition of the female *Bildungsroman* much in vogue since the 1960s, but it is noteworthy that the 'liberation' of Hetty requires leaving Britain for the vast unknown of continental Europe.

The British engagement with the rest of the world on the conditions of an immediately post-imperial situation has, in a literary perspective, been very much a question of market possibilities, less a question of actually accommodating that world of equal nations as the subject matter or themes of British literature. Towards the end of the century, though, there were definite signs of British fiction opening up and out to the rest of the world and using foreign cultures for a whole range of purposes. The downright fascination with 'ethnographica' and 'exotica', which may be seen in abundance in the literature of the imperial period, is of rare occurrence. As a compositional resource, however, literary constructions of meetings of cultures have proved of great value both as regards setting to resituate Britain in a post-imperial world and as a thematic device to enhance the scope for individual potential in a world being pulled closer together by political and technological developments.

The challenge of the foreign is a challenge common to all national literatures, of course. But in the case of Britain the challenge seems all the more exacting since it involves a readjustment in terms of hegemonic cultural constructions taken for granted for centuries, which did not suddenly cease to be in force by 1947, and which, as a complex of imperial aftermath, still to large extent form the popular frame of things. The examples of fiction that employ the foreign as a central constituent of subject matter and/or thematics in British fiction typically puts on display a compound voice in which the attempts at articulating a 'foreign tongue' while speaking fluently in the native one is the mirror image of the compound voice examined in the previous chapter, by which 'foreigners' attempt to articulate *their* concerns within a British literary tradition. Both approaches are most interesting and liberating for modern fiction.

7
Adopting and Adapting Crime Fiction

> *The Moonstone* provides an interesting insight into many aspects of its age, particularly through the truth and variety of its characterization, and this reflection of social mores and social habits was to become one of the most important virtues of the well-written detective story.... The detective story, because clue-making demands an interest in the minutiae of everyday life, frequently tells us more about the age in which it was written than does more pretentious literature.... If we want to know what it was like to work in a commercial office in the city when £4 a week was a wage on which a copy-writer could live in comfort and even make some show of tagging along with the bright young things, we should read *Murder Must Advertise*. Similarly in our own age we could learn more about South Africa from the novels of James McClure than from many books on apartheid.
>
> (James, 1993:5, 8–9)

If measured by degree of detail with which concerns of everyday life, at public as well as private levels, are reflected in literature, generic fiction, notably crime fiction in its many varieties, stands out with a reflection dynamic resembling naturalism at its most penetrating. With its tradition of reflecting all the potentially significant elements of a banal and trivial everyday world for the solution of crimes, it records stirrings in the body politic like a seismograph. Although the bulk of crime fiction titles follow formulas established and virtually unchanged for decades, it is an essential characteristic of the formulas that they rely on and therefore accommodate an ever updated actuality. Just as the audience of crime fiction expects certain patterns to be honoured, they also expect a fictional universe recognisably their own. Allowing for the great variety of writing in the last decades of the twentieth century in Britain, and for the constant generic hybridisation taking place in general, it is safe to say that to get a true-to-life rendering of the social and political situation one can profitably turn to crime fiction.

In her introduction to the 1993 British Council exhibition, 'The Art of Murder: British Crime Fiction', P.D. James makes a point of relating the detective story to mainstream British fiction by its ethics:

> The British detective story is more firmly rooted in the soil of the British literary tradition than is any other popular genre. It shares the assumption, strong in English fiction, that we live in an intelligible and generally benevolent universe, that crime is the aberration, peace and tranquillity the norm, and that the proper preoccupation of man is the bringing of order out of chaos. Because of this affinity with mainstream fiction the detective story is a genre with which such writers as Jane Austen, Dickens, George Eliot, Trollope and Meredith almost certainly would have felt at home.
> (James, 1993:3)

James distinguishes between the detective novel and the more generally encompassing 'crime novel' on the one hand, and on the other the detective novel and the 'thriller' and the 'spy novel'. However, although the classic crime-and-clues detective novel is still eagerly cultivated by writers and has a wide audience, the development of the genre – at its most inclusive – over the last two decades of the twentieth century in Britain seems to have been towards a hybrid of crime novel and thriller, that is with less emphasis on the proper investigation of crime by tracing clues in what amounts most of all to an aesthetic game of its own. Also, James's other premises seem to have been called into doubt in the genre, questioning the alleged benevolence of universe, crime as aberration, and the possibility of the individual to bring order of chaos, if the notion of order is found to be a social construct, relative to its 'consumers'.

In this chapter I shall focus on the way the genre, true to its tradition of being a precisely recording social seismograph, reflects changes in late twentieth-century Britain.[1] Being a widely read and easily film-adaptable kind of writing, it seems fairly safe to assume that the genre contributes significantly to the attention towards and the consolidation in the public awareness of such changes and resulting new social conditions. We see it in the fiction that openly acknowledges a debt to the traditional British whodunit, as in the case of Ruth Rendell's Inspector Wexford, whose hunting ground in the fictitious, Sussex provincial town of Kingsmarkham offers an exemplary microcosm of Britain as a whole. Also Frances Fyfield follows well-established plot patterns, but abandons any aesthetisation of her subject by setting her stories in inner-city London, haunted by social problems. The London of modern crime fiction is very much a city of many regions, the part of the city south of the river looming large with its tendency towards social and ethnic ghettoisation. But although the city is the seat of the legendary London CID, Scotland Yard, most British crime fiction has been set outside the metropolis. P.D. James has this to offer:

> Again in the tradition of mainstream fiction the detective story has a strong pastoral influence. Even Sherlock Holmes found his most baffling cases out of London. As he commented to Watson as they travelled by train through England's green and pleasant land, 'Not all the vilest alleys of the city can produce more horrifying crimes than can this smiling and beautiful countryside'.
>
> (James, 1993:3)

The tendency of modern crime fiction is perhaps not so much to demonise the countryside as a kind of compensation for expected metropolitan vice but to function as a simple *donnée* for writers belonging locally, just as in the case of much modern poetry. This new local optic applies to London as a regionalised city as it does to the rest of England and Britain as a regionalised 'confederation'. Mark Timlin, Stella Duffy, Ann Granger and Victor Headley offer regionalised representations of a London hardly recognisable by those who go by the myths so eagerly cultivated and marketed by tourists boards. Out of London, John Harvey sets his stories in Nottingham, Judith Cutler in Birmingham, Colin Dexter in Oxford, Ruth Rendell in Sussex and Ian Rankin in Edinburgh. By a kind of displaced regionalism, Michael Dibdin moves all the way to Italy, and Philip Kerr has gone to Germany and Russia.

If regionalisation is very much on the agenda of the modern crime story, it also highlights and problematises the issues of gender and of ethnicity very much part of the current British social scene. P.D. James's Byronic hero Adam Dalgliesh retains a certain masculinity, as does Colin Dexter's increasingly misanthropic Endeavour Morse and Ruth Rendell's Inspector Wexford, but to speak of 'male chauvinist pigs' would certainly be quite beside the point. The macho hero à la Dashiell Hammett's Sam Spade or Raymond Chandler's Philip Marlowe is found in the more hard-boiled specimens of the genre, but it is noteworthy that ex-policeman Sharman of Mark Timlin's action-packed crime stories is very much aware of his role as split-marriage father. A strong awareness of a specifically female identity is clearly discernible in the crime fiction of Judith Cutler, and the heterosexual barrier is jumped by such writers as Dan Kavanagh, whose protagonist is triumphantly and pragmatically bisexual, and the fictional universe of Stella Duffy is oriented completely by lesbian coordinates.

Attention to social conditions is where the genre as a whole has moved on most conspicuously since its so-called Golden Age, with its taking for granted of a social universe of fixed and immutable ranking. In modern crime fiction the tendency is to see crime in terms of the social and not, as in earlier fiction, in terms of a 'criminal personality'. In fact, the very notion of crime has come in for problematisation in the genre for which it is a basis. In modern crime fiction the ethnic claims as much attention as the social, and the two areas are frequently considered as complementary to one another. As the social has come to occupy more and more space in crime fiction in the classic English tradition, we see this attention shifted towards the ethnic, reflecting a distinct sense of the ethnically marked – the first or further generation immigrant – as the 'other' in WASP Britain. Such is the case in, for instance, Ruth Rendell, Judith Cutler or Mark Timlin. But in the crime fiction of Victor Headley or Mike Phillips the tables have been turned and the perspective here is that of the 'other', with the representatives of the host population marginalised to various extents.

Crime in an intercultural society

P.D. James in the introduction to the British Council exhibition referred to above prefers to distinguish between, on the one hand, the detective novel with its particular affinity to the English novel tradition, a taking for granted of a well-ordered body politic, and with a strong emphasis on the detection process, and, on the other, crime fiction and thrillers. This seems to be a distinction recognised generally by critics of the genre. The detective story, also listed as 'mystery' in publishers' lists, is a well-entrenched genre in the great British tradition of 'light reading', whose admirers may draw their entertainment from a canon for which names like Agatha Christie, Margery Allingham, Ngaio Marsh and Dorothy L. Sayers may be said to be centrally representative. Their heirs among writers born in the mid-twentieth century or later, such as Liza Cody, Lindsey Davis, Michael Dipdin, Frances Fyfield, Lesley Grant-Adamson, Tim Heald, Philip Kerr, Susan Moody, Magdalen Nabb, Mike Phillips and Joan Smith, seem to be exploring the potential of the detection plot pattern, with the intermediate generation – Edmund Crispin, Colin Dexter, Peter Dickinson, Dick Francis, Nicolas Freeling, Reginald Hill, H.R.F. Keating, Ruth Rendell and P.D. James herself – consolidating the form in contemporary settings.

While sophisticated plotting is at the very centre of the tradition of the detective story, the genre seems to have developed generally in the direction of the less plot-focusing but psychologically and sociologically interested crime novel. In the last couple of decades of the twentieth century the detection plot even proved strong and flexible enough to accommodate a range of contemporary issues, some of them supposedly quite controversial in the views of those who expect aesthetically organised and genteel murder puzzles from the genre.

State-of-the-art detective fiction, regarding both quality of plot and capacity to respond productively, in literary–aesthetic terms, to contemporary society, is in ample supply, so the selection of Ruth Rendell, Frances Fyfield and Judith Cutler is purely illustrative of recent developments rather than particular praise.

The settings chosen by the three writers form a neat symmetry: Ruth Rendell's southern English home county (but fictitious) Kingsmarkham stands in contrast to the London inner-city deprived areas that form the stamping ground of Frances Fyfield's stories, and both, as south of England/Metropolitan Area stand in contrast to the provincial or regional England of Judith Cutler's Brummie stories. So, as regards setting, England is covered and, what is more, setting appears to be of considerable significance to the plot-making events in the stories of all three.

Along with setting, interpersonal relations not germane to the plot are prominent to an extent not acceptable to uncompromising adherents of Ronald Knox's 1929 Ten Rules for detective fiction. Inspector Wexford's family and married life, bourgeois as it may superficially seem, is not without its kinks. The professional competition between Queen's Counsel Helen West and CID inspector Geoffrey Bailey clearly makes a less than ideal basis for their amorous relations in their private lives. In Judith Cutler's stories about further education college teacher Sophie Rivers and CID sergeant Kate Powers the fending off of unwanted sexual attentions and the desire for fulfilling love relationships play quite a part, in and out of whatever criminal investigations may be under way.

In social terms we are a long way away from the murder-in-the-vicarage stories with their middle-class gaze upon a strictly stratified society. Stratified it may still be, but as approached by a Rendell, a Fyfield or a Cutler, the very notion of social class is endemic to crime.

Guyana-born Mike Phillips introduced his immigrant freelance journalist and private sleuth Sam (Samson) Dean in *Blood Rights*, published in 1989, which was turned immediately into a BBC TV production in 1990 and followed by other Sam Dean stories.

This first story could have been plotted by a Ruth Rendell, with its critical focus on façade-cultivating establishment people of power, generation problems and skeletons in cupboards from a past conveniently repressed. But the difference from the contemporary mainstream English crime story is not just a matter of style – the Raymond Chandler streak is, however, less pronounced than the hype quote on the back from *Today*'s reviewer would have it – but also of a radically different point of cultural orientation. In the framework of a genre traditionally relying on generally recognised norms and values, Phillips explores the very foundation of a society which, in terms of ethnicity and cultural diversification, is a long way ahead of such inertia-driven norms. Sam remembers having interviewed a Conservative minister not very long ago, who on concluding the interview told him:

> 'Go back', he said to my astonishment. 'Go back and tell your people that we bear them nothing but good will.'
> For a moment I almost replied, 'Yes bwana.' But that was the kind of joke I had learned might blow the whole story.
>
> (Phillips, 1990:13)

Coaxed into looking for the disappeared daughter of Grenville Baker, a career-conscious Tory MP, by slack trade in his chosen profession, mild curiosity and an acute need for money, Sam Dean is drawn into the case increasingly motivated by the likeness he sees between Roy Akimbola/Baker, the MP's 'half-caste' son by a black woman wooed in his student days in Manchester and his own son by the white woman with whom he is no longer together. This parallel concern is what drives Sam on, even when he is told to get off the case when it begins to prove potentially embarrassing to the MP and his wife Tess:

> 'Or perhaps we thought it was absolutely none of your business', Tess said. Her tone was preoccupied, abstracted.
> 'You're probably right', I said. 'I'm not here because I care much about Virginia or you. No. I think your daughter, being who she is, if she survives, will most likely put all this behind her. It's Roy I'm worried about. See, I've got this little boy who's mixed, like him, and I suppose I've got them confused somehow, but I kept thinking about Roy being desperate and lonely and getting deeper and deeper into some kind of trouble he'd never get out of.'
>
> (Phillips, 1990:84)

Not that his concern is any different from what all parents feel in situations where their children are exposed to danger or exploitation, of which he is fully aware, although of course the situation is different because of ethnic and social circumstances. As the story progresses, Sam becomes increasingly aware of his obligation as a person specially equipped and trained to analyse and see through what seems to be a racial deadlock:

> There were so many times and places, I thought, where blacks and whites met in a desperate whirlpool of rage, exploitation and fear. Roy had experienced his life in the middle of all this. I knew what it was like and perhaps I could do something about it. But even if I couldn't I had to try.
> (Phillips, 1990:152)

Blood Rights is seen through the eyes of the other, the black presence in British society. Sam Dean combines powers of sophisticated intellectual analysis with the application of street wisdom acquired the hard way. His – often kindly ironic – appreciation of British customs and mores pays back in kind the familiar Eurocentric gaze of wonder at the exotic, as here in the scene where Sam is invited to dinner with the MP and his wife:

> The pine refectory table was laid for three, with two bowls of salad in the middle. We were having grilled pork chops and new potatoes, and the Bakers tucked into the meal with gusto. The upper and middle classes in England still loved to eat like schoolkids. Sausages, peas, bacon, chops, puddings. Like cheese to a mouse.
> (Phillips, 1990:10)

With an ability, or perhaps a will, to distinguish between the varieties of the darker hues of skin, Sam mostly recognises exponents of white British culture by their fair hair and blue eyes only, a reversal of the Eurocentric all-Africans/Chinese/Japanese/and-so-on-look-the-same.[2]

In Phillips's crime story the plot is there not so much for its suspense function as for its service as a catalyst to make the native British and the immigrant other interact, a ploy signalled clearly in the passage when Sam calls on the Bakers' house just south of Wandsworth Road to discuss the case over the dinner:

> As I rang the doorbell I looked around the square. When my family arrived in London more than twenty years before, we'd lived in a little street like this, in a house exactly like Baker's. But in our house a different family lived on every floor and we thought of it as a crumbling slum. All through my boyhood I had longed to get away from houses like this and live in a neat suburban box smelling of new paint and varnish.
> (Phillips, 1990:8)

Linking this to Engels's observation on the workers in Manchester living behind the street-lining façades of the houses of the employers, Sam is uncertain if Baker would appreciate the historical irony. Having to live the life of the exile, 'not wanting to be where you were, but having nowhere else you wanted to be' (ibid.:29), he finds himself situated in a white majority society from which reactions range from uncertainty, over studied toleration, to contempt, even fear.

Through his eyes the reader begins to see the differences in a population segment usually lumped together in generalised otherness: not only are there black crooks and honest blacks, but sub-segments of black otherness intersect with codes of behaviour, relevant or irrelevant for penal code perspective. It is quite telling that, instructed by his father on street behaviour in the black community, his son observes that 'People still get attacked though, Dad. Not us. But it's happening to Asians all the time' (ibid.:33). The reminding that oppression on ethnic grounds is not an either–or but a graded, fast-changing and therefore relative affair is underlined by the presence of the missing girl's college instructor Sophie, a half-black Argentinian whose textual function is that of the foil serving to throw ethnic problems in Britain into relief by comparison with her own background: '"All of you in this country", she said, "talk about violence and terror and poverty as if it were a story in a book. Believe me, there are places where such things happen all the time"' (ibid.:40–1).

Blood Rights is a crime story obviously energised by considerable bitterness caused by the ethnic situation in Britain at the height of the Thatcher–Major era. But its value is in its author's refusal to think in categorical terms, although such are frequently what he encounters in real-life Britain. While a lot of irony is spent on description of the white majority, the black community is far from idealised. Internal strife, misunderstanding, prejudice – all thrive in the black community as it does in the white, with a few scattered beacons of hope discernible, mostly in the form of the exchange of small, everyday kindnesses.

Victor Headley's *Yardie* from 1992 was a quite new departure in generic fiction of the whodunit variety, featuring an all-Jamaican immigrant London setting. A reversed crime story seen from the perspective of the crooks, in this case the illegal drug import and distribution trade, its plot is based on gang rivalry and not the usual fare of the solution of crime. Clearly, Victor Headley's concern is not just for the construction of a suspense story, but rather to use the format of the suspense story as an instrument to probe into the social problems of inner London, of which ethnic communities is a major factor.

The protagonist of *Yardie* is D., a courier who has just arrived in Heathrow Airport with a kilo of cocaine strapped to his body and a decision to go it alone rather than hand over as he is supposed to do. D.'s motivation is simple:

> D. knew that he was in no hurry to get back to Jamaica and the hardship of day-to-day living in the ghetto. . . . He had waited for his break for years. The break out of the dusty, hungry streets and into the bright lights of big cities with their flash cars and large houses.
>
> (Headley, 1992:6)

The novel offers considerable light on the sociology of urban gang structure and a particular kind of youth culture. An existence in an immigrant community offers few possibilities of social improvement, although at any time better than what may be offered back home:

> For anyone coming from a poor background in Kingston's tenements, England, no matter how tight things were getting, was still a more comfortable environment to live in.
>
> (Headley, 1992:27)

Not only is *Yardie* a reversed crime story, it also offers a perspective generally of the immigrant Jamaicans, and of D. in particular. White Englishmen appear only rarely and then only as threatening authorities, as in this scene in a police station: 'The policeman towered over Barry, shirt sleeves rolled up, his large stomach protuding over his trousers belt' (Headley, 1992:120).

Headley's *Yardie* is really ambivalent in its attitude: it partly glamorises the entrepreneurial spirit of the protagonist bent on making his way in the drug trade, partly puts on display the dismal aspects of ghetto life in London and the bleak possibilities for those who want to make good in a socially acceptable way. This is probably an ambivalence that will determine its potential audiences. To the 'yardie' audience it will probably appeal in its capacity for vicarious compensation of frustration, whereas to a more conventional crime fiction audience its cultivation of the ethnic element may be taken either as just another 'exotic' setting or as just another crime novel with a, by now generically *de rigueur*, social emphasis.

Metropolitan and regional

Although by most readers – and movie-watchers – London is thought of as the *locus classicus* setting of traditional crime fiction, this is hardly true. Conan Doyle's Sherlock Holmes had a central London address, but Holmes found his scenes of crime mostly away from 221B Baker Street, and from the time of the Great Sleuth central London has featured sparingly as the setting of the kinds of violent crime favoured by fictional private and police investigators.

In modern British crime fiction, London has become very much regionalised into many fractions, each with their own problems, although there seems to be a general boundary between inner-city destitution and suburban comfort. On the map of present-day fictional crime, affluent West End Chelsea and Mayfair and business City figure less prominently than Islington, Finsbury, Camden and Brixton. Crime fiction seems to have shed its attachment to genteel and socially contextless crime to follow in the footsteps of the changing social and ethnic demography that changes crime from P.D. James's aberration from a social norm to something exposing the nature of such a norm.

In the 'middle generation' of established crime fiction writers, crime is ubiquitous, and certain localities away from the metropolis have come to the attention not only of the British reading public, but of the international reading public as well, since both books and the film/TV tie-ins that seem to follow automatically in the wake of a popular whodunit are so eminently exportable. Thanks to the substantial success of Colin Dexter, the Oxford of Inspector Endeavour Morse from the Thames Valley is no longer just a famous place of great learning but also very much a modern city with its proportion of social and human problems and its fair share of crime. Crime writer John Harvey has drawn attention to today's Nottingham, known to most people outside Britain as the mediaeval city-cum-castle, with its incumbent evil sheriff threatening the famous green-clad outlaws of Sherwood Forest bent on social redistribution. Ruth Rendell has chosen to create a home county provincial city for her Inspector Wexford, who both fights local crime and acts as an authorial spokesman of social criticism generally, while Ian Rankin sets his stories in a very real Edinburgh, though not the city known to tourists with its romantic castle and picturesque pubs.

If the metropolitan domain of the classic English detective story is traditionally London's West End, the focus of criminal interest moved elsewhere within the Greater London area during the last couple of decades of the twentieth century. Yardie-centred stories have Brixton as geographical centre, as in Victor Headley and Mark Timlin. Ann Granger in her stories about Fran (Francesca) Varady, daughter of a Hungarian refugee going to Britain at the age of five after the 1956 revolution, writes about one of London's many homeless, moving from squat to squat. Her preferred environment is the brick-and-asphalt-scape of the large city. Returning from the countryside at the end of *Asking for Trouble* (1997), Fran Varady draws a sigh of relief:

> We quit the motorway and negotiated the network of roads through suburbs which seemed never-ending, running into one another, linked by scraps of tired greenery, scrappy workshops and car-sale forecourts. At last respectability, or at least a façade of it, began to give way to a jumble of grimy streets. I was back where I belonged. I never thought I'd be so pleased to

> see grubby shops offering 'fire-damaged goods' or 'closing down sales', gutters filled with debris, vandalised telephone kiosks festooned with cards advertising the services of local prostitutes, spray-can graffiti from the hand of someone called Gaz. All the things which to me spelled home ... with not a horse or a chicken or a cow in sight.
>
> (Granger, 1997:268)

Although welcoming a future of continued squatting, Fran Varady at the end of her rural adventure is grateful for the offer of a basement flat in NW1, but mostly because the owner–resident of the house is a retired librarian and Fran's literary interests are beginning to stir.

Although Ann Granger's Fran Varady stories suggest the invention of an interesting, with-it heroine rather than, perhaps, first-hand experience, an impression due first and foremost to a too neat reversal of social role clichés combined with voice and plotting reminding the reader of Enid Blyton's Famous Five books, there is a certain cultural significance in the fact of literary acceptance of punks and squatters as part of the reality resource from which a whodunit writer may get her material. However, Granger gives a voice to a London community south of the river, constituted of old workers and immigrants, equally unable to do something about their social situation and for that reason involuntarily victimised allies:

> Most of the people round here had no more chance of making it across the great divide to the affluent part of the area than they could sprout wings and fly.
> It was the older ones who were bewildered. Old men who'd worked all their lives down at the docks before the work disappeared and the wharves became tourist sights. Old women who'd lived here all through the Blitz and who still scrubbed their front doorsteps. People like Ganesh's parents, who'd come here thinking that it would be upward and onward in a new country and who had worked hard to achieve success, but who had found themselves trapped now in this urban wilderness, a far cry from anything they'd ever imagined.
>
> (Granger, 1997:48)

The close friendship between Fran and Ganesh, the son of an Indian corner-shop owner, between the innocent victim, as it were, of familial dysfunction combined with a social system not geared to care for the individual[3] and one whose future hopes are still premised on the idea of a well-functioning and just social fabric, is symbolic of a changing Britain.

In Fran's perspective, the main tension of values is not between ethnically or socially defined groupings, but between those whose world only makes sense if neatly categorised and those who accept it with all its imperfections. In a conversation with an elderly woman, the death of whose niece she is investigating, Fran is lectured to the effect that a 'beautiful thing, once damaged beyond recall, is better destroyed' (ibid.:245), to which she inwardly responds:

> I wanted to cry out that she was wrong. That she misunderstood what life was about. That it wasn't a world just for the young and beautiful and rich. It was a world with a place in it for me, Squib and Mad Edna, too. That the faceless planners who had decided to demolish our squat had reasoned as she was reasoning. That it couldn't be saved, wasn't worth saving, was too far gone. But we'd loved that house with all its peeling plaster and leaking rooftiles, and given a chance, we'd have saved it.
> (Granger, 1997:245)

In this light the setting of the story in a metropolis divided between the powerless and the powerful in the form of squatters versus developers lends another facet to the 'narrative' of a London changing by ethnical demography alone.

Mark Timlin's thrillers may be a bit too much for many readers. In a tradition harking back to Dashiell Hammett, Raymond Chandler and Ross MacDonald, with a heavy admixture of Mickey Spillane, the amount of gore and dead bodies seems to stand in inverse proportion to the ex-policeman hero's conscience compunctions. The addition of a cocaine habit does not alleviate the general impression of an unstable person bent on violence, with a considerable amount of racism and sexism to go with it. Although it is quite understandable that Nicholas Sharman is willing to go to extremes, as he does in *A Street That Rhymed at 3 AM* (the street is Neate Street, London SE: Timlin, 1998: 201), to investigate a plane crash that involves the death of his ex-wife, the body count ends up nauseating. The investigation soon turns into a revenge scheme, but is put back on a justifiable track when Sharman's daughter Judith is kidnapped by the opposition.

Although we may be allowed to question the ethics that drive Sharman and to be disgusted at the hero's cynicism, it is interesting for the purposes of this study to note that Timlin's criminal London is very much a city given over to gang warfare between various immigrant groupings, who seem more or less in possession of the metropolis south of the river, and that this situation seems to be taken for granted: '"Where are we going?" "The independent state of Brixton," he replied, pronouncing it *Brix-tun*"' (Timlin, 1998:100). When Sharman is taken to see the boss of one of the leading black gangs, the protagonist who did not 'relish being a chauffeur for the black detective' (ibid.:56) is subjected to being lectured on the issue of ethnic superiority:

> 'You expected a cockroach-infested slum full of young men in bobble hats. But we're not all like that, although some are. We can be as civilized as the best of you. Often more so. Our culture goes back to a time when this cold little island was populated by nothing more than savages. You should remember that.'
>
> (Timlin, 1998:104–5)

And when he realises that the Yardies routinely refer to white people like himself as 'grey meat' (ibid.:119), Sharman, who is not ungenerous with derogative ethnic epithets himself, is somewhat taken aback.

Mark Timlin's tough hero is a person in a social no-man's land, trying to make up for his losses with the Establishment that has decided to get rid of him by negotiating an alliance with those to whom his possession of a bag of cocaine makes him an asset, although a merely temporary one. By purely literary standards, Mark Timlin has projected the American urban thriller of long standing to the London setting, for which this kind of thriller with its DIY ethics has always been somewhat alien.

Judith Cutler's series which started in 1995 about further education college teacher and amateur choir soprano Sophie Rivers, and her series which started in 1998 about DS Kate Power, in many ways signal changes in the genre conceding to the realities of a late twentieth-century Britain: gendered, regional and social in its implications of awareness, but still retaining a firm grip on plot and several of the elements cumulated through almost a century of genre development and consolidation. When Kate Power moves from London CID to the corresponding unit in Birmingham, she moves into a job environment saturated by macho bluntness and locker room sexism and a residential area with a percentage of immigrant citizens which seems typical of most British larger cities. Kate does not seem a racially prejudiced person, but the implied narrator obviously has some fun confronting Kate with her expectations, as in this scene, where the local GP knocks on her door: 'The front door bell. Kate responded to the chimes: a sari-wearing woman in her late fifties with the kindest eyes Kate had seen for years. She carried an old-fashioned doctor's bag' (Cutler, 1998:90); or here, when she first says hello to her new neighbour, Mrs Mackenzie: 'Her accent was more Barbados than Jamaica but mostly Brum. . . . Kate wondered how many years she'd been over here' (ibid.:18). It is quite striking that it is the Birmingham accent, that is the touch of the local, that reopens London-weaned Kate's eyes to the multicultural composition of British society: 'Funny to hear Asians with a Brummie accent. No funnier than with a Sheffield or with a London one, she supposed' (ibid.:16).

In complementary contrast to Kate Power, Sophie Rivers is a Brummie native, with friendships and acquaintances dating back to her childhood. To her, Birmingham presents a gradually changing environment, some of it in perfect continuity with the great monuments of civic pride built during the nineteenth century, such as the erection of the new concert hall complex, the scene of crime in *Dying Fall*:

> Birmingham's city fathers had at last decided to build a prestige concert hall, the Music Centre. There were some who said it sounded more like something on a shelf in your living room, and others who insisted it looked like it. But it was a

huge improvement technically on the dear old Town Hall, and there were vastly improved facilities for musicians and audience alike.

(Cutler, 1995:30)

To Sophie Rivers, the ethnic composition of the large provincial city is just part of her everyday scenery. When Rivers is questioned about the violent death that sets the plot in motion, she has to explain to the investigating officers:

Look, a lot of our kids are deprived. They come from rough backgrounds. Inner-city estates, inner-city schools. A lot are poor. They can't get grants, and there's no point saying they should go and get a decent job because there aren't any decent jobs. So some dabble where they shouldn't.

(Cutler, 1995:5)

This is the message of a person right at the cutting edge of things and of one to whom the analytical message of her principal must sound not only tautological but also indicative of the kind of attitude that tends to separate rather than to integrate: 'You have to remember that we draw our clients from a wide variety of social, cultural and ethnic backgrounds' (ibid.:126).

If the kind of plot is in no essential way different from what we encounter in most mainstream English detective stories, and if the setting and dramatis personae are representative of the population of Birmingham so familiar to the protagonist, we might expect the differences to do with various social, cultural and ethnic backgrounds to go rather unnoticed because they are part of the familiar townscape. Yet Cutler tends to draw attention to region, gender, class and ethnicity, as we shall see below.

A fondness for Birmingham in particular and for the West Midlands in general is unmistakable in Judith Cutler's crime novels about Sophie Rivers and Kate Power. The fondness, however, is qualified by a well-developed sense of both the decline due to the closing of the mining and related industries and the contemporary urban problems common to large cities all over the world. Kate Power, assigned to the Birmingham CID after personal problems in London, is conveniently placed as the stranger able to see the local from a critical distance, as it emerges from these two observations: 'Alan Butler let her in. He'd found some manual work somewhere in this city of a thousand dying trades: there was oil round his finger nails' (Cutler, 1998:89); and

> She picked up the M6, and then peeled off on to the M5. Spectacular view of the once industrial, still tatty West Midlands. Someone somewhere ought to be pouring money into the area. It was the heart of the industrial revolution, if not the birthplace – that honour belonged to Ironbridge, didn't it? Mecca for school trips.
> (Cutler, 1998:160)

Sophie Rivers, a Brummie native, is apt to consider the now very much decrepit and dilapidated city in terms of possibilities of improval. She has no illusions about the short-sightedness of post-war town planning, a result of which is the ugly and hardly functional high-riser further education William Murdock College, but, as observed above, she sees the erection of the Music Centre to be continuous with what Joseph Chamberlain and other civic-minded city politicians and administrators achieved in the heyday of Birmingham. Also the canals, on the basis of which the tourist trade tries to market Birmingham as a kind of Venice of Britain, presents an object for improvement rather than regret, although the protagonist is acutely aware of a working-class culture subsiding to a quite different kind of culture, in which the canals are decorative, not functional:

> What was once a nice, cheap mooring in Gas Street Basin, ... was now being developed, much to the dismay of the narrowboat owners. And the early-nineteenth-century bridges, elegant cast-iron affairs, were being lovingly restored and repainted.
> (Cutler, 1995:128)

As in the case of the novel generally, also crime fiction shows the tendencies explored in Chapters 5 and 6, a centripetal one of embracing a British tradition, and a centrifugal one of seeking out new domains abroad. The followers all over the world of the British tradition in crime fiction are far too numerous to even begin to think of enumerating. The Golden Age British whodunit writers have, arguably, more epigones than any other writers at any time in literary history. It will suffice here to draw attention to the American writer Elizabeth George, who has cleverly adopted the long and character-focusing P.D. James format, while catering to ingrained ideas derived largely from the Golden Age writers in terms of the snob appeal which has not infrequently been a conspicuous element in the genre.

More interesting than market-sensitive epigones are surely the attempts on the part of British writers to set their fiction far away from the cosy vicarages at home. H.R.F. Keating's Inspector Ghote crime fiction set in India (Ghote is with the Bombay CID) and featuring an all-indian investigating team is a rather early initiative of this kind. Philip Kerr, in his Berlin Noir trilogy (*March Violets*, *A Pale Criminal*, *A German Requiem*), writes evocatively and uncannily about the tribulations of a police officer in Berlin just before, during and after World War Two. Michail Dibdin has preferred an all-Italian setting for his slightly surrealistic stories about Inspector Aurelio Zen, whereas Lindsey Davis in her detective stories set in ancient Rome combines geographical and historical displacement.

Upstaging gender

The classic, mainstream English crime novel features as its successful investigator, private or officially employed, a male to be admired for his brawn and/or brain, sexual attraction having been efficiently neutralised in the rare case of a female counterpart, by age and (non-) marital status of Miss Marple in Agatha Christie's uncannily idyllic universe. When sexually attractive women feature in that branch of fiction, they are either on the opponent's side or act as the great investigator's helper(s) and, in not a few cases, his reward also. The more we move into the violent world of the thriller, the more this distribution of role characteristics seems to be the case.

In the detective fiction developed in deliberate reaction to the classic form, and in the wake of the general shift of essential points of orientation in post-World War Two culture, a marked development has been the introduction of female sleuths, characters with gender role agendas conforming with post-war women's liberation. Although hardly a development directly attributable to imperial aftermath in Britain, the general climate of conventions questioning and stereotype probing has no doubt facilitated the introduction of a more equal balance in terms of gender in this genre traditionally enjoyed by female readers, but with some notable exceptions upholding a male-oriented order of things.

As for direct influence, role models for the character and plot creations of British gender-conscious whodunit writers are certainly to be found in American writers such as Sara Paretsky, Sue Grafton, Abigail Padgett, Janet Evanovich, Linda Barnes and Patricia D. Cornwell, who represent radical resettings of the conventions of literary scene of crime, making a point of tracing criminals as well as redressing gender-imposed injustice in the body politic. In Britain, Inspector Jane Tennison in Lynda La Plante's three *Prime Suspect* stories has to fight daily rounds just to be allowed presence at the police station, and the situation deteriorates for down-and-out ex-cop Lorraine Page in La Plante's *Cold Shoulder* (1996). That it is a lousy job out there among the criminals with no badge or uniform for protection is the experience of enterprising Hannah Wolfe in Sarah Dunant's private investigator series, as it is of the wrestler and private eye Eva Wylie in Liza Cody's successor to her Anna-Lee series. P.D. James has preferred to write in the all-male tradition in her Adam Dalgliesh novels, while lending an eye to the peculiarly female aspects of solving crime in her novels about Cordelia Gray. A special and psychologically highly-charged situation as far as gender is concerned is built by Frances Fyfield's (herself an experienced barrister) depressingly realistic inner-London crime stories. The interdepartmental jealousy between squadroom and courtroom spills over into the private relations between counsel for the prosecution Helen West and her high-ranking policeman lover Geoffrey Bailey.

In the case of Judith Cutler's Birmingham crime stories, the female protagonists make no bones about sexual desire. It is definitely there if a personable male is within view. Visual impact ('When he rehearsed us, he wore an enormous sloppy T-shirt, so this was the first time I could observe the perfection of his buttocks' – Cutler, 1995:48) and subsequent gland reactions accompanied by deliberations on condom-buying strategies (ibid.:111) are communicated in non-euphemistic prose, this being only a modest payback for the extensive sexism cultivated in the more or less direct ways traditional of the genre. But the really interesting feature in Cutler's fiction is the way she couples gender to ethnicity, and does it in such a way as to tease the traditionally minded reader, as in this introduction of Aberlene in the Duke of Clarence bar just outside the Music Centre:

> Aberlene van der Poele is just turned thirty and five foot eleven inches tall. She has a figure any woman would covet and walks like a goddess. She is also black. She has the most difficult job in the whole orchestra – she is the leader – and does it well. Even the men in the heavy brass agree about that.
> (Cutler, 1995:31)

Age, height, figure, impact. Then ethnic characteristic. Then occupation, not only placing her high in the orchestral hierarchy but also implying the status of a violinist of considerable abilities, a combination that draws the respect of the supposedly most-chauvinist group in the whole orchestra (elsewhere in the novel described as spending their intervals reading girlie magazines). The identical narrative surprise strategy is employed when the protagonist visits a Pakistani family she knows from her teaching:

> We talked about Khalid's degree and Fatima's job. She taught Law at Birmingham University, and was sour about the increase in student numbers without corresponding cash injections. I thought darkly a spell at William Murdock might be a salutary experience, but could hardly say that.
> (Cutler, 1995:158)

Dan Kavanagh introduced his private sleuth Duffy in the eponymously entitled detective novel in 1980.[4] Having been set up by a superior officer at London's West Central police station four years previously, the bisexual and mildly neurotic character with a diamond stud in his left ear living in a mews in Paddington has acted as security consultant and private investigator. Having worked in the vice department, Duffy knows the area round Shaftesbury Avenue down to the last square inch, knowledge that comes in handy when investigating the blackmail case of *Duffy*. The degree of outspokenness and the detail of description when it comes to matters of sexuality, whether of a commercial or a private kind, is quite unprecedented. Despite the fact that adultery and jealousy probably score highest regarding motive, the genre has traditionally preferred a rather high threshold in such matters. But it is not in the matter of sexual explicitness that Kavanagh's first Duffy novel is really noteworthy. In this respect it seems to follow the standards of tolerance epitomised by a booming London Soho in the wake of a generally more liberal climate in the area. Rather, it is the presentation of a character that rejoices in his gendered ambiguity and who takes obvious pleasure in sexual activities as a natural part of his life.

Introducing Saz Martin as female gumshoe in *Calendar Girl* (1994), Stella Duffy at the same time introduces the reader to a universe gendered in lesbian terms. Supposedly, this should not affect the sequence of events forming the plot line. But in the same way that events in an apparently gender-unmarked fictional universe could be said to be tacitly subjected to a male dynamic – the case in most crime fiction – and explicitly or implicitly contribute to the formation of the narrative, the lesbian orientation is of deliberately compositional significance in the Saz Martin stories.

In *Calendar Girl*, Ms Martin, located in south-east London (Duffy, 1994:101) accepts an assignment to trace a young woman who has disappeared, carrying with her a loan of significant proportions from her rather older and quite infatuated male friend, whose future depends on being repaid. As events progress – the story is told from two perspectives simultaneously involving from the start what the reader gradually identifies as the person Saz is hunting down by way of her partner, stand-up comedian Maggie, who keeps referring to her as 'The Woman with the Kelly McGillis Body' – most of the characters involved turn out to be from the gay and lesbian communities, and the bias of observation that controls the shopping experience in the local Sainsbury's is synecdochical of the total bias of the book:

> Looking for the other gay couples – easy to spot, their hands only just touching as they steered the trolleys together. The lesbians mostly in the direction of the pulses and the grains

and as far from the fresh meat as possible, the gays over to the Lean Cuisine fridge.

(Duffy, 1994:162–3)

In this carefully gendered discourse heterosexuals live, at best, marginal lives as mere cogs in the machinery of conventionalism or, at worst, as participators in a gigantic anti-female conspiracy. This latter role comes out clearly in a scene completely superfluous to the plot, where the as yet unrealised target of Saz Martin's investigation is taken by her girlfriend to worship at the grave of Sylvia Plath, close to the Brontë parsonage in Yorkshire. When it proves impossible for the girl at the Haworth Tourist Information Centre to direct them to the grave until she identifies Plath by her marriage, Maggie reacts in a way serving most of all to indicate the gender politics of the narrative:

'Well yes, we do have a note here. Under Hughes. He's a poet, don't know about her. A Mrs Hughes buried in the Old Church – is that the one you mean?'
I turned red. 'Her name was Sylvia Plath. She was a great poet. A very great poet in her own right. You illiterate cow.'
The Woman with the Kelly McGillis Body led me, blind with rage, from the office.
I was livid. Red, white and blue for America Sylvia had left and the distant sky was black for the shoes of the man listed instead of her.

(Duffy, 1994:31)

But it would be unjust to treat Stella Duffy's story as a hard-liner contribution to the gender battle. It takes it upon itself to problematise black-and-white issues and make space for perspectives that transcend traditional boundaries, as here when Maggie confronts an ex-boyfriend of her girlfriend who has foolishly assumed that the lesbian couple would find it attractive to do a threesome with him. Having grilled him for a while, Maggie reflects:

He was deflating in front of me. And the more I pushed home my point, the further he moved away from me. Not that it's even a point I believe in. There's a big myth surrounding 'women-loving-women', it sells a lot of books. No one can ever really know how another person feels. But it's a great argument when dealing with a Neanderthal.

(Duffy, 1994:58)

The merit of Stella Duffy's crime fiction placing the lesbian community centre stage is not so much the daring of exposing one of society's traditionally backstaged activities as it is the effort to desensationalise and present in a well-proven market-successful genre a universe of experiences gendered differently.

Intercultural crime

In Ruth Rendell's *Simisola* (1994), the well-tried plotting device of mistaken identity is given a startling twist when Chief Inspector Wexford has to realise that he has committed a serious forensic error as well as unnecessarily hurt citizens of his Kingsmarkham beat. In its crude essence, Wexford has unwittingly and unintentionally subscribed to the traditionally colonialist attitude of all blacks looking alike, neglecting to carry out the usual identification routines, because he has been looking for a black body in or in the vicinity of his white majority Sussex town: 'Melanie Akande's being black was to their advantage. In a place where there were very few black people, she was known, remembered, even by those who had never spoken to her' (Rendell, 1994:33).[5]

Simisola is a detective novel pivoted on immigration and ethnicity in contemporary southern England, in a fictitious town in most ways representative of the region, but perhaps not of all of England, and definitely not of all Britain. It is ironic that a mistake of this kind should be committed by Wexford, since seldom do we come across a person, in real life or in fiction, who is more scrupulously conscientious about his own attitudes and reactions to the ethnically other. Wexford's range of perception comes out clearly in a conversation with Detective Inspector Burden on this issue when Burden claims that people such as they cannot really be accused of harbouring racist prejudice. Wexford clinches his argument in this way:

> 'My son-in-law said to me the other day that he no longer noticed the difference between a black person and a white one. I said, you don't notice the difference between fair and

dark, then? You don't notice if one person's fat and another's thin? What possible help to overcoming racism is that? We'll be getting somewhere when one person says to another of someone black, "Which one is he?" and the other one says, "That chap in the red tie".'

(Rendell, 1994:12)

But more surprises are in store for the candid and self-critical chief inspector when he learns that ethnic prejudice works both ways, as in this conversation when Dr Akande, a Nigerian physician and the father of a young woman who has disappeared, is asked about his daughter's boyfriend:

'My wife and I ... well, we wouldn't care for the idea of Melanie taking up with a ... well, a white man. Oh, I know things are changing every day, they don't even use words like "miscegenation" any more and, of course, there was no question of *marriage* but still ...'

(Rendell, 1994:71)

And Wexford finds himself even more at sea when exposed to the council election campaign of rich and studiedly English Anouk Khoori, recently settled in the town with her Arab husband, owner of a supermarket chain store. The reader senses a degree of relief on the part of Wexford and his colleagues when it emerges that fellow citizens with an ethnic background different from that of the WASP may display what seems to be standard human foibles. Melanie's disappearance turns out to owe some of its explanation to the girl's feeling under excessive pressure by over-ambitious parents – her father a Fellow of the Royal College of Surgeons but earning his living as a GP, her mother a physics graduate from University College, Ibadan, now working as a nurse – a problem which does not respect ethnic boundaries:

'So they were ambitious for you?'
'Are you kidding?' said Melanie. 'You know what they call people like them? The Ebony Elite. The black *crème de la crème*. Our futures were all mapped out for us before we were ten.'

(Rendell, 1994:262–3)

And the ambitions certainly come out clearly when parental relief quickly gives way to energetic career planning.[6]

When the girl found dead is identified as an illegal immigrant 'imported' for 'slave' labour, verbal skirmishes concerning racism and the finer shades of conscience probing take on a less immediate importance. Still, Rendell has managed to paint what seems a true picture of the south of England in which the non-WASP presence is marginal – says Nigerian Dr Akande, 'After all, there aren't many people like us down here. Only one of my patients is black' (ibid.:193) – but in which at the same time the general attention is in line with Wexford's thoughtful attitude.

Judith Cutler's Birmingham setting with its ethnically composite population is a fact of life to the extent that, in cases where the reader is not meant to profit from information about ethnic relations, there will be no distinctive markers in the form of information about skin colour and so on, except of course for names when they are revealed. All the same, there are passages revealing an awareness of difference despite assumed familiarity. When, for instance, the protagonist and her colleague and friend Shahida visit a local branch of the International Commercial Bank, a 'young woman in *kameez* and *salwar* brought in tea' (Cutler, 1995:108). The italics in the text about clothes draw attention to these as out of the ordinary, conveyed in writerly terms by a change in orthography. That intercultural understanding is not always perfect, even between those supposed to know about essential cultural differences in order to carry out their jobs optimally, emerges from a short exchange of information between a female, Pakistani college teacher and one of the investigating officers. A Pakistani father does not want to send his daughter to college as long as the murder inquiry is under way. Instead he wants to send her to Pakistan for a holiday, which causes the teacher to erupt with excessive force. The sleuth cannot see the justification of such vehemence, since it seems like a good idea and like sensible parents. So he will have to be lectured:

> 'But you wouldn't marry her off just to make sure. A holiday in Pakistan is all too often a euphemism for an arranged marriage, officer. These poor girls end up with country cousins, real hicks some of them.'
>
> (Cutler, 1995:11)

Intercultural Britain certainly made its way into the crime fiction of the last decades of the twentieth century. But, as in the quotation above from a regionally conscious whodunit, issues of ethnicity cannot be isolated from other social issues that have to do with the individual's situation in contemporary society, notably those having to do with gender. A popular kind of literature like crime fiction is usually said to follow very closely the standards of the society within which it constructs crimes and their solutions. But perhaps this is to be more modest on behalf of the genre than it really deserves. By reaching a great number of readers, and most of them situated at a safe distance from both crimes and their usually sordid social contexts, the genre has a large potential for determining attitudes that will in turn have their effects on the business of everyday life. British crime fiction has clearly accepted the fact of the intercultural British society with its continuing major social and cultural upheavals. It also helps considerably to naturalise and come to terms with them in turn.

8
Critical Perspective

> It is a question whether the majority of writers between Canada and New Zealand actually share a major interest in anti-colonial discourse and transcultural hybridity or are at least just as interested in the situation of the individual in her or his immediate surroundings and against the background of the changing modern world in which such concerns are only of secondary importance.
> (Eberhard Kreuzer, in Nünning, 1998:437)[1]

It is, admittedly, somewhat unusual for a critical study of the present kind not to start off with a detailed and exhaustive consideration of its own rigidly theoretical premises, according to which the literature under consideration may be approached. The reason for my choice of a less common procedure was, however, prompted by my curiosity to see what kinds of theoretical issues would be brought up with the focus on specifically literary reactions to Britain in the process of social and cultural change attributable largely to the 'implosion' of Empire. Mass immigration, remnants of Empire ties, a tendency for Britain to be splitting up into regions, enhancement of gender issues and the development of a social structure too complex to be thought of in terms of class are all part of the same picture, that of a country having formerly imposed its own stamp of a well-ordered and ruly body politic on large parts of a more or less willing world but now having to cope with imperial aftermath from a much-reduced platform of power and within a much-reduced world order.

One premise of this study is that over the last few decades the designation 'Britain' has been a topic for often quite animated discussion. With Great Britain and the United Kingdom designating well-defined political unions entered into a long time ago, in 1707 and 1801, respectively, 'Britain/British' and 'England/English', despite the indisputable geographical precision of the last pair, have been comparatively much more emotional in their application. With the tendency towards the regionalisation of the United Kingdom into her four constituent parts, England is again, after hundreds of years, current as a neutral geographical term. The trouble seems to be at the other extreme, when it comes to finding a suitable collective name for the large archipelago separating the North Sea from the Atlantic Ocean. The British Isles has been suggested, but hardly to the satisfaction of the Irish Republic, for which reason Davies has suggested The Isles only (Davies, 1999). It is worthy of note, however, that immigrants and descendants of immigrants from the former Empire seem to endorse 'British' as an acceptable common denominator while being unhappy about 'English', although they may be actual citizens of English locations, such as London or Manchester. What is interesting in that respect, and also from a literary perspective, is the extent to which the otherwise quite dated use of Britain/British in connection with Empire holds a considerable sway over writers.

In this study I have used the somewhat vague expression 'British or related to Britain' on a number of occasions, when the focus has been on literature in (British) English by writers not settled in the UK, but perhaps born there and having emigrated or having just preferred to publish their work there to acknowledge some kind of relationship. In such cases their Britishness will appear from their language – orthography, grammar and general stylistic cadences – and their sharing in traditions of context and literary conventions indicating this relationship clearly. In this sense Britain is perhaps more a frame of mind than a geographical or even historical presence, an elective affinity that may have a purely personal motivation. It may, alternatively, be considered an attractive catalyst when it comes to giving expression to experiences and imaginings of identity as the product of an unchangeable past and a presence of multiple facets. From that perspective modern Britain is a geographical place on its way to becoming a literary place, a topos.

Above I have indicated and explored areas and ways a literary awareness is propped up by reliance on tradition and suspended between the incoming literary energies of the English-speaking post-imperial world outside Britain and the literary energies set free by a heightened awareness of belonging on a level less general and abstract than the nation state. It seemed only logical and fair to let these speak their different voices rather than curtailing them beforehand with a detailed theoretical framework. There are a number of areas in which literature written by authors related in a great variety of ways to Britain have broken with the past or have adapted conventional approaches to suit new urgencies of message, address and expression. But of course there are theoretical issues involved as soon as we begin to sift through a large number of texts to sort out the ones we want to examine, and it is an illusion of a classic kind to claim a purely inductive approach not affected by deduction. Certain theoretical assumptions will inevitably and implicitly have been made, such as the existence of a literary mode of discourse distinct from but related to other kinds of discourse: history, journalism and so on.[2]

Another tacit theoretical assumption is for literature to manifest itself through genre, of which the lyrical and the epic (fictional) have been in the foreground here. But other and less evident theoretical assumptions as well will have been made, the most important of which seems to have been the nature of the reading audience or, more to the point, audiences. To speak of a 'general reader', as I have done by implication in the study, is a matter of traditional convenience which, for all that, may always have been fallacious, but in the present circumstances perhaps in many cases directly misleading. So the constitution of the reading audience would have to have been problematised as an essential part of the concept of literary implosion, had this been a critical study of a more literary–sociological bent. Cultural audience segmentation is very much part of the picture of cultural marketing, but also in areas where deliberate marketing does not play a prominent role, we may find nexus to exist between producers and recipients to the extent of closed circuits. And then again, even where we may be able to document such closed circuits – a case in point would be the Jamaican reggae/dub poetry scene in south central London – the closed circuit may be found to be constantly short-circuited by the availability of the products in electronic forms universally available.

A localised and 'genuine' sub-culture may thus find itself removed over a considerable distance, geographically as well as socially and culturally, away from its point of origin and natural producer–audience nexus and into being part of the general culture scene, with the ephemerality of popular culture phenomena or perhaps the cultivation of cult culture as results. Since so much of the literature examined here was written by authors facing the British tradition either from positions as outsiders, as is the case of immigrants or those choosing Britain as a kind of spiritual or intellectual *pied-à-terre*, or from positions as insiders deliberately choosing alternative viewpoints, it would be tempting to apply the critical and theoretical perspective of post-colonial theory and post-colonial studies. While the insights and procedures of post-colonial theory and studies have been invaluable for large parts of contemporary literature, and, of course, not only literatures written in English, it is equally obvious that the ideological and methodological assumptions of post-colonial criticism only go part of the way to throwing light on the literature under scrutiny in this study.

In what follows I shall discuss briefly the potentials and limitations of currently available and popular critical paradigms for the literature of 'implosion' I have dealt with in my study. Not that there seems to be an overall critical alternative providing some sort of master key, a critical 'grand' or 'master' narrative. Rather, I wish to argue for the desirability of being able to provide the kind of critical 'small narratives', *in casu* the subjects of the preceding chapters, that seem so much more rewarding than the Procrustean dynamics of the grand ones, since present-day literature itself seems to prefer the status of 'small narratives'.

In comparison with the speed and adaptability with which the media respond to a world in which constant change seems the only certainty, and with which creative writing and the arts in general seem to be in happy rhythm, literary criticism has found it difficult to leave or to problematise positions consolidated at a time when technology-enhanced globalisation and technology saturation of life at all levels was still a future scenario, and one feared at that rather than welcomed. The approaches offering themselves to the literary critic are, roughly speaking, the perspectives of cultural studies, post-colonial studies, and theory – roughly speaking, since this categorisation cannot be said to do full justice to the nature of present-day critical exegesis. Cultural studies are leaving the strictly empirical mode of the Birmingham days to be increasingly theorised. Post-colonial studies have their roots in a cross-disciplinary concept of criticism drawing considerably on and generating theoretical issues. Theory itself, as a field acknowledging its roots in literary criticism and linguistics but more and more coming into its own as an area of academic discipline with its peculiar distinctions and with an impact on general modes of thought, is of a comprehensive nature. But despite the tendency towards theorising all kinds of empirical approaches, it is probably fair and of practical relevance still to assume a division of interests in literature into critical studies – cultural and post-colonial studies – and meta-critical studies: theory.

The difference between the implications for literary studies of cultural studies and post-colonial studies, on the one hand, and of theory, on the other, is for the first two a tendency to think in terms of reductive dichotomies and material first causes, whereas for the second the object of attention is the very nature of such reductive dichotomies, dealing with verbal signifiers rather than material signifieds. In modern critical practice, of course, it hardly makes sense to put the three kinds of approach, cultural studies, post-colonial criticism and theory, into watertight compartments separate from each other. They intermingle, drawing on each other, in the same postmodern manner of endless combination and intertextuality that we find in modern literature, to which, indeed, the transition is often quite seamless. Robert Crawford, Scottish spokesman for devolution, outstanding scholar and very active poet, in his poem 'The Saltcoats Structuralists' provides a model example of the way that a text unequivocally signalling itself as conventionally literary – unrhymed two-verse stanzas in loose iambic pentameter – draws on the lessons of recent theory to make for a tragicomic vista depending for its success on familiarity also with the material subject matter of cultural and post-colonial studies.

Crawford's poem plays with the way that post-structuralism as a literary–critical reaction has called into question the cognitive Empire building of structuralism with all its cultivation of a kind of classic rationality. Where structuralism had posited objectivity and order, post-structuralism has responded with subjectivity and chaos. It is this bewildering situation of chaos following cosmos that Scottish engineers and workmen, who used to be the British Empire's 'structuralists' when building railways in Egypt, feel on their retirement back into a society now post-Iron Age and deep into the IT revolution. In his ingenious poem, Crawford manages to make some essential points about the contemporary post-industrial world in general, and specifically about the Industrial Revolution on which the British Empire built, the aftermath of that Empire and, not least, about the Scottish stake in Empire building. The theory on which the poem depends for its point overlaps with its subject matter of the replacement of a mechanical and solid world – 'a world still made from girders' (Hulse, Kennedy and Morley, 1993:278) – by a digitalised and virtual world ('Kids zapped the videogames in big arcades' – ibid.) with which it is at one. The poem clearly demonstrates the inadequacy of the application of any one critical approach for the appreciation of the full potential of the poem. A cultural studies reading would have found it difficult to create a space for the non-material play at the meta-critical level, a post-colonial critical consideration would have focused wholly on the connections between industrial age and Empire, whereas theory alone would have tended to have reduced to rhetoric the solid realities behind the Saltcoats structuralists now (and not understanding for what material reason) turning into post-structuralists.

I am fully aware of the drastic simplification in the present discussion of some of the major critical industries at the turn of two millennia. I am also aware of the high degree of 'crossovers' between post-colonial criticism and gender criticism and cultural studies in general, and the extent to which all draw on elements common in the post-structuralist climate. All the same, my major point for these critical reflections is that most of the literature under scrutiny in the above chapters by its complexity of contexts defies attempts at getting squeezed into the hegemonic paradigms applied by kinds of criticism whose aim is to reveal and highlight ways in which literature enters into various power dynamics. In the following, before I proceed to a summation of my study, I shall argue why post-colonial criticism, although apparently cut out for a subject like the one of this study, is nonetheless of limited help seen in a perspective of the effects on literature from the implosion of Empire.

I find a quotation from Homi K. Bhabha highly illustrative of the reductive tendency often found in post-colonial studies and criticism. About the English weather considered as cultural stereotype it invokes, he writes, associations with more general cultural stereotype images:

> It encourages memories of the 'deep' nations crafted in chalk and limestone: the quilted downs; the moors menaced by the wind; the quiet cathedral towns; that corner of a foreign field that is forever England. The English weather also revives memories of its daemonic double: the heat and dust of India; the dark emptiness of Africa; the tropical chaos that was deemed despotic and ungovernable and therefore worthy of the civilizing mission.
>
> (Bhabha, 1994:169)

The argument is hinged on the simple Britain-versus-colonial-other dichotomy on which post-colonial criticism builds, with the tacit assumption that the English weather cultural stereotype, despite its hardly attractive implications, has nonetheless been dominant, its naturalness denaturing and turning into cultural stereotypes other kinds of weather conditions, at the same time making them inferior to the weather of the dominant culture. A formulation like Bhabha's with its invitation to the reconsideration of familiar images is an essential part of the orthodoxy of post-colonial criticism and central to its grand narrative of the positioning and revalidations of assumed dichotomies. But does it bear closer scrutiny? 'Deep' has been put in quotation marks. Do they signal irony or do they indicate a quotation? And, in the latter case, from where? The word 'crafted' usually carries positive overtones, but here such overtones seem to be ironically negated without any alternative offered. Surely, crafts as part of colonial-other cultures must be praiseworthy. The unacknowledged Rupert Brooke quotation has a quite familiar and generally accepted history of devalidation ever since the war atrocities became the object of a much-sobered British kind of patriotism with the slaughterhouse deadlock of 1916. In other words, the dominant side of the cultural stereotype part of the dichotomy seems to fall apart as an assumption of a geographically and epochally fixed set of values. Neither can the three cultural stereotype characteristics of the colonial other – Indian heat and dust, African emptiness and general tropical chaos – be said to be representative of the image awareness of a British nation, dominant as it was but always keen on cataloguing and being familiar with the details of its Empire.[3] Bhabha's bridge between the two poles of the dichotomy ('revives memories of its daemonic double') works as a statement rather than an argument. Whose memories are these? Does one have a memory of a cultural stereotypes image? And how is 'daemonic' suddenly introduced? We may appreciate why it is introduced, because it points the dichotomy in the desired direction, but 'daemonic' is certainly a leap to conclusions.

This is, of course, hardly a fair dismissal of the work of Homi K. Bhabha, since the passage from the chapter 'DissemiNation: Time, narrative and the margins of the modern nation' in *The Location of Culture* is meant as a light-relief coda concluding an exacting chapter requiring considerable attention and post-structuralist training on the part of the reader. Nonetheless, Susan Bassnett considered the passage characteristic enough of this particular approach to cite it in her introduction to *Studying British Cultures: An Introduction* (Bassnett, 1997:xxii–xxiii). The adoption of post-structuralist positions in post-colonial theory, notably by Bhabha and Gayatri Chakravorty Spivak, has indeed served to sharpen the tools of analysis considerably. But in the same way as the most wonderfully wrought weapons are typically meant for ritual and display, not for actual use, the reader is often left with a sense of aporia when it comes to applying the theoretical finesse rewardingly to the texts in the first place giving occasion for the theoretical elaborations. To theorise along the lines devised by Derrida, Lacan, Foucault, de Man and so on is of course quite legitimate, if that is what the thinker/writer sets out to do. But if the focus is on the literary text – literaryness being of course a highly problematic issue in a framework of post-structuralist theory, which prefers the more inclusive notion of text – the reader is arguably better served by such less text-distant deliberations as we find in Edward W. Said's insistence on 'worldliness' or 'locatedness', that is the refusal to be drawn away from the issues opened up, for, in and by the (literary) text. Said's suggestion of 'contrapuntal' readings to take into account 'affiliations' of a given text, in terms of what the text openly articulates or about what it remains silent, ensures a concern, even a respect for the text as a particularly charged enunciation: not more valid ('better') than other kinds of textual enunciation, but of a special kind, with a history and a traditional set of conventions to follow or to break away from. However, Said's recommendation of an 'amateur' attitude, that is an engagement with all relevant contexts of which some may lie outside the reader's/analyst's areas of specialist competence, seems to be liable to the criticism of superficiality frequently levelled at cross-disciplinary approaches generally.

Also in his dismissal of a 'rhetoric of blame' Said distances himself from much run-of-the-mill post-colonial criticism which sees its ultimate justification in auditing ethical accounts accrued since the start of colonisation. But Said sides with mainstream post-colonial criticism in his Foucault-derived view of the text as power, in his 'use of the concept of discourse, which he readily admits is partial, emphasizes dominance and power over cultural interaction' (Ashcroft and Ahluwahlia, 2001:70). Dominance presupposes agency, and agency, to have a meaning at all, is a question of a dichotomy of power and lack of power. Literature, indeed all texts are about power in this basic sense in so far as they relate to reality, however we wish to define it. Literature, indeed all texts, also exert power over those who read them. This amounts to a critical truism and is a feature of texts with which no one would wish to quarrel. And it is not in this trivial sense that Said, and other post-colonial critics with him, should be read. We need to specify power and dominance in political, social, ethnic, temporal and geographical terms. But the simple dichotomy prevails, and shifts the location of criticism from the domain of the text to the domain of politics, a deliberate politics of liberation. There is no doubt that the seamless transition from literary criticism into politics is justified in a number of specific cases and that to ignore the power in and of the text is to overlook an important textual aspect. But the forcing of a hermeneutical straitjacket on all texts and all textual situations is hardly the most illuminating critical procedure in all cases.

Post-colonial (discourse) theory, studies or criticism rely, arguably, on a refinement of given constituent elements into dichotomous patterns of dominance, calling out, on analysis, for resistance in terms of politics. One would be utterly blind and insensitive not to realise the amount of wrong done in the name of colonialism and imperialism since the first voyages of discovery, indeed since the ancient Roman and pre-Roman empires. And it is both right and timely that attention is called to the wrongs, ranging from genocide to mimicry, caused by those, in the past and present, committed to Empire. But if the critic sees her or his task in analysing relationships of power, turning them, Derrida-wise, into their opposites, with the ultimate aim of making a political demonstration, the critic should not stop at empire and its aftermaths, since all relations can be shown to be manifestations of power: between siblings, within families, between spouses, between genders, between social classes and so on. In other words, post-colonial (discourse) theory, studies or criticism are parts of a larger critical whole committed to a view of the (literary) text as a symptom of something larger than the (literary) text, but of which the (literary) text is a reflection and indeed, in some cases, also a motor.

If one could level criticism at post-colonial criticism, as at any other critical approach, for constructing its object according to its aim, one could also suggest that, by its having by now developed into a critical institution, this kind of criticism has crossed the threshold from the inductive to the deductive, that is from insights gained on the basis of texts drawing attention to themselves for their exhibition of certain features, either to mechanistic applications of a ready-made critical apparatus on any text, with results to be foreseen because prescribed, or to catapulting into further theorisation, leaving the literary text far behind. The latter we have seen in Homi K. Bhabha's attempts at wedding postcolonial theory to poststructuralism generally, the former in the many applications of Edward Said's technique of counterpuntal readings of canonical or canon-attached literature, in extension of his analysis of Jane Austen's *Mansfield Park* in his *Culture and Imperialism* (1993). This reading technique presupposes a view of the literary text as a simple reflection of a material reality. Furthermore, it prescribes a method to lay bare all the material affiliations that will illuminate the goings-on in the action of the text. It is hard to set any limit to this kind of affiliation study: how much is needed to 'understand' the material dynamics of a given text? In Charlotte Brontë's *Jane Eyre*, for instance, how much do we need to know about the material provenance of the deux-ex-machina inheritance from the Madeira wine-trading uncle? Does the exhibition of a 'false consciousness', as Marxist criticism dubbed it, compromise the situation and decisions on the part of Ms Eyre, or Ms Brontë? Certainly, if that is what the study set out to be in aid of. But surely many readers would feel this to be a misrepresenting of the narrative as a whole. Post-colonial criticism, from this aspect, tends to see literature (and this partly explains the endeavour to wipe out any distinctions between literary and non-literary texts) as so many signifiers attached firmly to their signifieds: the literary text, like any other, is a simple reflection of material reality. This in itself is problematic, since a case can be made both for the unique ontology of the literary and, in consequence, for the special ways literature 'processes' reality, whatever that is. It furthermore tends towards a situation of infinite regress in terms of political, economic, cultural, social and gender contexts, in which the literary work obtains a more and more marginal position and in which contextualisation takes over as critical dynamic. If this kind of 'counterpuntal' intervention can work, as indeed it can, compare my remarks on Graham Swift's *Last Orders*, in Chapter 5: there must be some invitation in the text that both justifies such an intervention and, not least, proposes its limitations.

In his development of a post-colonial discourse poetics in his 1988 Birkbeck College conference paper 'Articulating the Archaic: Notes on Colonial Nonsense', Homi K. Bhabha proposes as the key to understanding the post-colonial experience that 'It is in the enunciatory act of splitting that the colonial signifier creates its strategies of differentiation that produce an undecidability between contraries or oppositions' (Collier and Geyer-Ryan, 1990:208). If I understand this correctly as meaning the enunciation of an attitude brought about by the former colonial writer's uncertainty stemming from problematised cultural belonging in terms of relations with the British Empire, this attitude, when enunciated by the post-colonial writer writing back to (the aftermath of) the British Empire, is furthermore complicated since the contraries or oppositions are no longer reducible to a simple dominance dichotomy, but has had the (aftermath of) Empire in its national origin (Britain) and globalism added to it. In other words, the relative innocence of dichotomous undecidability in question has been replaced by an experience of a complexity to which reduction to a simple centre and margin approach would hardly do full justice. To spot the exact nature of undecidability in a given (literary) text, if that is indeed the object of one's reading, one could do worse than accept the text on its own premises and find out to what degree of complexity of undecidability, if that element seems to apply, the text invites.

In the preface to his informative and perceptive survey of British poetry in the period 1980–94, David Kennedy, as touched upon in Chapters 3 and 4 above, makes a somewhat contradictory statement regarding omissions. Having suggested that Irish poetry seems a critically well-covered area and therefore not in any particular need of inclusion in his critical survey, Kennedy goes on to explain why he has omitted Black British or Afro-Caribbean poetry 'not only because it seems inappropriate for a white critic to do so but because these poetries are still being theorised through perspectives of language and difference' (Kennedy, 1996:8). Having said this, Kennedy gives as his reason for not including women's poetry that 'to do so seems to me complicit with consigning women poets to a literary ghetto and with perpetuating conceptions of poetry by women as a kind of cultural sideshow' (ibid.). By the criterion for not including women's poetry – 'ghettoisation' – as a separate category, as seems to be the rule rather than the exception, Kennedy should have refused 'ghettoisation' for Black British and Afro-Caribbean poetry as well.

There seems to be absolutely no reason why the principle of integrated and non-gendered treatment of poetry by women could not have been extended to Black British and Afro-Caribbean poetry as well. But whereas 'ghettoisation' is found to do less than justice to poetry written by women, the right of separate treatment is accorded to the ethnically distinct group for two reasons: out of bounds for white critics, and the privileged domain of a particular critical approach ('still being theorised through perspective of language and difference'). The first reason, though, is in turn contradicted by subsequent and generalising comments made by Kennedy on the inadmissibility of the criterion of firsthand experience by poets and critics.[4] But the fact that Kennedy's first statement is later radically modified is not, in my opinion, as important as the special treatment almost routinely demanded by and accorded to groupings considering themselves especially vulnerable or deserving because of minority status.

Whereas the discussion about privileged position seems to reverberate between poles of integration and distinction in gender criticism, with a tendency to opt for the integrative move proposed and practised by Kennedy, another situation obtains when it comes to ethnically marked writing and post-colonial theory and studies. Kennedy's position is indeed typical of an attitude often encountered among critics and literary historians, respecting claims made by minority groups in relation to the majority culture which they have been made to accept or suffer. Such claims may be considered well-founded and just, and they may be expressed by literary means. But once made literary, such means have ventured into a domain whose very nature is public and whose dynamic is dissemination.

The kind of 'politically correct' situation that Kennedy is eager to put himself in is due to a simple categorical mistake which emerges as a failure to appreciate the difference between the signified of events and the signifier of their communication. Admittedly, a poem may be written to address a specific group, but once released with other poems, say on a CD for public purchase, the event it describes is no longer just the matter for the original intended audience. Once in the public domain, it is inevitable that it will be compared to other similar products, and that its thematic substance and artistic execution will be made the subject of critical discussion. It would indeed amount to a contradiction in terms to choose a literary medium and not to expect its dissemination.

It is understandable that the injustice suffered by subjects of imperialistic oppression demands a special kind of sympathy towards the sufferers on the part of those who acknowledge the injustice, and I have no quarrel with those who try to redress wrongs committed by sheer political force in the past or the present. My quarrel is with those, however, who attempt to establish a certain privileged position for texts dealing with such matters and, by extension, for the criticism they invite.

Unfortunately, there has been a tendency concerning the literature of 'subaltern' populations for criticism to mistake the medium for the message, and to pay routine homage to such literature by making special concessions in the way of implying moral superiority over the dominating culture's allegedly moral shortcomings. The tendency is by now so entrenched that most critics dealing with these matters expect a ritual guilt assumption as the ticket on the part of the representative of the dominant culture to enter the subaltern domain. The assumption of guilt may take a variety of forms, from the downright excuses made for imperialistic crimes of the past that became popular with Western statesmen in the 1990s, to more or less displaced verbal or pictorial forms. An illustrative case in point would be the image adorning Elleke Boehmer's *Empire Writing: An Anthology of Colonial Literature 1870–1918* in the Oxford World's Classics Series (1998). The cover illustration is taken from an *ABC for Baby Patriots* by Mrs Ernest Ames, a book published by Dean and Son in 1890. It shows a little girl on a toy horse on wheels, wearing toy helmet and breastplate and holding a drawn toy sabre. Under the toy horse's head stands a toy soldier at rigid attention, just the way emulated by the girl. The girl sits astraddle a Union Jack on the horse's back. The whole image is drawn in a deliberately simplistic manner. The implications of this image, whether the reader is aware of its origin or not, impose a kind of filter through which the contents of the anthology – a virtual goldmine of a great variety of texts to do with the British Empire during the period in question and with an extremely competent and balanced introduction and a fine commentary – appear in a distinctly 'we-know-better-now' light.

The impact of post-colonial studies and criticism has been double: it has enhanced an awareness in former colonial nations of native identities, and of uncertainty towards established literary traditions among the former colonisers. If a literary work is to be considered both an aesthetic verbal construct and a reflection of existential (that is, ethical, political, social) concerns, the value-questioning approach of post-colonial criticism will be able to point to gaps and inconsistencies in literary works which have been quite naturalised as the unambiguous, national tradition of the colonising power. Once we begin to read 'great works' through the lens of post-colonial criticism, the premises of the fictional universe displayed will often have to be re-examined. Textbook examples are Jane Austen and the unacknowledged significance of the imperialist Napoleonic Wars for the contemporary social fabric, Charlotte Brontë and Jane Eyre's reversal of fortunes depending on the Empire-based wine trade with Madeira, and Charles Dickens's limited analysis of Victorian industrial England because he never painted the full picture of the imperial economy. Once the colonial context is invoked, we can see what was not apparent to the author, who will typically diagnose as 'fate', 'character' and so on what depends on a much more concretely material reality.

These are of course only crude examples to indicate some of the more basic lessons to be learnt from post-colonial criticism as applied to the scene of the coloniser. Of a much more general and far-ranging nature is Edward Said's now generally accepted demonstration of 'oriental' as a Western concept which does not elucidate anything about cultures east of the Mediterranean but, on the contrary, quite a lot about 'occidental' ways of approaching these cultures, first and foremost as a cultural construction by the colonising West. Said suggests persuasively that the concept of 'orientalism' has settled to such an extent that it is accepted as the 'natural' mode of thought by Westerners. Likewise Toni Morrison, who situates the post-colonial arena right within the USA itself:

> until very recently, and regardless of the race of the author, the readers of virtually all of American fiction have been positioned as white. I am interested to know what that assumption has meant to the literary imagination. When does racial 'unconsciousness' or awareness of race enrich interpretive language, and when does it impoverish it? What does positing one's writerly self, in the wholly racialized society that is the United States, as unraced and all others as raced entail? What happens to the writerly imagination of a black author who is at

some level *always* conscious of representing one's own race to, and in spite of, a race of readers that understands itself to be 'universal' or race-free? In other words, how is 'literary whiteness' and 'literary blackness' made, and what is the consequence of that construction? How do embedded assumptions of racial (not racist) language work in the literary enterprise that hopes and sometimes claims to be 'humanistic'? When, in a race-conscious culture, is that lofty goal actually approximated? When not and why?

(Morrison, 1993:xiv–xv)

Post-colonial studies and criticism has sent shock waves into not only aesthetically based literary and cultural criticism, but also into context-based kinds of criticism. It has forced Marxist critics to consider Marxist positions as inscribed in Empire, and not the other way round, just as deconstructionist criticism has suggested to us the primacy of textuality and its power of suppression and oppression. It has given inspiration to and been energised by gender studies.

In their introductory examination of the definition range and validity of 'post-colonial,' the authors of the pioneering *The Empire Writes Back: Theory and Practice in Postcolonial Literatures* (Ashcroft, Griffith and Tiffin, Routledge, 1989) acknowledge the possible application of the term to the period since colonial rule, on the basis of a distinction between colony and independent nation. But they prefer a much wider use: 'to cover all the culture affected by the Imperial process from the moment of colonisation to the present day' (ibid.:3). Most of the English-speaking world is consequently to be considered post-colonial, even including the USA – although the authors find that the old transatlantic colony was quick to assume colonial ambitions herself, with England – and not Great Britain or the UK – left as the sole non-post-colonial culture.

While it is tempting to accept a view of the world divided into colonisers and colonised – us and the Other – with corresponding effects of a dialectical kind on the cultures of both, closer inspection of historical facts makes for a more faceted impression.

What about England itself before it became a colonising power during the reigns of Henry VII, Henry VIII and Elizabeth I? The

England of the Tudors comprised a highly composite population, of Roman, Nordic, Teutonic and Norman descent. Or what about your typecast NCO in the Indian Army: a ruddy Irishman, himself a descendant of either native Gaelic stock – wherever that came from – or the English or Scottish conquerors of the Emerald Isle, or more than likely a hybrid of all of them? Or Scotland, united with England first though royal succession in 1603, and then through economic need in a regular merger in 1707. Or Ireland, coerced into cohabitation with England since the Middle Ages with the treaty of 1801 as the binding judicial arrangement. Either had no little impact on the progress and nature of colonisation. Scotland left its mark on New England commerce, and Ireland on metropolitan life in the USA. And then there is the fundamental paradox that precisely in the early-modern period, when England became a coloniser, it was itself in a post-colonial phase, having recently shaken off the cultural hegemony of Rome and France.

Perhaps the best indication of hybridisation is language, whose very nature is a flow of giving and taking. The English imposed upon the colonised was Anglo-Saxon with a heavy admixture of mediaeval French, quite a lot of Viking-Nordic, and a little Latin. Present-day English is very much a mixture, now under heavy influence from the former transatlantic colony, to which it exported its language originally.

To reduce the discussion of literatures outside England to the reactions of the colonial and ex-colonial others to Imperial supremacy, to Edward Said's Western civilisation sense of orientalism, is surely to create a handy analytical and interpretational space, but does it do full justice to the historical or the contemporary situation?

The problematising and deconstruction of what may be assumed to be a rather standard construction of post-colonial criticism dogma serves to demonstrate, I hope, not a revisionist approach to an area in which much valuable criticism has contributed to our general understanding of the past and its significance for the present globally, but the extent to which a grand critical narrative tends to replace old with new orthodoxies, but not necessarily more correct just because the spirit of the time has a way of subscribing to rather than questioning politically, hence critically, correct assumptions. Considering the literature written during the period towards the end of the twentieth century that saw a complete recasting of geopolitical relations and a revolutionary IT development, both of which had considerable effects on both the what and how of literature, it makes less and less sense to apply the tools of critical grand narratives, such as those of cultural studies or post-colonial criticism, without, at least, considerable adjustment. The situation of British literature during these couple of decades could be said to present the best possible evidence for a problematisation of these two critical grand narratives.

We may assume that texts, literary or non-literary, remain stable as so many printed words and sentences. If a text is received differently by different readers, it is because their antennae have been tuned accordingly. If we apply an interpretive angle to literature from, say, India or Australia, which is geared to bring out the qualities in them which can be construed to derive from imperial or post-imperial Western suppression, then of course these are exactly the qualities we will find, results invariably predetermined by method. Certainly there is a deep need for this kind of criticism, especially with regard to minority ethnic groups trying to find a genuine voice of their own: aboriginal culture in contemporary Australia would be a case in point. But what about literature by writers from areas having been colonised for centuries, and for which the culture of the Empire has been a fact of life for generations? However alien the culture of the imperialists may have been, it has imposed itself to a degree which makes the longing for roots not only impossible, but also unrepresentative of the situation now. Take, for instance, the case of the African–American movement in the USA. We can all agree on the monstrosity of any civilisation supporting itself on slave labour. But the fact remains that imported slaves were an essential part of the construction of an English transatlantic colony over a period of about two hundred years, also after the colony became independent. However unsuccessful attempts at the full integration of the descendants of the slaves may have been, there is no way back. Resettling in Nigeria or other countries on the West African coast is a romantic and unrealistic dream. The black community in the USA is part and parcel of that larger community, which significantly, owes its coming into being to almost one hundred per cent (though voluntary for the majority) immigration.[5]

The critic imposing the concept 'post-colonial' on the literature of blacks (or of native Americans, or of the Irish, the Germans, the Swedes, the Jews and so on) in the USA, is bound to run into methodological and ideological difficulties even before he or she starts. While we all agree that it was an injustice that native Americans were deprived of their land, the 'criminals' who did it were not a well-defined ethnic army of conquest despite a predominant WASPishness: it consisted of immigrants from all over the Old World, who in many cases themselves suffered under such social conditions that emigration was the only way out. So in the first place we have to sort out the relationship between oppression in social terms within a given nation state in Europe and oppression in terms of coloniser/colonised. In the second place we shall have to construct some kind of culture which has been destroyed and lost and which constituted the 'purity' of what came before the conquerors. Both ventures pose difficulties of considerable dimensions.

But then, if we discard any facile view of post-colonial as implying cultural and literary criticism dedicated to a simplistic and reductive binarism, what can we do instead? After all, we have a lot of literature written in English, written partly in England, partly – and increasingly – outside the former hub of the Empire. In his 1972 address to an Indian audience, 'After Marabar: Britain and India, A Post-Forsterian View', Paul Scott, author of the *Raj Quartet*, faces the fact of colonisation and decolonisation by urging the two sides to accept a shared destiny:

> Once again, as between Britain and India, as between my own British generation and the Indian generation that corresponds with it, I see more clearly what connects than what divides. For instance that there must surely be an emotional correspondence between our giving you up or losing you and your kicking us out, or anyway persuading us in the light of incontrovertible evidence that it was time we went; an emotional correspondence in the shape of a shared moment, possibly a prolonged one, of hiatus, as together we found one kind of occupation gone and one kind of ideal fulfilled – whichever way it was, whichever way one chooses, but leaving an

emotional vacuum to be filled, and occasions of immediate and pressing demands on our stores of energy, ingenuity and idealism. In neither case can the past be discounted. We have both inherited it even if we didn't personally make it. And in many subtle ways it still connects us. Why should it not? It was a human experience. Another thing that connects us is the fact that the world into which we both floated off, as from an abandoned Imperial shore, was one for which neither of us was fully prepared, but that was more our fault than yours.

(Scott, 1986:128)

Fred D'Aguiar in his introduction to the Black British Poetry section of *the new british poetry* (sic!) from 1988 is also worth quoting at length, since he strikes the same chord:

It is becoming increasingly difficult to marginalise a poet on the basis of his or her racial origin or thematic concerns. This is perhaps due to a shared commitment to a notion of craft, to being engaged in an art form which cuts across race and class and shares a wide and borderless imaginative terrain.... Two black poets in Britain today are likely to have less in common than two poets picked out of a hat. This means that an examination of Black British poetry is at once a scrutiny of what is happening to poetry in Britain as a whole. Dualisms such as oral and literary, European and African no longer define the work of *individual* poets, much less explain the differences between them.

(Allnut *et al.*, 1988:xx)

The present-day writer is situated in the centre of a cultural dynamic, whatever her or his origin. When the Guyana-born British poet, dramatist and cultural studies academic David Dabydeen writes an elegy occasioned by his sense of alienation on the part of immigrants from the Caribbean now living the metropolitan life in Britain, he is well aware that there is no returning, but this does not mean simple acceptance of the predominantly British culture. In the introductory lines of his poem 'Coolie Odyssey *(for Ma, d. 1985)*' he at first quips at a Seamus Heaney and then at a Tony Harrison:

> Now that peasantry is in vogue,
> Poetry bubbles from peat bogs,
> People strain for the old folk's fatal gobs
> Coughed up in grates North or North East
> 'Tween bouts o'livin dialect.
>
>   (Allnut *et al.*, 1988:27)

Anyone can see that however tempting it may be at first glance to establish a dichotomy between, on the one hand, Dabydeen with his post-colonial background, and on the other, British consensus culture, this distinction does not hold up to critical scrutiny. Dabydeen is, by his situatedness, part of a variegated culture in the British Isles, as are Heaney and Harrison, who are, in their turn, as far from each other as both are from Dabydeen in most respects except for the shared literary medium of the poem. When Dabydeen pays his tribute to his place of origin, he has to carve a niche for himself in a house of poetry already in existence. In an effort reminding the reader of a dynamics of patricide as formulated in Harold Bloom's axiom of the anxiety of influence Dabydeen earns his place somewhere in that house too.

The focus in this study has been on literary texts written, on the whole, according to formal traditions familiar to a British audience but which at the same time display in their choices of subject matter and thematic concerns preoccupations resulting from a historic moment of important cultural intersections. The aftermath of Empire in the form of an influx of immigrants and a widespread feeling of London and Britain as the cultural meeting point has manifested itself in a significant widening in terms of subject matter. It is true that it is possible to trace what might be called an English 'core curriculum' in British literature, seemingly unaffected by the post-imperial situation. The fiction of Anita Brookner does not display much in the way of influence from a changing British demography. And it could indeed be argued that the fiction of Joanna Trollope and Rosamund Pilcher cleverly exploits a longing on the part of a segment of the reading audience for an England undisturbed by any retreat from global power. But apart from such 'time pockets' most fiction, seismograph-like, reports changes in the make-up of British society in consequence of the need for the nation to have to find a new role during the last half of the twentieth century.

It would, of course, be wrong to attribute all changes in British society and culture to an awareness of an Empire 'won' over centuries and 'lost' almost overnight. As in the case of all Western countries, there have been forces at work overriding 'local' British problems deriving from Empire. Ambivalent relations with a continental Europe bent on closer cooperation, with Germany and France not deferring in any way to the former leading workshop of Europe, adaptation to a world for forty years held in the deadlock of an arms race with Britain pleading a special relationship with the USA but in terms of a decidedly younger brother, and cultural innovation, at popular and avant-garde levels alike and increasingly at the mercy of the global market – in all these it is hardly possible to see Britain as an actor with decisive influence due to former Empire status. The concerns aired in the novels by Nick Hornby are hardly dependent on geographical location. If the reader makes a mental change of place names to New York or Munich, one would suspect that the rest of his novels would remain valid, since the subject of this kind of novel transcends nationality as a widely practised genre of urban fiction. The same applies to the Scottish writer Irvine Welsh, whose use of Low Scots does not disguise the fact that also here we have to do with thematic concerns of urban life generally imposed by forces of a more international range.

The world of literature is fast developing into world literature, with the market the sole arbitrator and the media powerful enough to the raise the poor and mediocre to star status and to bury the not immediately accessible or otherwise forbidding to the entertainment-craving masses by simply ignoring it. But internationalisation has not meant the ironing out of national and regional differences in favour of a neutral literary product, no matter how similar the news stand book shelves in airports all over the world may look. Readers seem to be craving that which has a distinct flavour and atmosphere. There may be a lot of different reasons for the international success of J.K. Rowling's Harry Potter stories, but surely their very English ambience is a charm for most readers abroad, and perhaps also for large reader segments in Britain, to whom this Englishness remains a construction. Generic fiction of the whodunit variety remains firmly located, because crime and its solution is a locale-conditioned phenomenon. So-called worldwide bestsellers of American provenance often make a point of displaying Americanness as a distinctly integral part of their narratives: they get their international appeal because there is a global desire to read about American phenomena.

So globalisation in literature is more about markets than about nationally neutral fictional universes created by writers. But globalisation is also a question of intersections of traditions, conventions, locales and provenances of writers. Latin American Magic Realism had tremendous effects in literature generally in the latter half of the twentieth century. American New Journalism, which came into its own in the 1970s, is a blend of fiction and discourses usually associated with factual writing that proved a challenge to writers everywhere, although its success in Britain must be said to have been limited.

Britain has been in a peculiar situation in this globalisation of literature in terms of intersections, since the country, like any other country, is reorienting itself in the 'global village', at the same time as it is attempting to cope with a situation determined by its former status as leading imperial nation. This peculiar situation of globalisation at two levels, so to speak, naturally results in far more cultural interfaces than those of most other countries. Whereas, in most countries, the discussion about sex roles and gender constructions reflects the way these issues are discussed with a global input but in relation to local – 'native' – women, an extra dimension is added in Britain with its demographic aftermath of Empire, in which 'native' means intercultural rather than monocultural. This creates the 'compound voice' so characteristic of the climate in British letters towards the end of the twentieth century: the frequent presence of the sense of an 'other', in terms of narrative or thematic structure, in terms of locales of reference, or in terms of displacements of such an 'other', a displacement most often carried out by historical projection or perspective.

In this study I have identified – or, as some would no doubt prefer it, constructed – the compound voice in a number of literary–historical 'small narratives' which overlap and complement one another. I believe there is a point in this non-systematic method reflecting the lack of willingness on the part of the literature related to Britain of the last couple of decades of the twentieth century, so it seems to be the shared opinion of critical observers, to unite in movements, schools or under manifestos. I hope to have demonstrated that, far from this being a state of confusion, we have to do with a tremendously energetic and extremely variegated epoch in British literature, rich in talent and empowered by an awareness of intercultural potentiality.

Notes

1 Literary Britain between Imperial Legacy and Regional Devolution

1 My translation from the French: 'Alors que les Français se laissent séduire par les illusions du Moi ou par l'assurance-vie que représente la tradition historique, l'histoire réside chez ces écrivains de langue anglaise dans une relation polémique entre "leurs" deux cultures' (Mongin, 1992:2).

2 For a brief discussion, see Chapter 2 in Sauerberg (1997).

3 Whereas the attitude of former imperial nations in the post-colonial atmosphere of the last two or three decades of the twentieth century has been to prefer the apologetic, the reconception of Englishness after an imperial epoch identity overlap with Britishness seems to necessitate a 'baby-and-bathwater' awareness. Colley concludes her No. 10 Downing Street talk (1999) by saying so explicitly, and so does Ann Leslie when she warns against identity neutralisation by a liberal opinion favouring a constant demand for *mea culpas* over the past (Leslie, 1998:19).

4 As the tendency in the 1990s seems to have been to take more or less gracious leave of 'British' as a designation of more than diplomatic convenience (cp. Linda Colley's recommendation of a British citizen nation above) in favour of more local–specific points of geographical reference (cp. A.S. Byatt's account of an Irish friend addressing her as a Yorkshirewoman, 1998b:1), it is curious to note that Peter Childs and Mike Storry have chosen to entitle their encyclopedia for Routledge *Encyclopedia of Contemporary British Culture* (1999).

5 'As it happens, she not only manages to weed out Maugham with admirable tact ("a little too mechanical"), but gives the chop to writers whom we might confidently have expected to encounter, preferring those who have been less frequently anthologised. Be warned that this is an anthology with Ronald Fairbank but no E.M. Forster, J.G. Ballard but no Arnold Bennett, Ian McEwan but no George Eliot.... Elizabeth Bowen is left out, presumably because she was Anglo-Irish. And no, Henry James and Joseph Conrad do not get in, although Byatt does not say whether this is due to an accident of birth, or because both were really practitioners of the novella rather than the short-story form. Other writers omitted either on critical grounds or because of lack of space include Elizabeth Gaskell, Walter de la Mare, Doris Lessing (all too long), and E.M. Forster (too whimsical)' (Lowry, 1998:24).

6 In her 6 April 1998 *Sunday Times* article on 'What it means to be English', A.S. Byatt does not talk about whimsy, but about wickedness: 'We are interested in small spites and large malfeasances' (1998b:3). In this article she also elaborates on the way that Englishness is symptomatically that which there is a reaction against, so existing as an implicitly given, manifested by a great many explicit others, and she singles out the 1997 volume of essays *Studying British Cultures*, edited by Susan Bassnett, from which 'you get the feeling that the English exist only to be discarded and "challenged"' (1998b:1). Another piece of evidence regarding the implicitness, even the absence of Englishness, appears in a poignant passage in an essay by Ann Leslie, after she has interviewed a group of young people hanging around outside a shopping centre about their sense of national identity: 'The English have woken up to the fact that the Scots and the Welsh increasingly call themselves "nations", not regions, as we have always called them. Well, if Scotland is a nation, and Wales is a nation, and Ireland is a nation, what is England? The English, having been complacently boss nation for so long – first over all other Britons, and secondly over much of the world – do not know what they are any more' (1998:18).
7 Cp. 'There is no fixed, unchanging entity called Englishness, or Britishness, or Jamaicanness. Each of these cultural identities, like that of Scotland, is in constant evolution, continually re-manufacturing itself' (Crawford, 1992:14).
8 As a chapter in Crawford (1992) and as major topic in Crawford (1998).
9 'Nynorsk' (New Norwegian) is based on a dialect from central Norway.

2 Imperial Aftermath in British Post-World War Two Fiction

1 The tendency to question the given 'truths' and values implied in the British literary canon has not been confined to post-colonial writings, but can be seen in, for instance, works which critically 'continue' more or less open-ended literary works of established popular or canonical standing. We see this typically in Susan Hill's *Mrs de Winter* (1993), which confers poetic justice on the events told by Daphne du Maurier in *Rebecca* (1938) and, in Elaine Feinstein's *Lady Chatterley's Confessions* (1995), Mellors is allowed to develop consistently according to his crypto-fascist *Blut und Boden* inclinations and Lady Chatterley is given a chance to emerge as a human being in her own right.
2 Cp. 'The order of the procession seemed to Dacres and, more fearfully and less philosophically, to Sligh, to be not so much a symbol as the objective reality of the order in which they were to live'

(Sisson, 1953:73) with the administrators at the back of the cavalcade, and with the NCO ahead of them, liaising with the horsemen of the prince's guard.
3 Cp. 'Sir Bertram was delighted with the prospect of the mission. Any other mission would have pleased him equally, for it was a matter of temperament as well as of professional training that he ignored the content and purpose of any task he undertook. If the subject was sufficiently complicated, so that there was some point in a man of his calibre having a go at it, he was satisfied. His whole body shrivelled in fear and disdain if a discussion in which he was taking part was spoilt by a fool alluding to the remoter consequences of what was being planned' (Sisson, 1953:85).
4 See Sauerberg (1984).

3 Verbal (Pre)Occupations

1 In this connection one may note W.N. Herbert's humorously intertextual updating of Robert Burns's 'To a Mouse'. Herbert's 'To a Mousse', prosodically true to its model, begins: 'O queen o sludge, maist royal mousse,/yer minions bear ye ben thi hoose,/O quakin sheikess, lavish, loose,/dessert o fable:/ye pit thi bumps back oan ma goose/and shauk ma table' (Astley, 1999:72).
2 That this sense of being in a kind of no-man's land has other dimensions emerges from Joanne Limburg's 'Seder Night With My Ancestors' (Astley, 1999:232–3) which introduces the theme of the diaspora Jew as a likewise regional theme.
3 The post-World War Two immigration by Caribbeans since the first docking of the *Empire Windrush* at Tilbury in 1948 is recorded with engaging empathy by Mike Phillips and Trevor Phillips in their *Windrush: The Irresistible Rise of Multi-Racial Britain* (1998).
4 It is quite curious to note that Kennedy seems to contradict himself when it comes to poetry written by women: 'I have not devoted a separate chapter to women's poetry: to do so seems to me complicit with consigning women poets to a literary ghetto and with perpetuating conceptions of poetry by women as a cultural sideshow' (Kennedy, 1996:8). Cp. discussions of Kennedy's problematic positions on these issues in Chapter 4 and 8.

4 Wholly Female, Partly Foreign

1 In an area notoriously slippery when it comes to generalising statements and subscriptions to convention and prejudice, though not in all cases intentional, Jeni Couzyn's poem may well stand as a reference text, in that it seems to offer a kind of highest common denominator of gender awareness at the same time as it uses imagery of an almost pedagogical clarity in this respect.

2 In her review of *The New Penguin Book of English Verse* (ed. Paul Keegan, 2000), Helen Dunmore notes that 'Keegan devotes 279 pages, out of 1,100-odd, to twentieth century poetry. Fewer than 30 poems by women feature on these pages, and none is a long poem. There is nothing by Fleur Adcock, U.A. Fanthorpe, Liz Lochhead, Selima Hill, E.J. Scovell, Elizabeth Jennings, Wendy Cope, Gillian Clarke, Anne Stevenson, Carol Rumens, Ruth Padel, Pauline Stainer, Kathleen Raine, Patricia Beer, Elaine Feinstein, Ruth Fainlight, Vicki Feaver, Penelope Shuttle, Gillian Allnut.... All this is such a loss to the reader. Vital registers and qualities of late twentieth-century poetry are missing. There's none of Cope's formal wit and play, Hill's ferocious originality, or Fanthorpe's Janus-faced monologues. Their absence is baffling and the anthology's representation of the twentieth century is diminished by it, as is the reader's pleasure' (*Observer* 12 November 2000, Review, p. 13). I might add that nor does Dunmore's list of notable omissions include immigrant women's poetry.

5 In the Great Tradition – but with a Difference

1 For a discussion of criteria of distinction between fictional and non-fictional texts, see Sauerberg (1991: chs 2 and 3).
2 But it is possible to put together an aetiology of Leavis's sense of values relating to the English nation: see Sauerberg (1997:64–98).
3 The year is not stated, but can be computed by comparing the reference to the birth date of June, Jack the butcher's daughter on 1 June 1939 at the time of her fiftieth birthday, which is then 1989 (Swift, 1999:83). Jack's widow decides to stop seeing the seriously retarded daughter on the day, 2 April, when the friends are taking Jack's ashes to Margate, and she refers to her age as fifty (Swift, 1999:276–7), which then has to be 1990.

6 Global Villagers

1 Barnes's novel is an excellent illustration of postmodernist fiction.
2 When the series stopped in 1943, 5800 titles by 800 authors had been published.
3 Cp. Sauerberg (1991).
4 The move was made by Spiller and others in their *Literary History of the United States* in 1948. Cp. Sauerberg (1997:14–17).

7 Adopting and Adapting Crime Fiction

1 This includes the currently popular problematisation of national stereotypes. Some good-humoured national stereotype nagging

appears, for instance, in Stella Duffy's *Calendar Girl*, when she has her heroine, when under cover in New York, actually succeed in taking American men's reputation for obsession with cleanliness for granted by avoiding intercourse by faking her period (Duffy, 1994: 122–3).
2. Cp. also 'An Indian girl was standing in the doorway. West Indian by her accent. Trinidad or Guyana. I couldn't be sure because living in England had rounded out and shortened her vowels' (Phillips, 1990:31) and 'He was from one of the small islands where a French patois was spoken, by the sound of him. They were usually friendly and polite people, but withdrawn and reserved according to Caribbean standards' (ibid.:32).
3. Fran's mother left her father, and when her father died, Fran lived with her increasingly senile Hungarian grandmother. A previous period at an exclusive girls' school only succeeded in strengthening her individualistic character (Granger, 1997:85, 115). For a brief and somewhat cavalier survey of 'female amateurs' in crime fiction up to the time of this study, see Binyon (1989:70–72).
4. Pseudonym of Julian Barnes.
5. Cp. 'He *had* assumed a black girl's body was that of a missing black girl and he has done so *because she was black*... This error had occurred through prejudice, through racism, through making an assumption he could never have made if the missing girl were white and the body white. In such a case he would merely have thought it likely the lost girl had been found, but he would have done a lot more rigorous research into appearance and statistics before summoning the parents to make an identification' (Rendell, 1994:178).
6. Dr Akande, who in successive Wexford stories remains the inspector's doctor, is an illustrative example of what sociologists since the 1980s have termed 'buppies', that is black, upwardly mobile middle class citizens belonging to ethnic minorities. Rendell uses him as an effective foil against which to test the reactions of Wexford – the representative type of sincere, middle-class Englishmen – in the area of racial relations.

8 Critical Perspective

1. My translation from the German: 'Es fragt sich, inwieweit die Mehrheit der Autoren zwischen Kanada un Neuseeland tatsächlich das Primärinteresse am anti-kolonialen Diskurs und an der transkulturellen Hybridität teilt oder ob sie nicht mindestens so sehr an der Problematik des Individuums in seiner unmittelbaren Umwelt und vor dem Hintergrund der sich wandelnden modernen Welt interessiert ist, in die solche Fragen nur sekundär hineinspielen' (Nünning, 1998:437).
2. For blending of fictional and factual modes of discourse in post-World War Two literature in English, see Sauerberg (1991).

3 See, for example, Richards (1993).
4 'Cults of the authentic and the personal do poets and poetry no favours' (Kennedy, 1996:13) and 'Peter Fuller, for example, was neither a painter nor a sculptor but this did not prevent him from writing with sympathy and insight about artists as diverse as Willem de Kooning, Jackson Pollock, Henry Moore and Cecil Collins' (ibid.:12).
5 The radical voices in post-colonial studies who urge a literal return to roots come up against the same difficulty as those advocating cultural – and literary – criticism on ecological grounds: the authentic seems an ever-vanishing phenomenon, as it refuses to be re-called into being or reconstructed.

References

Publication data indicate edition used.

Allnutt, G., F. D'Aguiar, K. Edwards and E. Mottram (eds) (1988). *the new british poetry*. London: Paladin.
Ashcroft, B. and P. Ahluwahlia (2001). *Edward Said*. London: Routledge.
Ashcroft, B., G. Griffith and H. Tiffin (1989). *The Empire Writes Back: Theory and Practice in Postcolonial Literatures*. London: Routledge.
Astley, N. (ed.) (1988). *Poetry with an Edge*. Newcastle upon Tyne: Bloodaxe Books Ltd. (2nd edn 1993).
Astley, N. (ed.) (1999). *New Blood*. Newcastle upon Tyne: Bloodaxe Books Ltd.
Barker, P. (1994). *The Eye in the Door*. London: Penguin.
Barnes, J. (1985). *Flaubert's Parrot*. London: Picador.
Barnes, J. (1996). *Cross Channel*. London: Picador.
Bassnett, S. (1997). *Studying British Cultures: An Introduction*. London: Routledge.
Bhabha, H.K. (1994). *The Location of Culture*. London: Routledge.
Binyon, T.J. (1989). *'Murder Will Out': The Detective in Fiction*. Oxford: Oxford University Press.
Boehmer, E. (ed.) (1998). *Empire Writing: An Anthology of Colonial Literature 1870–1918*. Oxford: Oxford University Press.
Britain 2000 (1999). *The Official Yearbook of the United Kingdom*. London: The Stationery Office.
Brooke, R. (1942). *The Collected Poems*. London: Sidgwick & Jackson.
Byatt, A.S. (1996) 'Parmenides and the contemporary British novel'. *Literature Matters: Newsletter of the British Council's Literature Department*. Issue no. 21, 6–8 December.
Byatt, A.S. (1998a). *The Oxford Book of English Short Stories*. Oxford: Oxford University Press.
Byatt, A.S. (1998b). 'What it means to be English'. Http:///www.sundaytimes.co.uk/news/pages/tim/98/04/06/timfeafea01001.html?129, 1–3.
Childs, P. and M. Storry (eds) (1999). *Encyclopedia of Contemporary British Culture*. London: Routledge.
Coetzee, J.M. (1986). *Foe*. London: Secker & Warburg.
Coetzee, J.M. (1999). *Disgrace*. London: Secker & Warburg.
Colley, L. (1999). 'Britishness in the 21st Century'. http://www.number-10.gov.uk/public/news/features/feature-display.asp?id=848.
Colley, L. (1992). *Britons: Forging the Nation, 1707–1837*. New Haven: Yale University Press.

Collier, P. and H. Geyer-Ryan (eds) (1990). *Literary Theory Today*. Cambridge: Polity Press.
Crawford, R. (ed.) (1992). *Devolving English Literature*. Oxford: Oxford University Press.
Crawford, R. (1993). *Identifying Poets: Self and Territory in Twentieth-Century Poetry*. Edinburgh: Edinburgh University Press.
Crawford, R. (1998). *The Scottish Invention of English Literature*. Cambridge: Cambridge University Press.
Cutler, J. (1995). *Dying Fall*. London: Piatkus Publishers.
Cutler, J. (1998). *Power on Her Own*. London: Hodder & Stoughton.
Dabydeen, D. (1994). *Turner: New and Selected Poems*. London: Jonathan Cape.
Davies, N. (1999). *The Isles: A History*. London: Macmillan.
Day, G. and B. Docherty (1997). *British Poetry from the 1950s to the 1990s: Politics and Art*. London: Macmillan.
Dooley, M. (1997). *Making for Planet Alice: New Women Poets*. Newcastle upon Tyne: Bloodaxe Books Ltd.
Duffy, C.A. (1990). *The Other Country*. London: Anvil Press Poetry.
Duffy, S. (1994). *Calendar Girl*. London: Serpent's Tail. 4 Blackstock Mews, London N4 2BT.
Dunn, D. (1994). 'Review of Dream State: The New Scottish Poets', in *Poetry Review*, New Generation Poets Special.
Eagleton, T. (1998). 'Revaluations: F.R. Leavis'. *The European English Messenger*, VII/2, 49–51.
Easthope, A. (1991). 'What is English about English Literature?' *British Council's Literature Matters*, December, issue no. 9, 6–7.
Farrell, J.G. (1973). *The Siege of Krishnapur*. London: Weidenfeld & Nicolson.
Fischer, T. and L. Norfolk. (1999). *New Writing*, 8. London: Vintage and English Council.
Fleming, I. (1956). *Moonraker*. London: Pan.
Fleming, I. (1959). *From Russia With Love*. London: Pan.
Fleming, I. (1965). *You Only Live Twice*. London: Pan.
Forbes, P. (1992) 'Poetry for the '90s'. *British Book News*, pp. 670–75, October.
Forbes, P. (1994) *Poetry Review (New Generation Poets: A Poetry Review Special Issue)*, pp. 4–6.
Fowles, J. (1964). 'On Being English but Not British'. *Texas Quarterly*, vol. 7, Autumn, 154–62.
France, L. (ed.) (1993). *Sixty Women Poets*. Newcastle upon Tyne: Bloodaxe Books Ltd.
Frye, N. (1971). *Anatomy of Criticism: Four Essays*. Princeton, NJ: Princeton University Press.
Granger, A. (1997). *Asking for Trouble*. London: Headline.
Harrison, T. (1994). *V*. Newcastle upon Tyne: Bloodaxe Books Ltd.
Headley, V. (1992). *Yardie*. London: Pan.
Heaney, S. (1980). *Preoccupations. Selected Prose 1968–1978*. London: Faber & Faber.

Hulse, M., D. Kennedy and D. Morley (1993). *The New Poetry*. Newcastle upon Tyne: Bloodaxe Books Ltd.
Ishiguro, K. (1989). *The Remains of the Day*. London: Faber.
James, P.D. (1993). Introduction to 'The Art of Murder: British Crime Fiction'. A British Council Exhibition, 2–12.
Kennedy, D. (1996). *New Relations: The Refashioning of British Poetry 1980–94*. Bridgend: Seren.
Kureishi, H. (1995). *The Black Album*. London: Faber & Faber.
Leavis, F.R. (1972). *The Great Tradition*. Harmondsworth: Penguin.
Leslie, A. (1998). 'English Identity', in *Postscript: Studies on Contemporary Britain*. London: The British Council.
Lowry, E. (1998). 'The nouvelle cuisine of the turnover', *Times Literary Supplement*, 26 June, 23–4.
Massie, A. (1997). *Shadows of Empire*. London: Sinclair-Stevenson.
Mathias, R. (1986). *Anglo-Welsh Literature: An Illustrated History*. Bridgend: Poetry Wales Press.
Matthews, D. (1999). 'Review of *The Oxford History of English Music* by John Caldwell', *Times Literary Supplement*, 19 November, 8.
Mo, T. (1997). *Sour Sweet*. London: Vintage.
Mongin, O. (1992). 'La France en mal de fiction', *Le Monde*, 3 July, 2.
Morrison, T. (1993). *Playing in the Dark: Whiteness and the Literary Imagination*. London: Picador.
Nünning, A. (ed.) (1998). *Metzler Lexikon: Literatur- und Kulturtheorie*, Stuttgart und Weimar: Metzler.
O'Brien, S. (1998). *The Deregulated Muse: Essays on Contemporary British and Irish Poetry*. Newcastle upon Tyne: Bloodaxe Books Ltd.
Observer, 1 November 1998, front page.
Observer, 5 March 2000, news section: 6.
Observer, 12 November 2000, review section: 13.
Paxman, J. (1998). *The English: A Portrait of a People*. London: Michael Joseph.
Phillips, M. (1990). *Blood Rights*. Harmondsworth: Penguin.
Phillips, M. and T. Phillips (1998). *Windrush: the Irresistible Rise of Multi-Racial Britain*. London: HarperCollins.
Rendell, R. (1994). *Simisola*. London: Hutchinson.
Rhys, J. (1966). *Wide Sargasso Sea*. London: André Deutsch.
Richards (1993). *The Imperial Archive: Knowledge and the Fantasy of Empire*. London: Verso.
Rushdie, S. (1994). *East, West*. London: Jonathan Cape.
Rutherfurd, E. (1997). *London: The Story of the Greatest City on Earth*. London: Century Publishing Co.
Said, E. (1993). *Culture and Imperialism*. London: Chatto & Windus.
Said, E. (1995). *Orientalism*. Harmondsworth: Penguin.
Sanders, A. (1994). *The Short Oxford History of English Literature*. Oxford: Oxford University Press.
Sauerberg, L.O. (1984). *Secret Agents in Fiction: Ian Fleming, John le Carré and Len Deighton*. London: Macmillan; New York: St Martin's Press.

Sauerberg, L.O. (1991). *Fact into Fiction: Documentary Realism in the Contemporary Novel*. London: Macmillan; New York: St Martin's Press.
Sauerberg, L.O. (1997). *Versions of the Past – Visions of the Future: The Canonical in the Criticism of T.S. Eliot, F.R. Leavis, Northrop Frye and Harold Bloom*. London: Macmillan; New York: St Martin's Press.
Scott, P. (1978). *The Jewel in the Crown*. London: Heinemann.
Scott, P. (1986). *My Appointment with the Muse: Essays and Lectures*, selected by Shelley C. Reece. London: Heinemann.
Shute, N. (1968). *Round the Bend*. London: Pan.
Sisson, C.H. (1953). *An Asiatic Romance*. London: Gaberbocchus.
Snow, C.P. (1962). *The Affair*. Harmondsworth: Penguin.
Storry, M. and P. Childs (1997). *British Cultural Identities*. London and New York: Routledge.
Swift, G. (1999). *Last Orders*. London: Picador.
Thomas, E. (1978). *The Collected Poems of Edward Thomas*. Oxford: Oxford University Press.
Timlin, M. (1998). *A Street that Rhymed at 3 AM*, London: Vista (Gollancz).
Wadham-Smith, N. (1999). 'Re-Inventing Britain: Introduction'. *British Council's Anthology Issues 6–10*. The British Council, pp. 107–9.

Index

Adcock, Fleur, 29, 84
Agard, John, 7, 63, 69
  'Half-caste', 70
  'Listen Mr Oxford Don', 69
Allingham, Margery, 166
Allnut, Gillian, 85
Alvi, Moniza, 7, 64, 65, 66, 71–3, 74, 97–9
  'The Bed', 71
  'Hindi Urdu Bol Chaal', 97
  'I Would Like to be a Dot in a Painting by Míro', 71
  'Presents from My Aunts in Pakistan', 71–2, 99
  'The Wedding', 97–8
Amis, Kingsley, 40, 115
Amis, Martin, 7, 10, 14, 29, 142, 150–1
  Time's Arrow, 153–5
anglocentricity, 25
Arnold, Matthew, 112–13
Ash, John, 28
Ashcroft, Bill, 7
Astley, Neil, 63, 65, 87
Atwood, Margaret, 156
Auden, W.H., 56, 64
Austen, Jane, 13, 14, 21, 35, 114, 125, 129, 135, 136, 203

Ballantyne, R.M., 35, 36, 158
Bakhtin, Michael, 22
Barker, Pat, 24, 49
Barnes, Julian, 7, 10, 14, 29, 110, 111–12, 142, 144–8, 217
  Cross Channel, 145–8
  Flaubert's Parrot, 144–5
Barnes, Linda, 181
Bassnett, Susan, 196, 214
Beckett, Samuel, 110, 114, 115, 155
Bennett, Arnold, 13, 110

Berger, John, 7, 10, 112, 142–3, 150–1, 152
Bhabha, Homi K., 7, 195–6, 198–201
Bhatt, Sujata, 63, 91, 100
  'Muliebrity', 100
  'Shérdi', 91
  'What Is Worth Knowing?', 93
Bishop, Elizabeth, 64
Blair, Tony, 3
Bloom, Harold, 146, 209
Bloom, Valerie, 70
  'Longsight Market', 71
Blyton, Enid, 174
Boyd, William, 7
Boehmer, Elleke, 34, 202
Boland, Eavan, 59
  'An Irish Childhood in England: 1951', 59
Booker Prize, 65, 111
Borges, Jorge Luis, 115
Breeze, Jean Binta, 70
  'I Poet', 93
  'For All Blue Notes', 93
  'Riddym Ravings (The Mad Woman's Poem)', 70
Britain/British, 2, 5, 32, 63, 125, 142, 190
Brontë, Charlotte, 35, 157, 199, 203
Brontës, the, 21, 35, 114
Brooke, Rupert, 23, 24, 195
Brooke-Rose, Christine, 110, 11
Brooks, Cleanth, 146
Brookner, Anita, 13, 114, 156, 209
Burton, Sir Richard, 138
Byatt, Antonia, 15–20, 22, 24, 115, 117, 118, 125, 136, 140, 213, 214
Byron, Lord George Gordon, 21

Caldwell, John, 16
Calvino, Italo, 115
Carré, John le, 157
Carter, Angela, 14
Chandler, Raymond, 165, 168, 175
Chatterjee, 63
Chatwin, Bruce, 10, 112, 138, 142, 150–1, 158
Chaucer, 110, 120
Childs, Peter and Mike Storry, 213
Christie, Agatha, 156, 166, 180
Cixous, Hélène, 84
Cleary, Brendan, 60
  'Sealink', 61
  'Slouch', 61
Cody, Liza, 166, 181
Coetzee, J.M., 36, 77, 83, 141–2
  Disgrace, 141–2
  Foe, 77, 83,
Colley, Linda, 15–16, 213
comedy of manners, 13
compound voice, 9, 11, 31, 65, 89, 161, 211–12
Conrad, Joseph, 113, 114, 118, 125, 129, 135, 136, 159
Cornwell, Patricia D., 181
Couzyn, Jeni, 85, 89, 93, 94, 103
  'The Message', 85, 89, 215
Crawford, Robert, 15, 24–9, 140–2, 193–4, 214
  'The Saltcoats Structuralists', 193–4
Crispin, Edmund, 166
cultural studies, 193
Curtis, Tony, 60
  'Thoughts from the Holiday Inn', 60
Cutler, Judith, 165, 166, 167, 177–9, 181, 187
  Dying Fall, 177–9, 181–2, 187
  Power on Her Own, 179

Dabydeen, David, 7, 64, 66, 74–9, 83, 208–9
  'The Canecutters' Song', 75
  'Catching Crabs', 75–6

'Coolie Mother', 75
'Coolie Odyssey (for Ma, d. 1985)', 74, 76
'Elegy', 75
'Nightmare', 75
'The Servants' Song', 75
'Turner', 77–9, 83
D'Aguiar, Fred, 70, 208
  'Mama Dot Warns Against an Easter Rising', 70
Davie, Donald, 22
Davies, Norman, 16, 190
Davis, Lindsey, 166, 180
Day, Gary, 81–2, 85
deconstructionist criticism, 204
Defoe, Daniel, 77, 139, 157, 158
Deighton, Len, 157
DeLillo, Don, 156
de Man, Paul, 27, 196
Derrida, Jacques, 145, 196
Desai, Anita, 156
Dexter, Colin, 165, 166, 173
Dharker, Imtiaz, 7, 54, 106, 108
  'Minority', 54, 106
  'Purdah (1)', 106
Dhomhnaill, Nuala Ní, 58, 96
  'The Language Issue', 96
Dickens, Charles, 13, 35, 114, 157, 203
Dickinson, Peter, 166
Dipdin, Michael, 166, 180
discourse approach, 34
Docherty, Brian, 81
Donaghy, Michael, 64
Donovan, Katie, 90
  'Underneath Our Skirts', 90
Dooley, Maura, 86–7
Douglas, Norman, 21
Dowson, Jane, 85
Doyle, Sir Arthur Conan, 156, 172
Drabble, Margaret, 13, 110, 115, 156
Duffy, Carol Ann, 63, 84, 94, 95
  'River', 94
Duffy, Maureen, 10, 142, 159, 160

Duffy, Stella, 165, 183–5,
    Calendar Girl, 183–5, 217
Dunant, Sarah, 181
Dunmore, Helen, 216
Dunn, Douglas, 27
Duran, Jane, 28
Durrell, Lawrence, 21, 36, 139, 140, 157

Eagleton, Terry, 116
Easthope, Anthony, 18
Eco, Umberto, 148, 149
EEC, 4
Eliot, George, 13, 35, 113, 114, 125–6, 129, 135
Eliot, T.S., 28, 56
England/English, 2, 3, 4, 15, 21, 27, 32, 59, 63, 125, 190
EU, 4
Evanovich, Janet, 181

Farrell, J.G., 45, 46, 48
    The Siege of Krishnapur, 47–8
Fenton, James, 55
Fielding, Henry, 21
Fleming, Ian, 42, 157
    Moonraker, 42
    You Only Live Twice, 42–3
Foden, Giles, 52
    Ladysmith, 52
Forbes, Peter, 54–6, 63–5
Forster, E.M., 21, 36, 40, 140
Foucault, Michel, 153, 196
Fowles, John, 20, 22, 110, 115
    The French Lieutenant's Woman, 110
France, Linda, 59, 86
    'North and South', 59
Francis, Dick, 166
Fraser, George Macdonald, 52
    Flashman epic, 52
Freud, Sigmund, 153
Freeling, Nicolas, 166
Frye, Northrop, 118
Fyfield, Frances, 164, 166, 167, 181

Gaarder, Jostein, 148
gender studies, 25, 204
generic fiction, 13, 149, 150, 162
George, Elizabeth, 180
Golding, William, 36, 115, 139, 158
Goldsmith, Oliver, 151
Grafton, Sue, 157, 181
Granger, Ann, 165, 173–5
    Asking for Trouble, 173–5
Grant-Adamson, Lesley, 166
Graves, Robert, 21
Greene, Graham, 139, 159
Griffith, Garreth, 7
Griffiths, Jane, 83, 107
    'Emigrants', 83
    'Migration', 107

Haggard, E. Rider, 35
Hammett, Dashiel, 165, 175
Harrison, Tony, 54, 62–3, 74, 208–9
    'V', 62
Harvey, John, 165, 173
Headley, Victor, 165, 166, 171–2, 173
    Yardie, 171–2
Heald, Tim, 166
Heaney, Seamus, 20, 21–2, 54, 56–7, 65, 74, 208–9
Henty, G.A., 35
Herbert, W.N., 58
    'The King and Queen of Dumfriesshire', 58
    'Riddle to my Wife in Brazil', 58
    'To a Mousse', 215
Hill, Geoffrey, 22, 54, 56–7
Hill, Reginald, 166
Høeg, Peter, 148
Hofmann, Michael, 64
Hornby, Nick, 136, 210
Hughes, Ted, 22, 54, 56–7

immigrant writers, 13–14
implosion, 11, 191, 192, 195

intercultural, 9, 10, 11, 31, 32, 91, 111, 119, 124, 188, 211–12
Ireland/Irish, 21, 27, 30, 32, 57–8, 59, 96
Ishiguro, Kazuo, 7, 14, 29, 49, 112, 119, 125, 126–8, 136, 142
  The Remains of the Day, 126–8

James, Henry, 28, 113, 114, 118, 125, 129, 135
James, P.D., 163–4, 165, 166, 181
Jastrzebska, Maria, 95
  'Bi-lingual', 95
Johnson, Linton Kwesi, 7, 63, 67, 70, 74
  'Bass Culture', 68–9
  'Mekkin Histri', 67–8
Joyce, James, 110, 114, 115

Kavanagh, Dan, 165, 182–3
  Duffy, 182–3
Kay, Jackie, 7, 63, 103–5
  Adoption Papers, 104–5
  'In My Country', 103–4
  'Pride', 104
Keating, H.R.F., 166, 180
Kennedy, David, 80–1, 200–1, 215
Kerr, Philip, 149, 165, 166, 180
Khalvati, Mimi, 7, 90, 91, 105–6
  'Amanuensis', 105
  'Blue Moon', 105–6
  'Rubaiyat', 105
  'Stone of Patience', 105
  'The Waiting House', 90
Kingsley, Charles, 35
Kinsella, John, 65
Knox, Ronald, 167
Kureishi, Hanif, 7, 14, 119–20, 128–30, 136
  The Black Album, 128–30, 132–3

La Plante, Lynda, 181
Lacan, Jacques, 153, 196
Latif, Tariq, 63

Larkin, Philip, 22, 23, 24, 56–7
Lawrence, D.H., 21, 113, 114, 118, 125–6, 1
Leavis, F.R., 10, 112–17, 129, 135–6, 216
Leslie, Ann, 213, 214
Lessing, Doris, 36
Levertov, Denise, 28
Levi, Primo, 153
Limburg, Joanne, 103, 104
  'Seder Night with My Ancestors', 103, 215
Lively, Penelope, 10, 14
Lodge, David, 118
Lomax, Marion, 102
  'Kith', 102
Lowry, Elizabeth, 17

MacDiarmid, Hugh, 58
MacDonald, Ross, 175
magic realism, 211
Mann, Thomas, 140
Marryat, Captain, 35
Marsh, Ngaio, 166
marxist criticism, 204
Massie, Allan, 49
  Shadows of Empire, 49–52
Masters, John, 43
Matthews, David, 16
Mathias, Roland, 27
Maugham, Somerset W., 139, 159
McEwan, Ian, 8, 10, 14, 140, 142
migration, 89
Mistry, Rohinton, 111
Mo, Timothy, 7, 120, 128, 130–2, 136, 143, 158
  Sour Sweet, 130–32
Mongin, Olivier, 13
monocultural, 119
Monsarrat, Nicholas, 43, 44
  The Tribe That Lost Its Head, 44
Morris, Jan, 138
Moody, Susan, 166
Morrison, Blake, 55

Morrison, Toni, 203–4
Motion, Andrew, 55
Muldoon, Paul, 58, 96
multicultural, 11, 14
Murray, Les, 54
muscular Christianity, 35, 40

Nabb, Magdalen, 166
Naipaul, V.S., 14, 111, 125, 136
New Generation poets, 56, 63–5
New Journalism, 211
Nichols, Grace, 91, 99–102
  'Abra-Cadabra', 99–100
  'Configurations', 91
  'My Northern-Sister', 101–2
  'Tropical Death', 100–1
  'Walking with My Brother in Georgetown', 101
Norfolk, Lawrence, 7, 110
Northern Ireland/Northern Irish, 2, 4, 5, 15

O'Brien, Sean, 84
O'Callaghan, Julie, 28
Ondaatje, Michael, 111, 150
Orwell, George, 36, 40

Padgett, Abigail, 181
Paretsky, Sara, 157, 181
Paxman, Jeremy, 16
pathetic fallacy, 121, 140
Phillips, Mike, 166, 167–71
  Blood Rights, 167–71
  Windrush: The Irresistible Rise of Multi-Racial Britain (with Trevor Phillips), 215
Pilcher, Rosamund, 110, 209
Poe, Edgar Allan, 156
Porteous, Katrina, 61, 102–3
  'Charlie Douglas', 61–2, 103
post-colonial studies/criticism, 6, 25–6, 28, 33, 36, 192, 193, 195–210
postmodern/postmodernism, 64, 87, 150, 153
postmodernist fiction, 110

post-structuralism/post-structuralist, 34, 87, 194
Pound, Ezra, 28
Proust, Marcel, 146
Pym, Barbara, 114

Raine, Craig, 55, 56
Rankin, Ian, 165, 173
realist novel, 13
regional/regionalism, 25–7, 102, 103
Reid, Christopher, 5
Rendell, Ruth, 164, 165, 166, 167, 173, 185–7
  Simisola, 185–7
Rhys, Jean, 35
Rouse, Anne, 28
Rowling, R.K., 210
Roy, Arundhati, 156
Rumens, Carol, 84
Rushdie, Salman, 7, 14, 111, 120, 13, 136
  'Chekov and Zulu', 133–5

Said, Edward, 7, 197–8, 203
Salzman, Eva, 28
Satyamurti, Carole, 91
  'Fear of Corpus Christi: Warsaw', 92
  'My First Cup of Coffee', 91–2
  'Sex Object', 92
Sayers, Dorothy L., 166
Scholes, Robert, 118
Scotland/Scottish, 2, 4, 5, 15, 21, 26–7, 32, 59, 65, 205
Scott, Paul, 44–5, 48, 207–8
  Jewel in the Crown, 46
Scott, Sir Walter, 13
Segal, Erich, 149
Seth, Vikram, 111, 136
  An Equal Music, 136
Shakespeare, Nicolas, 8, 10, 112, 142, 158, 159
Shute, Nevil, 37, 43
  Round the Bend, 37–9

Sisson, C.H., 40, 44
  An Asiatic Romance, 40–1
Smith, Joan, 166
Smollett, Tobias, 21, 137
Snow, C.P., 41
  The Affair, 41–2
social comedy, 13
Sontag, Susan, 150
Spillane, Mickey, 175
Spivak, Gayatri Chakravorty, 7, 196
Sterne Lawrence, 137
Swift, Graham, 14, 119, 120–25, 136
  Last Orders, 120–25, 199

Tauchnitz, 148
Thackeray, William, 13, 35, 145
theory, 193
Thomas, D.M., 10, 142, 143, 150–1, 152–5
  The White Hotel, 152–5
Thomas, Edward, 23, 24, 56
Thomas, R.S., 59, 60
  'Reservoirs', 60
Tiffin, Helen, 7
Timlin, Mark, 165, 166, 173, 175–6

A Street That Rhymed at 3 AM, 175–6
transcultural, 9, 31
transnational, 9, 31
travelogue, 138
Tremain, Rose, 140, 159
Trollope, Anthony, 13, 35, 110, 145
Trollope, Joanna, 110, 209

United Kingdom, 2, 4, 5, 15, 20, 21, 66
USA, 4, 14

Wain, John, 40
Walcott, Derek, 54
Wales/Welsh, 2, 4, 15, 21, 27, 32, 59
Waller, Robert James, 149
Waugh, Alec, 43
Welsh, Irvine, 210
Winterson, Jeanette, 110, 115, 140
Wolfe, Tom, 156
Woolf, Virginia, 84, 110, 120
Wordsworth, William, 56, 151

Yeats, W.B., 153